THE WEB OF POLITICS

THE WEB OF
POLITICS

The Internet's Impact on the
American Political System

Richard Davis

New York   Oxford

Oxford University Press

1999

Oxford University Press

Oxford   New York
Athens   Auckland   Bangkok   Bogotá   Buenos Aires   Calcutta
Cape Town   Chennai   Dar es Salaam   Delhi   Florence   Hong Kong   Istanbul
Karachi   Kuala Lumpur   Madrid   Melbourne   Mexico City   Mumbai
Nairobi   Paris   São Paulo   Singapore   Taipei   Tokyo   Toronto   Warsaw

and associated companies in

Berlin   Ibadan

Library of Congress Cataloging-in-Publication Data
Davis, Richard, 1955–
    The web of politics : the internet's impact on the American
political system / Richard Davis.
        p.   cm.
    Includes bibliographical references and index.
    ISBN 0-19-511484-1; 0-19-511485-X (pbk.)
    1. Political participation—United States—Computer network
resources.   2. Political planning—United States—Computer network resources.
3. Lobbying—United States—Computer network resources.   4. United States—
Politics and government—Computer network resources.   5. Internet (Computer
network)   6. World Wide Web (Information retrieval system)   I. Title.
JK1764.D38   1999
323'.042'0285—DC21   98-6872

To mentors and friends:
> Lee Farnsworth
> Ralph Barney
> Tom Patterson
> Dave Magleby
> Bill Daynes

Acknowledgments

My name appears on the front of this book, but this book is hardly a one-man production. I wish to acknowledge the assistance of Thomas LeBien at Oxford, who has been a source of good advice and direction. Thankfully, he expressed early and vigorous interest in the project. Montague Kern and Diana Owen reviewed the manuscript and offered helpful suggestions. The students of Political Science 410 also critiqued my ideas and forced me to defend myself.

Research help came at significant junctures. The College of Family, Home, and Social Sciences at Brigham Young University provided critical research support early on, as did a donor who insists on remaining anonymous. While conducting this research I have been blessed with the help of several research assistants. The two who contributed the most were Vincent James Strickler and Stephanie Ord. They kept the others, as well as me, on task. They were joined by Amy Bice, Hugh Brown, Nicole Carlisle, Katherine DeLapp, Allison Gilmour, Katie Hunt, Anna Nibley, Aaron Olsen, Jared Trent, Amy Wilda, and Kristen Winmill.

My family, as always, provided the essential refuge from writing block and helped prevent me from turning into a workaholic.

Contents

Foreword

On Friday, August 11, 1998, the full contents of Independent Counsel Kenneth Starr's report to the House of Representatives on the conduct of President Bill Clinton were released to the public—on the Internet. Experts feared the first serious bout of Net gridlock—a massive overload of demand exceeding the Net's capacity to respond. There were, in fact, several million "hits" on the various Web sites that contained the Starr Report, but no major glitches.

The Starr Report thus became historic in two ways. It was the first time after enactment of the law creating the independent counsel that a report on potential impeachment had been sent to the House. And it was the first time that a momentous document of this sort had been released directly to the public using the Internet as the conduit. To many, the latter consequence was more significant than the former—here was the Net unleashed, enabling citizens to get direct access to vital public information rather than being forced to rely on the press as the conduit and filter. This was the epitome of Net empowerment—the new wave of democracy, the herald of citizen rule.

Those predictions might prove true. But it was easy to be skeptical. The day after the Net release, major newspapers like the *Washington Post* and the *New York Times* printed the full text of the report as an insert, reaching more readers than the first Web package and in a much more easily digestible form. A book version emerged within three days and showed brisk sales, seemingly not affected by the easy and direct access on the Web. Moreover, it was not clear at all that the six million hits and downloads of the Starr Report meant that six million people were actually reading it. Nor was it clear who the millions of downloaders were. Were they largely highly educated elites or a representative slice of the electorate? Did they barely scratch the surface, or did they represent the full population of political junkies who will make up the core audience for any future Web release of important public affairs information?

The impact and implications of this innovation in information dissemination will be analyzed and debated for some time. That makes the publication of *The Web of Politics* even more timely and significant.

The early returns from the Starr Report were interesting. Politicians scrambled as the information spewed out to the country, but they did not seem to respond differently to the report's widespread availability than they would have if it had simply been printed and given away or sold. Journalists scrambled as well to get the information out instantly, both on their own Web pages and on the air, so as not to be scooped by their rivals. That meant some embarrassing moments, since there was no opportunity to filter or screen out unsuitable material, but it did not seem to demonstrate any fundamental differences from pre-Internet news gathering or dissemination. And if some citizens bypassed the gatekeepers to read off the Net, most appeared to get their information either from traditional sources or second hand from friends and acquaintances.

To be sure, the information in the Starr report affected the mass audience differently from the opinion-maker audience. Opinion leaders and makers were appalled by the portrait of Bill Clinton in the report and called in large numbers for his resignation or impeachment. The mass audience showed continued support for Clinton as president, albeit with a continuing decline in his image as a person and as a moral leader, and indicated in large numbers that they wanted him to continue as president. But this gap between mass and elite opinion had been evident for eight months before the Starr Report and could not be easily attributed to the unfiltered access provided by the Net. The release of the Starr Report on the Net may yet prove to be a revolutionary harbinger. But the early evidence supports Richard Davis's central thesis—that the Web will not fundamentally transform American politics: that it will not change passive citizens who wait for information to come to them into activists eagerly exploiting the freedom and resources of the Internet; that politicians and policy makers will adapt to the flood of messages and information coming to them via the Web and will use the ability to reach voters in return, but not in ways sharply different from their information give-and-take now; and that the main impact will affect the most active, data-rich elite consumers of information.

Davis makes a persuasive case, backed by history, literature, and logic. But a caution is still in order. The advent of the Internet has thrilled and excited a core of populist and direct democracy advocates, who have become the leading proponents of cyberdemocracy. The Net, they say, is the key to freeing citizens from the bonds of so-called representative democracy, the key to making the old model of town-hall democracy work across 3000 miles and 250 million people. It can take the existing initiative and referendum process, now allowed in 24 states, and make it universal to enable citizens to make decisions that override their legislature and legislators. It can take the nascent movement toward voting by mail, which had its first statewide effort in Oregon's Senate election in 1995 and eliminated the stamps and delays.

This idea first resonated with a non-elite population when H. Ross Perot pledged during the 1992 presidential campaign that if elected president, he would use "electronic town meetings" as a central forum to guide national policy decisions. Perot did not spell out what he meant by electronic town meetings—perhaps just national television forums—and he did not get elected to implement his plan. But the idea of using technology to enhance democracy—to implement "cyberdemocracy"—gathered credence and momentum, especially as the technology has advanced.

Virtually all members of Congress now have their own Web pages. So do all significant presidential candidates; all think tanks; most daily newspapers and weekly magazines; nearly all federal agencies; the White House; Congress (its THOMAS Web page was the prime conduit for the Starr Report); and most states, counties, cities, state agencies, and other governmental units. Some of these units are emulating Colorado Springs' Citylink, which allows citizens to communicate with city managers and city council members. Other sites offer on-line debates with candidates for office. The Democracy Network, which started in California and has expanded to other states, offers debates, dialogues with candidates, and other election-related news in an interactive format.

Futurists have had a field day with these developments, projecting a rosy picture of democracy writ large. Lawrence Grossman, former president of NBC and PBS, has imagined Congress becoming a discussion chamber that waits for public instructions before making any decisions. Futurist Christine Slaton has suggested that we can scrap the concept of elected legislators, moving to a technology-driven participatory democracy where lawmakers are chosen by lot and rotated regularly. Alvin and Heidi Toffler, expanding on their "Third Wave," predict that today's political parties will disappear and that we will develop a new representative model. They suggest it may be one in which Americans choose representatives by lot, or at least go part way, dividing representation into half regularly elected officials, with the other half coming from a random sample of the public.

Almost all of these scenarios envision frequent national referendums over the Net, along with elections shifting from polling stations to home computer terminals or digital TVs with Web connections. People will shed the inconvenience of leaving their homes, waiting in lines, speaking to others, much less having policy choices made by a small group of Washington-based political elites.

The scenarios assume an electorate unleashed, eager and willing to take on this reponsibility, freed from the shackles of the media gatekeepers and the professional political class. This means an electorate also eager and willing to spend time seeking out information and taking some of their leisure or work time to study issues and vote on policy choices. Davis, however, offers a strong antidote to that thesis. There is no reason to believe that citizens juggling job, family, and other responsibilities will decide to shirk those duties to spend time studying or acting on public policy. Passive individuals who today consume news inadvertently or intermittently are unlikely to change into policy wonks no matter how convenient the Net makes it to access information or play a direct role as policy actor.

Starting with C-SPAN and punctuated by the World Wide Web, the explosion of public affairs information has created a two-tiered system. It has provided more access to more information and political activity than anyone has had in the history of the world to a sliver of the populace—for instance, junkies like me. But most others have been largely oblivious to the information cyber-revolution. The division is certainly related to education, gender, race, and income; surveys show vast gaps in regular Internet use between college graduates and high school graduates, men and women, whites and latinos and blacks, and those with incomes of $50,000 and more and those at $20,000 or less. While these gaps will undoubtedly narrow, a skew toward the well-to-do and highly educated, and probably toward the more ideologically driven, is inevitable.

To be sure, the President's initiative to wire the nation's schools and classrooms could eventually make the technology available to everybody (although not necessarily in their homes). But there is reason to believe that even if there were universal service, there would not be universal interest. Lloyd Morrisett, recently retired president of the Markle Foundation, studied California's experience with referendums and projected his findings to the era of cyberdemocracy. Morrisett found that as the California ballot became overloaded with complex and lengthy initiatives, it discouraged people from going out to the polls rather than motivating them to offer their judgment. His observations suggest that voting on the Net would fall into the same pattern, replicating what has happened with voting at the polls.

Even if we could be assured that all would participate, there is a greater danger in the expansion of cyberdemocracy—its challenge to the deliberation process in government. The Framers designed the American political system not to be a "pure" or direct democracy where citizens "assemble and administer the government in person." They did not want the government to reflect directly public opinion or public emotions, and they feared the prospect of a tyranny of a majority. Instead, they chose a republican, or representative, form of democracy, where citizens choose representatives who meet face to face and make and execute laws.

The idea of the Framers was to produce a public judgment, reached after extensive discussion, disagreement, and debate, that would enlarge and refine public views. Reaching a judgment requires time and effort. The slow and deliberate process of debate and give-and-take, done face to face by representatives from different areas and disparate constituencies, allows all perspectives and interests to be weighed. The process of persuasion and building laborious coalitions, the Framers thought, would result in decisions more just and more likely to stand the tests of time and legitimacy with citizens. Deliberation and cyberdemocracy are not easily compatible. Consider the difference between laws passed by referendums and laws passed in legislatures. Legislative deliberation does not always work as intended, but the process encourages informed debate among informed and semi-informed individuals with different partisan, regional, and philosophical differences, who go through a gauntlet of subcommittee and committee hearings, bill markups, and floor debate, with amendments usually allowed and occurring at all levels, in each of two houses of Congress. Few if any bills emerge at the end as they were drafted at the beginning, or emerge in identical form from the House and the Senate.

There is debate, to be sure, in some state referendum campaigns, but usually through major media campaigns arranged by proponents and/or opponents. The debate, such as it is, involves two sides, pro and con, and is usually played out via slick thirty-second commericials in black-and-white terms. There is no face-to-face debate, much less the perspectives of dozens or hundreds of interests reflected in representatives from various constituencies. There is no amendment process—just a final up-or-down vote. In California, the initiatives to be voted on often run to hundreds or thousands of pages, available for voters to digest before they cast their "thumbs up" or "thumbs down" votes. Few if any voters spend much time studying the issues, much less actually reading the provisions and language of the referendums. The process would only deteriorate and the deliberative quality decline if the referendums were moved to the electronic venue and expanded dramatically in number.

Of course, there is the related question of who writes the referendums or gets them on the ballot for consideration. The process is anything but a democratic one. Small groups of elites, often ideological ones, dominate the process, relying on a new breed of high-paid political consultant specializing in initiatives, including how best to frame a complex issue into a simple yes or no vote. In reality, most referendums become more a high-priced clash among special interests and less a reflection of any real form of democracy.

That is not to say that the advent of the electronic town square is entirely negative or necessarily antideliberative. There are ways to make a larger mass of voters a constructive part of the deliberative framework. Political scientist James Fishkin, with the cooperation of PBS, brought a random sample of 600 citizens together in Austin, Texas, in January 1996 for three days of discussion, moderated by independent experts, on important issues of the day. The process was an admirable if extraordinarily expensive one—and probably not an example that would or could be regularly emulated in the digital age.

Realistically, the "deliberative poll" or "electronic town meeting," if applied on a larger scale, would be more likely to evolve into a new version of a contemporary television talk show, a cross between Oprah Winfrey and CNN's "Talk Back Live."

As an avid consumer of public affairs information, I could not be more delighted by the cornucopia of information available on my computer, there at the stroke of a key without requiring me to leave my desk. But I am uneasy about the dangers represented by a combustible combination of cynical distrust of institutions, populistic glorification of "pure" democracy, and the accelerating advance of information technology.

Consider what Newt Gingrich, who rode a wave of voter cynicism and populism to the Speakership of the House of Representatives in 1994, said to one of his college classes:

> Direct democracy says, Okay, how do we feel this week? We all raise our hand. Let's rush off and do it. The concept of republican representation, which is very clear in the Founding Fathers, is you hire somebody who you send to a central place. . . . They, by definition, learn things you don't learn, because you don't want to—you want to live your life. They are supposed to use their judgment to represent you. . . . [The Founders] feared the passion of the moment.

Preserving the Founders' vision and protecting against the passion of the moment won't be so easy in the age of the Web.

Norman Ornstein
The American Enterprise Institute

THE WEB OF POLITICS

Introduction
Enter the Internet

On July 17, 1996, an explosion rocked TWA's Flight 800 shortly after it departed from JFK airport. The plane plummeted to the earth in pieces. Months later, after extensive search operations and testing by various governmental organizations, the mystery of what downed the Paris-bound flight remained.

Nearly four months later, Pierre Salinger, former Kennedy White House press secretary and ABC News reporter, announced that he had solved the puzzle. Using a document he had obtained from a French intelligence source, Salinger announced that the U.S. government had covered up an accidental shooting down of the plane by a Navy ship in training exercises.

Salinger's revelation was new to most of the world, but not to many Internet users. Salinger's "original" secret document actually was an e-mail message written on America Online by a former airline pilot and distributed on the Internet for several months before Salinger's pronouncement.[1]

Thanks to the Internet, a private speculation had been posted as near-fact and then legitimated by a respected news reporter. Salinger's report was taken seriously enough by the Pentagon that a press conference was held to refute the accusation.

The Internet—a term that was not even in the public lexicon a decade ago—has captured the attention of the media, the government, and many of the public. It has changed the way many Americans receive information and communicate.[2] Even the term "Internet" has become interchangeable with a variety of expressions, such as "new information highway" or "information superhighway."[3]

Increasing numbers of Americans are logging onto the Internet, going "online." To meet demand, a flourishing cottage industry in Internet-related literature, how-to books to cyberspace, has appeared. Perhaps the most popular aspect of the Internet, e-mail, has revolutionized correspondence—both business and personal. An estimated 50 million people used e-mail in 1997, up from an estimated 37 million in 1996.[4]

Internet use has reached astounding proportions in a remarkably short period of time. Estimates of the number of Internet users vary widely since measurement is difficult. For example, in early 1994, the Times Mirror Center for the People and the Press estimated Internet use at 11 million.[5] Surveys in 1995 estimated approximately 10 million Internet users.[6]

But by 1996 an estimated 46 million Americans had access to the Internet, with three-fourths of those actually using it, which would produce a user total of approximately 34 million. Using 21 surveys of Internet usage, one market research company claimed the Internet user population grew by 132 percent in one nine-month period.[7] By 1998, two surveys showed that about one out of every two adults in the United States are on the Internet.[8] While survey numbers have fluctuated, a constant has been the rapid growth in public use of the Internet.

As public notice and use has increased, the Internet increasingly has been accorded an eminent status as the technology of revolutionary change. It has been called "a revolution as profound as the invention of printing" and an invention "as important as the invention of movable type."[9] Political scientist Ithiel de Sola Pool boldly proclaimed electronic communication, of which the Internet is the primary force, the fourth stage in human communications development, following speech, writing, printing, and broadcasting.[10]

Accordingly, the potential political role of the Internet has been extensively speculated upon. The future of American politics has been called an "age of Internet democracy," and the residents of that new political system will be known as "netizens." This new medium has been predicted as the beginnings of true direct democracy—a vehicle for enabling common citizens, rather than distant elected representatives, to make ongoing policy decisions. Anthony Corrado suggests future citizens of the wired republic "will have the capacity to take legislative decision-making into their own hands by initiating proposals and considering public referendums electronically."[11]

However, the anticipated promise of the Internet as a revolutionary vehicle for political participation has prompted not only ecstasy, but also consternation. Ted Koppel predicts "the country may be moving in the direction of a purer democracy than anything the ancient Greeks envisioned. It promises to be a fiasco."[12] Leaders, it is argued, can be too closely tied to the public. Howard Fineman put the question this way: "What if our presidents become nothing more than the sum of our whims and misinformation? The netizens of the future will have to take their jobs seriously. Are we ready for this much democracy? Let's hope so."[13]

The thesis of this book is that neither scenario concerning the Internet is accurate. Rather than acting as a revolutionary tool rearranging political power and instigating direct democracy, the Internet is destined to become dominated by the same actors in American politics who currently utilize other mediums. Undoubtedly, public expression will become more common and policy makers will be expected to respond hastily. But the mobilization of public expression will still largely be the creation of groups and individuals who currently dominate the political landscape. And the information that the public will obtain electronically will come primarily from the same sources on which they currently rely and will not feature interaction by more people than currently exists via other means. Today, the production of political news and information is the result of the interaction among official entities, interest group representatives, and the news media. Such interaction also will govern the Internet's presentation of news and information.

This argument does not assume that all information will be channeled through the structures established by these forces. That is not true today *offline*. Any individual or group can publish a newsletter or magazine, develop their own mailing list, and, therefore, reach other people. The Internet, as discussed above, facilitates that activity. That will not change.

Rather, the argument is that the current forces dominating political news delivery, who dwarf the independent efforts, also will overshadow them on the Internet. The news organizations, interest groups, and government entities with the most influence on the mass news dissemination business will transfer that role to the

Internet. Their information will become the primary information sources for Internet users of the future.

They will offer organization for the vast majority of users, an organization these users sorely want and need. The small minority of highly sophisticated computer users, of course, may bypass that organization. But most users will welcome quick, ready, and structured access to news and information.

For their daily dose of news, they will want to go to the *New York Times,* the *Washington Post* or, more likely, a local newspaper site. For information on specialized topics of interest to them, they will go to sites of groups they already belong to or at least are familiar with. These will include the AFL-CIO for union members, the Sierra Club for environmentalists, or the National Rifle Association for gun enthusiasts.

Internet users will write down and/or seek out the addresses of known companies rather than new businesses they have never heard of. (While there, they may read or hear, or even see, the company's take on not only the corporate world, but also the political world as well.)

Unlike in the case of radio or television, it is not necessarily the government providing boundaries (although that is a probable future outcome), rather it is the interest groups, the news media, and the politicians who will do so through offering structure and familiarity. The sites established by these dominant players in the existing distribution of news and information will become the way stations for weary Internet surfers who want to organize their interests simply and effectively.

It is true that Internet users will have a range of information choices once they are at a Web site. There will be no need to sit through a half hour evening news broadcast to hear all the news to be presented. Nor will it be required to pour through the entire front news section of a newspaper in order to reach stories of interest. Users will be able to chose the stories they wish to see, hear, or read from a menu. In that sense, these organizations will have less control over what news people receive from among the news available on the site.

But such choice really does not matter. Whether users read a story about floods in the Midwest, peruse an electronic newsletter of a group, or watch a video clip of the president's latest speech, what they read or see will still be the news and information presentation of that media outlet, group, or politician on which users are relying. And although there will be many other options available to them, most people will choose these because such sites will be ones most readily advertised for them, will already hold an affiliation for and interest in them, and will cater to their information gathering and processing needs.

New sources, originating with the Internet, will find the inherent problem with information overload, that is, that "each item of information produced faces more competition in gaining an audience."[14] As a result, the audience will gravitate to those sources most capable of winning such a competition.

That is what this book is all about—to show how that dominance by existing players is occurring and why and how it will continue to happen in the future. The object of this book is not to suggest whether it should or should not happen, only to point out that it is and that this constitutes the future of the Internet in American political life.

Also, before preceding further, it is important to note what this book is not about. This is not a technical book describing how the Internet works or how it will change technologically in the future. It is not a discussion of how the Internet is or should be regulated by government. Also, this is not a book discussing the application of the First Amendment or privacy issues. Nor is it a how-to book describing relevant sites of interest to surfers or offering tips on how to deal with the Internet. Such books have already been written and many more will be written in the future.

This book is about the effect of the Internet on American political power: How the Internet already has changed the shape of political processes and institutions, but also how current political actors have adapted to the Internet's presence and growing role and are using the Internet much as they have used other new media technology in the past.

The following chapters will explain the overtaking of the Internet by players who have dominated other mass media forms. Those chapters following will describe the changes each of these players have made to shape this new medium in order to maintain power in American politics and prevent the very diffusion of power to other players the Internet is supposed to encourage.

The next chapter links the Internet to previous technologies and demonstrates how the existence of new media has resulted in adaption by existing political players rather than a revolution in political activism. Chapter 2 demonstrates how news media organizations have supplemented traditional media forums with the Internet and how the audience has responded. Chapter 3 turns to interest groups, players who have moved onto the Web to carry on, perhaps even more effectively, the functions they have long performed in American politics. Chapter 4 analyzes campaigns and demonstrates how candidates, particularly incumbents, incorporated the Internet during the 1996 campaign and how they will do so in coming elections. Chapter 5 shows how government officials in the legislative, executive, and judicial branches are employing the Web to interact with constituents. Chapter 6 focuses on the ordinary Internet user and demonstrates how the most populist forum of the Internet, Usenet, is ineffective as a forum for gauging public opinion. Chapter 7 offers conclusions about the Internet's place in American politics today and points to what will be its future role.

ONE

Communications Technology and Democracy

Like other new technologies, the Internet has been pro-claimed the instigator of a social revolution.[1] "Today we are witnessing the early, turbulent days of a revolution as signifi-cant as any other in human history," one industry executive opines. "A new medium of human communications is emerging, one that may prove to surpass all previous revolutions—the printing press, the telephone, the television, the computer—in its impact on our economic and social life."[2] Admittedly, the Internet has already in-fluenced American life.

The most coveted activity of most Americans—leisure—in-creasingly has included the Web. Time spent online has increased dramatically. By 1997, 85 percent of users said they go online at least daily.[3] In 1996, half of users said they were online at least 10 hours a week. One-fifth said they stayed online more than 20 hours per week. Indeed, use can exceed access: America Online was se-verely criticized and even sued by some of its customers for dump-ing millions of disks in direct mail campaigns and offering unlim-ited access time without sufficiently increasing their ability to handle new customers.[4] Online services are rushing to increase telephone connections to meet the growing demand.

Though initial use centered on the workplace, where corporate or academic users utilized the Internet for business or research pur-poses, home use has grown. Now people are more likely to go online at home than at work.[5] The Internet has gone from a tool for labor to a leisure activity.[6] Since the amount of leisure time has not in-creased, many people are logging on in lieu of other past activities. For example, 37 percent of Internet users say they go online instead of watching television.[7]

A portent of its future role is the age group to which it most appeals. The Internet has caught the attention of younger people, particularly. According to a Newsweek poll, 61 percent of teenagers say they surf the Net.[8] This fact may be related to the integration of the Internet into colleges and, increasingly, elementary and secondary schools. At many higher education institutions students are expected to own personal computers. Not surprisingly, people under 30 are the most likely to have access to the Internet.[9]

A prerequisite for such growth outside the workplace is the flourishing use of home computers. According to the U.S. Census Bureau, the number of households with computers grew from 6.9 million in 1984 to over 22 million by 1993.[10] By May 1994, one survey estimated one-third of American homes had a personal computer.[11] And by the end of 1997, one survey suggested 43 percent of U.S. households, or over 40 million households, had a personal computer. Also over 50 percent of households with children had a computer in the home.[12]

Sales of computers for home use have increased at a rapid rate. In 1997, sales jumped 76 percent for that market. Computers are moving into homes for personal use at a rapid rate.

Dramatic growth may continue with the introduction of Web TV.[14] The change to digital television will force television set owners to purchase new receivers. That transition could stimulate Internet use if new sets are accessible to Web TV.

The Web does have a more limited appeal than television as a leisure time activity because, in its present form, it is an interactive form of entertainment. Television, on the other hand, is passive. One critic argues that this cardinal difference will limit its appeal because "the consumer doesn't want to work to be entertained."[15] But it has been predicted by Everett Rogers that the Internet will change people's behavior meaning "the era of the passive media audience is gone, or at least going."[16]

Growth in the Web's usage has been directly proportional to the uses the public perceives for it, as evidenced by the range of activities possible on the Web. There has been a dramatic increase in the amount of information available on the Web. The number of Internet domains has mushroomed.[17] Over a four year period (1993–1997) the number of Internet hosts jumped from 1.3 million to just over 16 million. Nearly seven million hosts were added in 1996 alone.[18] Users are far more likely now than in the early

1990s to find sites of interest to them, such as online stores, travel agents, or financial news.

Publicity about the Internet probably sparks escalated interest in getting online. The Internet has become a popular news topic. Coverage by major newspapers increased quickly from an average of two stories per month in September 1992 in 15 leading newspapers to nearly 50 stories monthly by September 1993.[19] The term "Internet" appeared in 157 stories in those major newspapers between September 1 and November 5, 1994. During the same period in 1996, the term was used in 739 stories.[20]

The Internet is no longer a novelty news item for the news media. Rather, it has become a standard news beat and a stock feature of news. Print and broadcast media now have regular cyberspace or Internet related columns or features. The *New York Times* contains in its weekly computer section news articles on Internet-related news. *Time* and *Newsweek* have regular columns on Internet-related developments. *Newsweek*'s column, "Cyberscope," gives information on Internet and other computer-related news. *Time*'s frequent "Netly News" contains news on the Internet specifically. Moreover, knowing that an increasing number of readers are Internet users, news media stories have documented the problems of online services, such as slow service, customer dissatisfaction, or their treatment of pornography. Feature stories highlight the Web's impact on business, culture, and politics.[21]

The Societal Impact

The Internet and Business

Home use is not the only sphere of life affected by the Internet. The corporate world has become a connected world via the Internet. The Internet has affected fundamental functions in the corporate world such as inter- and intracorporate communication and relationships with consumers.

The Internet is reshaping the corporate workplace. Today, many corporations are telling some of their employees not to come into the office for work. Via the Internet, workers can connect to the main office, send e-mail, prepare files, and even attend virtual meetings and conferences, without ever leaving home. The corporation saves on housing an employee in an office and even on benefits when the employee is transferred to an independent contractor relationship. There may be effects on job security, employee morale, or an individual's ability to obtain fringe benefits in such situations, but the bottom line for companies is improved. Many companies also find employees through the Internet by listing job openings on their own site or posting on career placement sites.[22]

The relationship with the consumer is also undergoing change, and there the Internet is making inroads as a sales tool. Consumer shopping is a growing online activity. According to one market study, 73 percent of Web users spend some portion of online time seeking product or service information. That compares with 55 percent who did so in 1995.[23] The Net offers a new way to reach those consumers. Banks are increasingly offering their services online, allowing customers to check their balances or transfer funds across accounts.[24] Airlines list their schedules, auto companies display their latest models, travel agencies offer special tourist packages, bookstores list their stocks, stockbrokers advertise investments—all using the Net to complete the sale.

Another intersection of the Web and business is the growth of display advertising, which now characterizes many Web sites. Many companies are using the Internet as another forum for display advertising. In 1997, advertising revenue on the Web reached $906 million.[25]

Additionally, the Internet has spawned a growing list of exclusively online businesses, such as travel agents, stores, periodicals, bookstores, and even banks.[26] All of this is supplemental to the online access services and Web site developers who find expanding demand for their services.

Such online businesses are flourishing partly because overhead for online businesses is lower than for off-line business. Hence, stockbrokers, for example, can take smaller commissions on online transactions than on traditional ones.[27] Increasingly, entrepreneurs, although wary of a tool unfamiliar to them, are seeking a presence and, even more, a new method for making money.[28] Given the amount of time many users spend online, the corporate world has found a new mechanism for reaching tens of millions of potential customers. In 1996, Internet-based sales reached $733 million, and one market research firm expects Internet-based sales will exceed $2 billion by the year 2000.[29]

Workplace use of the Internet currently is dominated by professionals and managers. In a 1997 survey, 39 percent of users were professionals or managers. This was a decline from 1995, where 50 percent of the Internet users were in this category. But it was still well above the national average—25 percent—for this occupational category.[30] For example, psychiatrists conduct research over the Internet and diagnose patients by obtaining electronic access to files and doctor-patient communication over the Internet.[31] Health professionals are exchanging information over discussion lists and newsgroups.[32] Family physicians can view human anatomy images or multimedia presentations of patient cases.[33]

Pedagogy on the Net

Perhaps the area of greatest interest in employing the Internet is as a tool for education. The Internet has been touted as the new, unprecedented educational agent. According to President Clinton, "The Internet will be the most profoundly revolutionary tool for educating our children in generations. I want to see the day when computers are as much a part of a classroom as blackboards, and we put the future at the fingertips of every American child."[34] Diane Ravitch, an education trends researcher, has described a new world of learning via the Internet: "In this new world of pedagogical plenty, children and adults will be able to dial up a program on their home television to learn whatever they want to know, at their own convenience. If little Eva cannot sleep, she can learn algebra instead."[35]

Universities, particularly research institutions, have long been at the forefront of Internet use, even since the days of the defense department's network. But such usage was a function of research, first military-related and then more broadly defined, and it was limited to faculty and other researchers.

Now the Internet has been discovered as a teaching tool at all levels. Universities are connecting classrooms, establishing etherports in dormitories, and facilitating off-campus usage by students. Some small private colleges are requiring students to purchase personal computers, which now are equipped with modems and Internet services. Increasingly, colleges are offering distance learning courses via the Internet.[36]

More recent has been the movement of the Internet into primary and secondary education. Primary and secondary schoolteachers are clamoring for Internet connections, raising another expenditure issue for school boards and administrators often already straining under budget cuts. Computer hardware expenditures already are an expensive component of school budgets, and the costs of connecting have added more pressure.

The demand is growing because the Net is offering multimedia teaching opportunities educators have only dreamed of. Education oriented sites are proliferating. Teachers can take students on virtual tours of museums, participate in online discussions with experts, and communicate with other students in distant countries. Students are using the Internet to conduct research for term papers, thus expanding their access to resources far beyond their high school or local public libraries. Moreover, many official governmental sites, such as the White House, some government agencies, and state government bureaus, are including educational sections for children.

Social Effects

The social ramifications of the Net are only now being explored. It has forged new relationships by creating so called virtual communities.[37] Enthusiasts for various activities, ideologies, and interests are finding each other through Usenet groups. Some elderly persons are finding the Internet an avenue for communicating with others while still being homebound. Users are developing new online personal relationships, many of which they continue offline.[38] Other users are able to make frequent contact with geographically distant family and friends at a low cost. Still others are locating long, lost friends through online address or e-mail databases.

These activities are transpiring particularly at a time when common public areas, such as town commons and public halls, are no longer the venues for public debate they once were. These virtual communities are "not defined by many of the boundaries that sociologists and others traditionally have used to define communities, especially geography and political boundaries."[39] Moreover, many users find they now can communicate with people who share their interests but whom they would have never met before going online.[40]

Technological innovations do not arise suddenly and acquire a niche in public life without sparking concerns about the effects of that sudden emergence on society. Like television before it, the Web has not come without such public fears.[41] One psychoanalyst of the computer age has warned that "computers don't just do things for us, they do things to us, including to our ways of thinking about ourselves and other people."[42] The Internet has created fears about how this technology will shape our future.

A popular movie called *The Net* was released in 1995. The film describes the story of a young woman whose social life is primarily the virtual community of the Internet, but who finds her identity has been wiped away. Using the Net, villains destroy any evidence of her existence. Though strictly fiction, the film raised compelling questions about where the Internet was going. Was this new technology, if placed in the wrong hands, really capable of ruining our lives? Or, somewhat less nefariously, could our privacy be erased by central information databases possibly accessible to virtually anyone?

News reports of a prison inmate who was able to store a list of thousands of children for a child pornography ring fed public fears that privacy, even for children, is readily violated on the Internet.[43] How much information on us is at anyone's disposal?

These stories, real or imagined, have produced fears of the implications of Internet and e-mail. Reports of unwanted e-mail messages lead to concerns that too many predators are using the Internet to find unsuspecting people. A majority of Americans say they are "very concerned" that activities such as giving out their e-mail address on the Internet or joining various discussion groups or chat rooms can lead to unwanted advances or "virtual" stalking. Many Internet users fear invasion of privacy by a "cookie," a feature that allows a site you visit to monitor your Web activity, not only on their site but other sites as well. As a result, by visiting a site you can give away information about your interests and, in some circumstances, even your e-mail address. This is particularly useful information for junk e-mail distributors.[44]

Yet, access to many sites requires handing over personal information—e-mail addresses, regular mail addresses, telephone numbers, and profiles of our interests, hobbies, and activities. To make purchases on the Net, even credit card information is demanded. The accumulation of such data offers a portrait of each individual that that person may not want online.

In May 1998, Vice President Al Gore proposed an electronic bill of rights designed to protect privacy of Internet users. This came in response to the fact that many Americans fear the Internet will offer too much private information to other people. [45] A Federal Trade Commission survey found that 82 percent of Americans are concerned their privacy will be threatened by the Internet. [46] While a 1996 survey found 39 percent of Internet users shop for products, more than twice the number only one year earlier, only 15 percent say they actually buy items online. [47] According to market surveys, the main reason more people do not make online purchases is "lack of trust in the security of electronic payments." [48] A computer network with so much information accessible to so many individuals may well include information that individuals do not want made public.

Another fear with even greater public visibility has been the extent to which the Internet is a venue to peddle pornography. The accessibility of cyber-pornography to young children has become a major issue for policy makers. Moreover, Internet use by children is expected to mushroom. An estimated 10 million children and teenagers are expected to be online by the year 2002. [49]

The issue has been most acute as Internet use enters the schoolhouse. Some parents object to the use of the Internet as an educational tool for fear students will be exposed to pornography while in school. News reports of online pornography sites feed fears of widespread moral corruption caused by the Internet.

One mother sued America Online for allowing child pornography to be sold via open chat rooms. [50] However, many worried parents are turning instead to filtering products, such as Cyber Patrol and SurfWatch, to screen out undesirable content.

But even the extent to which cyberpornography exists on the Internet is hotly debated. According to some estimates, pornography is only a tiny fraction of the information available on the Net. [51] Out of the thousands of existing news groups, an estimated 250 are sexual related. [52] Yet, Internet pornography is easy to access, no matter the age of the user.

Clearly, the public has come to believe it is a danger, not only to children but also to adults who are vulnerable to sexual exploitation. [53] Critics of the Net point to the story of a young woman who used an Internet chat room to become acquainted with a man who allegedly murdered her after they met in person. *U.S. News and World*

Report opined that "the Internet is a perfect breeding ground for victims looking to be victimized."[54] At the behest of morality groups such as the Family Research Council and the Christian Coalition, Congress passed anti-computer obscenity legislation as part of an omnibus telecommunications bill. President Clinton signed the bill on February 8, 1996. However, in 1997 the U.S. Supreme Court overturned the bill as restrictive of free speech.[55]

In turn, this issue has mobilized a newly existent group—Internet users who perceive any content restrictions to be a violation of their right to transmit and receive any information they desire. During and immediately following discussion of the bill, sympathetic Webmasters adorned their sites with blue ribbons to protest government censorship of the Internet.

News media coverage has highlighted the Internet presence of groups not within the traditional mainstream. Socialists "chat" on "SocNet: The Socialist Party Online," the discussion group for American Socialists. Right wing use of the Internet has proliferated as well. Users who tap into the Stormfront White Nationalists home page, which has as its slogan "white pride world wide," can download images of a Nazi flag. In militia newsgroups, subscribers discuss the mystery of unmarked black helicopters at U.S. military bases and the virtues of various types of semiautomatic weapons. The news media message is blunt: The Internet could be used by extremists to get someone you love to join a fringe religious group, a terrorist organization, a militia group, or even just a group with an extreme political ideology.

Still another worry is the potential addictive nature of Internet use. Reports circulate of individuals becoming hooked through "going online" and spending hours browsing through Web sites or reading and posting messages on Usenet groups. Spouses are complaining that Internet use has captured their husbands or wives. Students reportedly spend hours in front of computer terminals, miss classes, and flunk out of school. One physician described it as "a silent addiction that sort of creeps into your home. It's just a computer and it seems so harmless."[56]

Another fear is that the addiction of gambling, coupled with the Internet, will create an unregulated casino gambling culture. Gaming sites have been proliferating outside of legal supervision or control.[57]

Separate from the cyberporn issue, parental concern is rising over children's use of the Internet. Similar to the video game craze of a previous decade, when critics contended youth were rotting their minds and atrophying their bodies spending hour upon hour playing Nintendo or Sega games, parents worry that too much time on the Internet is not healthy for children.[58]

Tellingly, these new social problems have spawned a literature of self-help Internet-related books. These new offerings give tips on how to avoid Internet-related problems, such as commercial scams, false romances, electronic junk mail, and cyberpornography.[59]

A major social cost of the Internet is the growing tendency toward social isolation. The Internet may connect us virtually with the far reaches of the globe, but leave us with little *real* contact with those who live next door. As Stephen Doheny-Farina opines, the "net seduces us and further removes us from our localities." The Internet, he contends, can be a positive force within local communities, but not as substitutes for them.[60]

Yet, such a virtual world could be perceived as preferable to the real world. The Internet offers a world largely within our control. We can close our connection to a site or cut off a conversation anytime we wish. Social contact comes with protective gloves that screen us from the sometimes unpleasant task of dealing with certain other people in real world situations.

The Internet itself may feed the perception that the world is a scary place and online discussions are safer than real ones. As one analyst of the Internet concluded, "maybe that security is the allure, in a day and age when the man next door is as likely to pull out an automatic weapon as he is to come at you with a clever rebuttal."[61]

This social isolation is accompanied by a perception of virtual belonging. People believe they are connected with others, even when they really are geographically distant, such as a couple in a rural town in Colorado: "Although we are six hours from Denver, with our computers, telephones, fax machine, and Federal Express we are as in touch with the rest of the world as if we were in downtown Tokyo or London."[62]

In all fairness, the Internet is not the sole cause of such social isolationism. It is only the latest in a series of communications technology innovations, offering more individual control not only over the content of media messages, but also where and how such messages are delivered. Home entertainment centers—complete with big screen television monitors, video tape recorders, CD players, and video disc players—have lured people home and alone rather than away from home and in groups.

The Internet also has sparked another gender gap. Generally, men have embraced the Internet more than women.[63] Men are more likely to go online in the first place and to spend more time online. That gender gap may close in the future, however as, more and more women are going online, particularly younger women.[64] By 1997, between 38 and 42 percent of online users were women.[65]

Even if that chasm is bridged, there may be another gap between the sexes in the types of activities conducted on line. When both men and women go online they do so for different purposes.[66] Women do so more for personal e-mail communication, while men gather information from sites.

Another fear of the Internet, and one similar to that claimed when television spread across the United States as well as the world, is the creation of a single homogeneous culture both in the United States and in the world. The concern about cultural hegemony is not new, but the Internet has exacerbated the concern. Globally, the anxiety is over further hegemony by the West over indigenous cultures already affected by satellite television.

Moreover, the Internet possesses the potential to create even greater homogenization. While satellites are limited geographically, the Internet is not. The text-based nature of the Internet has already aided English, which is the language of most of the Internet, over other languages. The dominance of English on the Net is of particular concern to other nations, such as France, who are sensitive about preserving their own culture and language.[67]

Yet, as text-based Internet information is replaced by audio and visual images, the possibility for cultural dominance increases. Web TV may allow users across the globe to choose programming from any region of the world, which clearly offers an advantage to Western culture. Since Internet domains are most common in the United States and Western Europe, and these two areas will likely lead in the development of Web TV for some time to come, they could long remain the primary sites for users in other parts of the world.

The Internet has already affected commerce—national and international—both within and between corporations and in the relationship with consumers. It has facilitated information transfer for professionals. It offers opportunities, but also potential dangers, for our educational system. It is reshaping social relationships, yet with possible costs.

Yet, one area has not been discussed—politics. What are the predictions about the Internet's effect on our political system? That is our subject now.

The Promise of Political Participation

According to the predictions concerning its political role, the Internet holds great promise. *Newsweek* columnist Howard Fineman called it, "the new Louisiana Purchase, an uncharted west." The political role of new communication technology has been termed a "great transformation."[68]

The Internet is viewed as a vehicle for educating individuals, stimulating citizen participation, measuring public opinion, easing citizen access to government officials, offering a public forum, simplifying voter registration, and even facilitating actual voting.[69] It has been termed a "powerful technology for grassroots democracy" and one that by "facilitating discussion and collective action by citizens, strengthens democracy."[70] It also has been called potentially "the most powerful tool for political organizing developed in the past fifty years."[71] Some organizations are already attempting to implement Web-based voter information and participation systems.[72] Books, like *How to Access the Federal Government on the Internet 1997*, *Environmental Guide to the Internet*, and *Politics on the Net*, have appeared to guide Internet users to sites of interest to them in order to facilitate their roles as active citizens.[73]

Even more grandly, according to some observers, the Internet is imbued with a capability to restructure relations between people on the planet and solve vexing economic, social, and political problems. Repeatedly, Vice President Al Gore has painted a bright future with the Internet, or "Global Information Infrastructure," as a worldwide communications device:

> These highways . . . will allow us to share information, to connect, and to communicate as a global community. From these connections we will derive robust and sustainable economic progress, strong democracies, better solutions to global and local environmental

challenges, improved health care, and—ultimately—a greater sense of shared stewardship of our small planet.

The Global Information Infrastructure will help educate our children and allow us to exchange ideas within a community and among nations. It will be a means by which families and friends will transcend the barriers of time and distance. It will make possible a global information marketplace, where consumers can buy or sell products.[74]

As the Internet spokesperson for the Clinton administration, Gore claimed that the knowledge received from the information superhighway would "spread participatory democracy," thus granting people access to information essential for participating in a representative democracy. He envisioned a global conversation "in which everyone who wants can have his or her say."[75] Gore's statement reflects a widespread appellation for the Internet as the ultimate democracy because "no computer is 'above' any other . . . neither IBM nor the White House has any special advantage over a 15-year-old clever enough to set up his own connection. Class, hierarchy, and even physical location count for nothing on the Internet."[76]

Similarly, President Clinton views the Internet as "our new town square." "The day is coming when every home will be connected to it (the Internet) and it will be just as normal a part of our life as a telephone and a television."[77] And Senator John Ashcroft of Missouri suggests the information age "redefines the way citizens can communicate and participate in our democracy. As Washington resists change, new technologies and the Internet are providing new avenues for people to be involved in changing government."[78]

The claims of proponents of an Internet revolution in political participation can be sorted into three categories: citizen information, interaction between citizens and government, and policy making.

The most common promise of the Internet is twofold: an increase in information readily available to the average citizen, and more individual control over what information is received. Combined, these two promise true citizen awareness. Political scientist Anthony Corrado concludes that the result may well be "a revitalized democracy characterized by a more active and informed citizenry."[79] And

Howard Fineman has opined: "Access to political information is being radically democratized."[80]

Undoubtedly, the Web has already made accessible to users extensive amounts of information in electronic form. Previously, access to this material would have required extensive research and long hours in libraries. Furthermore, the future bodes well for more information appearing, much of which could be useful for political purposes.

The extent of such information currently available for free on the Net is astounding: data on PAC contributions to candidates for federal office; the voting records of individual members of Congress; the full texts of legislation, executive agreements, treaties, and speeches; transcripts of press conferences, and on and on. This is in addition to the plethora of news media sources that are now available online.

Citizens armed with such information, it is claimed, will then be able to interact intelligently with government officials to articulate their concerns.[81] Such electronic interaction is already becoming a common feature of communication between elected officials and interested constituents. On January 13, 1994, Vice President Al Gore was the first federal government official to conduct an online news conference with Internet users.[82] Other officials, including presidential candidates and state officials, have conducted similar sessions.[83]

According to former PBS president Lawrence Grossman, the Internet is making the previously passive into political activists: "In kitchens, living rooms, dens, bedrooms, and workplaces throughout the nation, citizens have begun to apply such electronic devices to political purposes, giving those who use them a degree of empowerment they never had before."[84]

Perhaps the greatest expectation of the Internet is its promise to help average citizens affect policy. Involvement by common citizens, it is predicted, will alter the policy-making process, thus enabling the citizenry to instantaneously communicate their wishes to their representatives. "By pushing a button, typing on-line, or talking to a computer, they will be able to tell their president, senators, members of Congress, and local leaders what they want them to do and in what priority order."[85]

In response to criticism that this kind of democratic participation is dangerous, proponents argue that, if properly informed, the citizenry are capable of serving in such a role. The solution is not to undo technology, but to educate the public to perform their essential democratic tasks.[86]

The Realities of Political Participation

The above scenario is appealing in an age of intense cynicism about the common person's ability to affect policy. Yet, plainly the realities of political participation intrude. These lofty predictions assume something quite unusual—dramatic changes in human behavior. Anthony Corrado admits that the success of new technology as a democratic tool depends on "the willingness of significant numbers of citizens to take advantage of these extraordinary new tools to engage in meaningful political discourse, become better informed voters, and get more involved in civic life."[87]

However, there is no evidence such a change will occur. The scenario of an active, informed electorate gathering information and expressing opinions electronically is accurate for some individuals—those who are already politically interested and motivated. For that group, the Internet will be a tremendous boon in the process of collecting information, interacting with policy makers, and, indeed, shaping policy.

But for the majority who are less politically interested, this scenario is unreal. These people will not be more likely, just because of a technological innovation, to suddenly acquire an interest in politics and follow the above scenario. As Russell Neuman has noted, "the mass citizenry, for most issues, simply will not take the time to learn more or understand more deeply, no matter how inexpensive or convenient further learning may be."[88]

Granted, some individuals do become mobilized. The portrait of the common citizen armed with information, capable of intelligently lobbying elected officials, and changing the course of policy is alluring. Greater citizen awareness and participation are ideal outcomes in democracies. Again, such interventions do occur in American politics. These sudden activists, such as Candy Lightner and John Walsh, have become transformed into political lobbyists usually as a result of some cataclysmic event in their lives.[89] Certainly, these actions should be encouraged, applauded, fostered.

But they are rare; they are truly exceptions, not the rule. Moreover, they did not occur because of the existence of a new technology or the ready availability of information.

Do not misunderstand. This is not an argument for dismantling the Internet, if that were possible. Rather, it is a reality check—placing the Internet in the light of human behavior.

Choice

First, it does not necessarily follow that making information more readily available to more people and allowing the individual more control over that information produces well-informed and politically engaged citizens. It may not occur to proponents of this Internet revolution that the latter change (control) may actually cancel out the supposed positive effects of the former (readily available information). That is because most Americans don't choose to become politically informed and engaged, except in rare circumstances. With the exception of the already politically interested, most people will not normally gravitate to political information, even if it is readily available. The majority of adult Americans do not watch national network television news regularly.[90] More than four in 10 adults do not read a newspaper daily.[91]

In the first place, for many people, having a choice will mean choosing not to go online, now or in the future. As indicated earlier, people in older age groups are less likely to be Internet users than younger people. One survey found that young people (ages 18–29) were four times as likely than older people to peruse political web sites. This suggests the newest generation is the most familiar with and interested in using the Web to gather political information.[92] Yet even among those under 30, over 60 percent do not use the Internet regularly. Even many in the "Internet generation" have chosen not to go online.[93]

It is quite probable that large segments of the populace will never go online. This has been true for cable television, where even though 91 percent, or 99 million households, have access to cable, one-third of the population declines to be connected.[94] The reasons for avoidance of the Internet may vary—lack of time, lack of perceived technological ability, unwillingness to pay—but the outcome will be the same.

Of course those who do go online may well find the Internet a useful tool, but not for political purposes. One 1996 survey taken during the presidential campaign, when political interest among citizens usually peaks, found that only 6 percent of voters visited political sites and less than 1 percent of voters used campaign-related information from the Internet.[95]

Undoubtedly these figures will grow. As Internet use increases, more people will use the Internet for political information. But as more people go online, the percentages of the total users who go online for news and information actually will likely decline. A new group of less politically interested users will appear. For example, the percentage of Internet users who were registered to vote slipped from 92 percent in early 1996 to 82 percent by December 1997.[96] While a majority of longtime users go online to follow up on a traditional media story, only 34 percent of new users (defined as people who have started using the Web only during the past six months) do so. New users are more interested than longtime users in sites featuring nonpolitical information such as sports and entertainment.[97] And these new users also are less likely than longtime users to use e-mail for political purposes.[98]

So, even among those who go online, many will choose to do so for other purposes than politics. For them, the Internet has work functions, personal communication advantages, or mere entertainment value, but it is not a tool for political participation.

Representation

Given what has just been said, it should come as no surprise to learn that Internet users are not representative of the general population. This is particularly true of those who use the Internet for political newsgathering. How politically different Internet users are from nonusers is unclear. But there is some evidence suggesting Internet users are substantially different. According to a Pew Research Center survey in 1996, 38 percent of online users made annual incomes of over $50,000, compared with 22 percent of the general population. Sixty-nine percent of users had at least some college education versus 44 percent of the general population. Rural dwellers constitute 21 percent of the population, but only 14 percent of the online usership.[99] Also, while one-third of the general public is under 35, 50 percent of Internet users are under 35. And there is the issue of gender as well. Fifty-seven percent of Internet users are male, while only 46 percent of the general public are.[100]

Evidence suggests users also are unrepresentative politically, yet it is unclear in what partisan direction. For example, according to one survey during the 1996 campaign, Internet users were more likely to be Republican or Independent and more supportive of Robert Dole than the public at large.[101] Yet, still other research points to a leftist or libertarian dominance.[102] Twenty-seven percent of users consider themselves "left-liberals" while one-quarter call themselves libertarians.[103]

Partisanship or ideology is not the only distinguishing factor. Internet users are more knowledgeable about politics. During 1996, 71 percent of Internet users could identify Bob Dole as the candidate proposing an across-the-board 15 percent tax cut, while only 59 percent of the general public could do so.[104] They are more politically active than the public at large. Internet users are far more likely than nonusers to discuss politics with family members or friends or contact a public official about a problem by writing a letter or sending e-mail. They are somewhat more likely to try to convince someone else to vote for a particular candidate. They are also more commonly registered voters than others. According to one survey, 86 percent of Internet users are registered to vote, more than 10 percent higher than the general population.[105] But since Internet users are drawn from a demographic more prone to be voters than the general public, such activity should be no surprise.

Another difference between users and nonusers is in respective feelings of internal political efficacy. Online users feel they have greater ability to affect the political process than nonusers. The fact that users fall in higher socioeconomic categories might account at least partially for this finding.[106]

A major drawback to the Internet user population as representative is the fact that certain populations are absent. Part of that limitation stems from the decision not to go online, especially for politics, as we just discussed. But there are also people who cannot go online for financial reasons. Virtual communities so far have disadvantaged certain groups, such as the inhabitants of most countries in the developing world, as well as the poor in already industrialized nations. Even within the United States, the poor, minorities, rural people, and the elderly are least likely to have access to the Net.[107] The existence of such neglected groups is common with new technologies.[108]

Accessibility for those least able to pay has long been a concern about new technology, including the Internet. For example, the Telecommunications Policy Roundtable, a consortium of 71 non-profit groups, recommended that policy makers designing the information highway assure, among other goals, that

1. There is free access to all.
2. There exists an "electronic commons" for public debate.
3. There is a marketplace of ideas accessible to all, not limited by commercial carriers.

Even if these goals could be achieved, it is doubtful there would be a flood of people rushing to participate in the "electronic commons" of public debate. It is hard to imagine that very many people who are in these disadvantaged groups will take the time or make the effort to become involved. This is true not because they might not wish to be involved if circumstances were different. Rather, it is because the value of such participation is not apparent, particularly given the fact that other demands of life—obtaining an income, raising a family, securing a modest standard of living—are of greater immediate importance.

Politics and the New Media

The Internet is the latest in a series of major mass communications technology innovations (which primarily appeared during the twenieth century). Each new innovation in turn has been similarly heralded as a major breakthrough in public information and political participation. One broadcast historian even concluded that "since the dawn of history, each new medium has tended to undermine an old monopoly, shift the definitions of goodness and greatness, and alter the climate of men's lives."[109]

The expectation of positive effects of the new media on American politics rests on an assumption of democratic politics, that is, that new mass communications technology enhances political participation by increasing the quantity of available information for mass participation and thereby stimulating mobilization. Interactive communications technology holds the greatest promise because it offers the potential for gauging public opinion and register-ing mass decisions. It decentralizes communication with the result of upsetting hierarchical relationships and fostering equality be-tween communicators.[110]

The implication of this thesis is that communications technol-ogy constructs the platform for a populist movement that will revo-lutionize mass political participation.[111] Granted, there have been dissenting voices who see new technology as destructive or at least possessed of traits producing negative effects.[112] But the historical picture has been one of high expectations of the beneficial influ-ences of new technology.

Newspapers were the first medium to be hailed as a major break-through in citizen information and, ultimately, participation. First published in the early 1600s, these broadsheets, as they appeared initially, were seen as technologies "that were to transform society, while bringing to the peoples of many lands an improved service of information. . . . The newspaper press . . . became the cutting edge in man's battle against ignorance, isolation, superstition, autoc-racy, drift and misunderstanding. It is only stating a fact to say that the printing press, and newspapers in particular, brought a new equality to men, and brought the world into focus."[113]

Similarly, Anne Ellsworth's first words on Samuel F. B. Morse's new invention, the telegraph, "What hath God wrought," signaled a major new era in the history of the human race.[114] The telegraph was a force designed to unite the nations. Morse himself predicted the invention would bring together the nation. " [I]t would not be long ere the whole surface of this country would be channelled for those nerves which are to diffuse, with the speed of thought, a knowledge of all that is occurring throughout the land; making, in fact, one neighborhood of the whole country."[115]

But it is the twentieth century which has been the most active in communications technology development. New innovations stepped over one another and won rapid public embrace, as well as acclaim, as new tools in the reshaping of power structures. Understandably, this age has been termed "the communications revolution."[116]

Early in the twenieth century, wireless radio was received with the same praise as had the newspaper and the telegraph. Radio's ar-rival was called a "new miracle."[117] The radio's potential went even further by transcending the literacy barrier. As radio receivers became more portable and transmitters proliferated across the globe, the radio was seen as a major advance in informing an uninformed public, and, with the aid of networks, in offering truly mass communication with reach to hundreds of millions simultaneously.

Television followed closely on the heels of radio. By allowing viewers to see with their own eyes, rather than merely hearing with their ears, television added another sense to radio—one certain to increase public comprehension and public enlightenment. Moreover, television would produce truth, as opposed to the filter of print. At the 1939 New York World's Fair, David Sarnoff called television "a torch of hope in a troubled world" and a local television broadcaster predicted that "the most outstanding of the contributions that television can be expected to make to further democracy ... will be its unique usefulness as a means of public information."[118]

Then came coaxial, the wire in the ground that gave television viewers not five or six channels, but 40 or 50, and eventually 100. In the early 1970s, cable was viewed, seemingly, as "about to effect a revolution in communications."[119]

In political terms, cable expanded the range of viewing options by offering, mainly through new networks such as CNN and C-SPAN, live, unfiltered access to politics and policy making. Congressional committee hearings, presidential candidates' speeches, candidate debates, and academic conferences all became viewable by millions of Americans across the country.

Cable was not a unique communication medium, like radio or television, since it was an extension of an existing medium, television. However, that extension, coupled with satellite broadcasting, had an enormous impact on broadcast television. These two—cable and satellite—should be treated in tandem because the past 20 years in television industry history has been the story of the combination of cable and satellite to expand broadcast television program offerings far beyond the narrow confines of a few allocated VHF frequencies in a market area.

In each case, the new media were viewed as upsetting the old order and establishing a new one based on the traits of the new technology. One essayist has called information technology "the quintessential engine of fractious, late twentieth century democracy, in which individuality is prized and people won't tolerate being pawns of big institutions or a mass marketplace."[120]

Yet that is not what really happened. Existing media did not fold in response. Power structures did not crumble. The public did not rise up and become suddenly powerful players vis-à-vis media or government.

Instead, the reaction was quite different. At each innovation in the history of mass communications, existing media and other actors adapted to the new technologies and incorporated them. Rather than losing power, they retained it. Some might even argue they extended it.

Radio

For example, when radio emerged as a new form of communications ready for consumer use, newspapers faced a dilemma. Radio's advantages were apparent; it could carry news faster than newspapers, offering late-breaking news that even newspapers with three editions a day could not do. Even more threatening, it was personal. Hearing the human voice was an appealing draw for a news audience accustomed to the dry, impersonal form of print. Moreover, rather than ending up as a gimmick, it became a commercial success, receiving the quick embrace of the public. In 1925, 10 percent of American families owned radio sets. A decade later, two thirds had radio receivers.[121] This growth occurred even in the midst of the Great Depression.

To existing media, particularly newspapers, this was perceived as bad news. Local radio stations were a financial threat. The formation of broadcast networks constituted an even greater danger. Newspapers first resisted the new medium, even attempting to boycott the printing of programming schedules and preventing radio stations from subscribing to the Associated Press wire.[122] Then newspapers, with the encouragement of the broadcast networks, took over the new medium. By late 1932, 239 radio stations were either owned by or affiliated with newspapers.[123] Broadcasters and print had formed such a strong alliance that further attempts to regulate broadcasting were opposed by both.[124]

Newspapers were not the only organizations determined to use this new medium. Religious organizations, department stores, hotels, and other businesses were early sponsors of new stations.[125] Many of these stations merely served as advertising bulletins for their sponsors.[126] (Much the same would be true with the corporate world's movement onto the Internet.)

Radio broadcasting posed a new dilemma for the federal government as well. The potential existed for this new medium to become a vehicle for populism. Many stations censored such views, but others became a forum for them.

A conflict arose about the extent to which public groups, other than commercial interests, would have access to the medium. For example, the Chicago Federation of Labor and the Paulist Fathers, a religious order of New York, operated radio stations in Chicago and New York, respectively, and sought to survive in the midst of competition from commercial interests.[127] The already established broadcasters, such as NBC and CBS, argued successfully for the complete commercialization of the medium. As a result, commercial enterprises dominated radio, with public broadcasting languishing.[128]

Rather than upsetting the existing balance of power, radio became a tool in the hands of already established players—newspapers, interest groups, business, and even government.

Television

The next innovation, television, received similar treatment as had radio. Television broadcasting, which emerged as a commercial entity in the late 1940s, was greeted as a counterweight to the power of radio and, especially, the print media. As radio had done to newspapers in the 1920s and 1930s, television became the major competitor for radio in terms of public interest and, in turn, advertising dollars. Television sets were in 33 percent of households within seven years of the first commercial sale of receivers.[129] Radio news and entertainment programs would move quickly into television.

But, in actuality, existing radio networks and ownership groups, usually dominated by newspapers, quickly expanded their influence into the new medium. The major networks—NBC, CBS, Dumont, and ABC—rapidly applied for, and were granted, local television licenses in major markets, many of which also included network-owned radio affiliates. Other regional groups already in the radio business, such as Storer Broadcasting, Cox Enterprises, Taft, and King, also joined in. Newspapers, such as the *Washington*

Post, the *Detroit Evening News,* and the *Washington Evening Star* also obtained initial licenses in their respective markets.[130]

By the mid-1970s, one-quarter of all VHF television stations in the nation were owned by newspaper-based groups, while another 21 percent were owned by broadcasting groups. And network owned and operated VHF stations constituted over one-third of stations in the top ten markets in the United States.[131]

Television's rapid expansion across the nation in the 1950s raised questions about election coverage. Minor party candidates saw this new vehicle as a means to gain exposure to a mass audience. But Congress wrote the Equal Time provision (known as Section 315) in such a way as to eliminate those candidates from airtime. While broadcasters were required to provide "equal access," it did not mean free time or even any time at all. As a result, broadcasters, understandably from their perspective, chose to sell time, rather than give it away. Since candidates other than Democrats or Republicans rarely possessed the financial resources to buy time, Section 315 effectively excluded minor party candidates. Moreover, news and documentaries were exempted from the equal time requirement.

Like radio, television was a medium with revolutionary expectations, but also like radio, it did not provoke a political, populist revolution.

Cable

Cable television began in 1949 when a Pennsylvania television set retailer decided to boost transmission to his rural community by setting up a master antenna connected to each subscriber's household by a coaxial cable. Other communities quickly followed suit. By 1960, there were an estimated 650 cable systems in the United States, although most were located in small, rural communities. By the early 1970s, cable had expanded to nearly 3,000 systems reaching 11 percent of homes.[132] Today cable access reaches more than 90 percent of homes.[133] Cable expanded the number of channels possible and reduced the interference associated with direct broadcasting via transmitters or satellite. Moreover, it offered consumers the advantage of receiving the service at a lower cost than having to purchase expensive satellite dishes.

Not surprisingly, broadcast networks and media conglomerates already owning local broadcast stations invested in cable systems.[134] In the early 1970s, one-half of cable systems were owned by other media companies.[135] By the early 1980s, the vast majority of cable systems were linked to media conglomerates. More than one-third of cable systems were connected to broadcast stations and another 16 percent to newspapers.[136]

One broadcast executive admitted the movement into new systems was an attempt to be on top of an anticipated revolution:

> I got into cable early because I saw it as another means of communication. . . . But we got into it for the same reason we got into . . . television. We feel that it will expand the opportunity for public service. It will be profitable, of course. It has to be if we're going to make it provide public service. And it's going to be the new world of communications. It will revolutionize everything we're doing today.[137]

With a multitude of available channels, cable's programming appetite was enormous. Because of the plethora of channels, the strategy of cable channels would be "narrowcasting," appealing to highly specific audiences—children, evangelical Christians, Spanish speakers, African Americans—rather than "broadcasting," which had been the method of network broadcasters.

However, local cable systems were not designed to compete with network production capabilities. They were the mechanics and technicians, not the producers. Thus, satellite channels were spawned to meet that programming need. HBO and CNN, offering entertainment and news respectively, were early entrants on the cable scene. Others came quickly, including superstations, such as WTBS (Atlanta) and WGN (Chicago); additional news and public affairs offerings such as the Financial News Network and C-SPAN; and niche entertainment programming such as the Christian Broadcasting Network, Nickelodeon, and the Discovery Channel.

The success of cable and satellite naturally drew the interest of media conglomerates. Existing media conglomerates invested in the new technologies. CNN and TBS were the creations of Ted Turner, who owned Atlanta station WTBS. Time Inc. financed the success of HBO. NBC started CNBC.

Groups also entered the cable market. Reverend Pat Robertson started Christian Broadcasting Network, which was later renamed the Family Channel. Hispanics started Univision, Galavision, and Telemundo, all Spanish language channels. BET targeted African

Americans. Cable channels became the domain of racial and ethnic groups.[138]

The story of cable's development eventually resembled other new media technologies. Like radio and television before it, cable was transformed into a forum for existing media players to continue their role in American society and politics.

Despite the historical trend, repeatedly each new communications medium has been hailed as a watershed for participatory democracy. The printing press transferred knowledge to the literate masses. The radio receiver transcended the literacy barrier and, with the aid of networks, offered truly mass communication with reach to hundreds of millions simultaneously. Television allowed viewers to see with their own eyes and reduced the filter of print or the single sensory nature of radio. Cable expanded the range of viewing options and through new networks such as CNN and C-SPAN offered live, often unfiltered access to politics and policy making.

The Newest Media

The most recent addition to this pantheon of communications technology innovations, the newest media, is the Internet. The Internet is not as new as it appears; in fact, it has a much longer history than is generally known. The Internet was established in 1969 at the University of Southern California, for national defense uses, as a way to connect various local computer networks through "gateways" or linking systems. The Department of Defense (DOD) became the backbone of the system early on, although other governmental bodies, such as the National Science Foundation and NASA, subsequently joined in. Research institutions, particularly those linked to national defense, participated as well.[139]

Separate private online services were started up in the 1970s to serve specialized customers. In 1973, Mead Data Central took their Lexis legal information service online for their clients. Westlaw provided a similar service in 1975. Five years later the Nexis news service, containing full texts of print media, was added to Lexis services.

CompuServe began the first online access service for customers in 1979.[140] Other services, including America Online, Prodigy, and

MSN (Microsoft Network) followed. By 1997, America Online boasted eight million subscribers, while CompuServe had over five million, and MSN had two million.[141] These online services were in turn succeeded by an array of local access providers.[142]

By the late 1980s, the DOD had set up a separate Net system for the network of military research sites. Simultaneously, but now independently, the nonmilitary side of the Internet began to flourish with the support of the National Science Foundation. In the late 1980s, academic institutions and research institutes constituted a large proportion of Internet users and supporters. However, soon thereafter commercial users began to sign on. By the mid-1990s, with the introduction of the World Wide Web (WWW), commercial users burgeoned and became the predominate users of the Internet. Government funding, which initially constituted the bulk of Internet support, was eliminated by the mid-1990s. A network of computer access providers then became the backbone of the Internet.

Yet, this newest media, given its multifaceted nature, is qualitatively different from previous technologies. It seems well suited as a forum for political participation because it possesses traits that have not appeared before and certainly not all together. One such characteristic is interactive simultaneous mass transmission and reception, which is much like a telephone, except on a very big party line. In "chat rooms," for example, people can "talk" interactively with potentially large groups of people participating.

The Net thus erases the distinctions between communication transmitter and receiver. Unlike the audience for newspapers, radio, TV5 cable, and satellite, Internet users can both send and receive mass messages. The term "self-publishing" has acquired a new meaning as users create Web pages with their own individual statements—social, religious, economic, or even political.

The Internet thus breaks down long-standing barriers between traditional media—print and broadcast, daily and weekly, general interest and narrow interest. The Internet integrates text, audio, and visual presentations on the same site. Which has far-reaching implications for the news media. On the Internet, the strict categories delineating types of mass media are fading.

Still another barrier removed by the Internet is the one between mass communication and interpersonal communication. Users can send a message one-on-one via private e-mail or instantaneously turn that message into mass communication through transmission to a discussion group.

The Internet is a range of mediums all in one. Morris and Ogan have succinctly summarized the Internet's simultaneous multiplicity of functions:

> Each point in the traditional model of the communication process can, in fact, vary from one to a few to many on the Internet. Sources of the messages can range from one person in E-mail communication, to a social group in a Listserve or Usenet group, to a group of professional journalists in a World Wide Web page. The messages themselves can be traditional journalistic news stories created by a reporter and editor, stories created over a long period of time by many people, or simply conversations. . . . The receivers, or audiences, of these messages can also number from one to potentially millions, and may or may not move fluidly from their role as audience members to producers of messages.[143]

Given these characteristics, it is logical to suggest that the Internet's power to revolutionize the relationship between citizen and government is greater than other traditional media. Most critically, each new technology offering in the past featured only unidirectional communication. For example, while radio and television offered new venues for information dissemination, they did not provide innate mechanisms for interactivity. Listeners or viewers could not respond via these media. Nor could they establish their own means of transmitting, due to excessive cost, government licensing, and the requirement of technical competence. Hence, those who controlled the gates of the media were alone capable of transmitting. Cable had the potential for two-way communication. But such experiments were limited to small communities and inevitably failed to catch on even within those areas.

As a two-way mass communications medium that allows users to receive news and information, as well as participate in information transmission and public discussion, the Internet potentially diffuses power over information dissemination and public debate. That ability even extends to overt lobbying by individuals in behalf of their own political interests. And the technology may even facilitate the most formal of public inputs—the vote.

Such capability has prompted observers to conclude that the Internet is the people's instrument. It will increase mass participation because of the ease not only of accessing news and information, but also the simplicity and rapidity of the process of communicating with policy makers or joining a public discussion group. In a democracy facing steep declines in voting and communal activity and immersed in a wave of rampant public cynicism toward governmental institutions and processes, greater mass participation in the political system, even via electronic means, is widely viewed as a public good.

Moreover, it is argued, this new electronic communication will shift power from elites to the common people. One advocate predicts that less active, less vocal citizens "have opinions too, and in a democracy they should have an equal right to have them heard. The new information technology could put them on an equal footing for the first time."[144]

This prediction will occur because the Internet is not structured. The Internet has been described as "an essentially unregulated, free speech environment, governed at best by ad hoc protocols and informal customs."[145] The very chaos of it offers the opportunity for real democracy. "The vision is that the net becomes so complex and decentralized that no power structure can control it."[146]

But in terms of the future role ascribed to it, the Internet is quite similar to earlier technological breakthroughs. It will be treated like other new technologies, that is, as a means for existing players to continue their roles.

The Internet and American Politics

Like other new communications technology, the Internet has created a vacuum that needs to be filled. That vacuum is the organization of this new technology. Since it is new and its purposes are yet undefined, a new communications technology offers the opportunity for existing players to define it and therefore shape it. As Kenneth Laudon has posited, " each technology imposes restrictions on who has access to the information potential and who controls its flow—what we call "the mode of organization."[147] The Internet's apparent chaos will produce a mode of organization benefitting those players capable of offering it structure and meaning for average citizens.

That vacuum is even larger in this case because of the way the Internet has grown. Though initially created under the auspices of the Department of Defense, the Internet soon became a free-wheeling network of networks with no central control or moderator. Anyone could establish a gopher or Web site. The rules were, essentially, "no rules." When some Internet regulars occasionally attempted to establish rules, they lacked any enforcement mechanism, a feature they themselves, incongruously, also lauded.

The Internet is similar to radio in its initial days. Entrepreneurs could establish stations and broadcast on any frequencies they wished. The rules of broadcasting did not exist. Only when the federal government stepped in was order created.

The anarchy of the Internet was viewed by longtime users as a cardinal virtue of the Internet. They sought to preserve the Internet as the "last frontier." They claimed the Internet would not be the Internet without such looseness. According to Sheizaf Rafaeli, due to the Internet's history, lack of structure is inherent. "[T]he organizing principle is to have no organization, or deliberate, orderly anarchy."[148] Moreover, many longtime users of the Net regard this disorganization as a means for evading centralized control, government intervention, and, ultimately, censorship.

However, that very lack of structure on the Internet constitutes a major complaint of new Internet users today. Users suffer from information overload. Many newer users consider the lack of organization to be a detraction. One analyst knowingly complained that "there's no map to all this clutter, not even a promontory where you can stand and get your bearings. . . . You have to grope and delve and sift your way along, learning by trial and error."[149]

Worse still, the chaos of the Internet, which is such a redeeming virtue for many Internet veterans, could become its downfall with the average user. It could relegate the Internet to the fate of eight-track tapes or the Edsel. The Internet's disarray is a huge barrier to its expansion, particularly as a political tool. For example, while Internet use has climbed, political use may not have. In January 1996, 8 percent of adults said they went online at least one to two days per week for current events and political information. Even in a presidential election year, that number had remained unchanged six months later.[150]

However, such a fate does not await this medium. Rather, the Internet will be imbued with structure. In fact, that process is already underway and will accelerate. One analyst has called the current period the "Internet's adolescent stage."[151] In this stage, it has thrived on chaos and rewarded primarily the most faithful computer afficionados, those who enjoy spending time surfing the Web and relying on serendipity to discover newer, more interesting bits of information. On the other hand, others seek to use it but do not have the time or inclination to spend hours surfing and may pass it by if they see no value there for them.

However, instead of cultivating such avoidance, the Internet will move into a responsible adulthood as it is refined and structured. Structure will be provided by the very players who offer structure to news and information dissemination offline. These are the traditional news media, established interest groups, candidates, and governmental institutions. Let's see how that is already occurring.

TWO

Surfing for News

> Imagine sitting in front of your wall-screen television in 2001 and seeing a news story about a fire swept out of control by the Santa Ana winds in southern California. Using your voice recognition TV response system, you ask for more video about the fires, which instantly comes up. But, acting as an assignment editor, you ask for information about the estimated cost of battling the fire, the communities affected, and the number of similar fires in the area in the past twenty years. . . . Your response is processed in a central news bureau, which receives similar questions from more than two thousand viewers. The bureau assigns a reporter to the story you have requested, and the next day that story is transmitted to your digital video recorder for later viewing.[1]

The scenario above is still futuristic, but probably not for long. Though use of the Internet for news retrieval still lags far behind other functions (such as entertainment and e-mail correspondence), news organizations have responded to a growing belief that users, like the hypothetical one above, will demand such services in the not-too-distant future. And the news business must be prepared for it. News organizations have moved onto the Web, partly to fill an expectation to be there. But, as they have in the past, news organizations have adapted to the Internet in order to maintain their role as the primary dispensers of news and information to the American public.[2]

The Displacement of Traditional Media?

Ironically, news media organizations were predicted to be among the first casualties of the Internet age. In the Internet age, it has been predicted that, "the future of the daily metro newspaper looks grim." That concern is understandable. The news media, after all, are in the news delivery business. If the Internet becomes a primary source for news and information, news media could lose large segments of their audiences.

As more and more readily accessible information is delivered to the home through the Internet, where does that leave traditional media? Does it leave the daily newspaper unread on the doorstep and the television turned off or connected to a computer hard drive hooked to a modem?

That news will be provided online is a given. The only question really is "by whom?" The Internet, then, raises the real possibility that consumers will look elsewhere for news and information and not look back, deserting the traditional news media outlets. Anthony Corrado predicts that, though traditional media will continue to play a role, there will be "neointermediaries" who will allow people to communicate with each other without reliance on the traditional gatekeepers of the media.[3] "Online, they are competing with nearly anyone who has a modem," laments one commentator.[4]

Another suggests any opinionated entrepreneur will be able to attract a wide audience:

> We've come a long way from the wild-eyed fanatic marching up and down Broadway in a sandwich board proclaiming "The End is Near." Nowadays, that guy is sitting at a keyboard somewhere, tapping out his loony prophecies and zap! As fast as he can think them up, they're available to millions of computer users all over the world.[5]

In some ways, Internet-based newcomers to the news reporting business may well be better able to capture audiences moving onto the Net. This is true because their background is the Net and not traditional news formats. Moreover, they lack the overhead of traditional newsgathering organizations. Their capital outlay is minuscule compared to large news media organizations such as CBS, Times Mirror, or Gannett. They have capital investment in computer hardware, software, and modem connections, instead of in printing presses, video production equipment, and bureau offices.

This problem becomes more acute when news organizations contemplate the possibility that people who move onto the Internet rather than allocate more time in their lives to news will choose the medium that best suits their needs. If equivalent information is available on the Internet in a format that gives people more control and choice (with a click of a button you can move between audio, video, and text), they may stop reading a newspaper or watching television news.

Because we often listen to the radio when we're not near a computer, such as during a commute, radio news and talk may be less affected. But the proliferation of radio channels available on the Internet may mean less direct radio listening while at work and more listening via the Internet. Also, cars in the future may feature Internet access, allowing Internet listening as well, particularly to stations not within the car antenna's range.

Even more dangerous for the traditional media, younger people, seemingly the most comfortable with the Net, are even less likely than their parents and grandparents to read newspapers. Newspaper reading among 18- to 25-year-olds has dropped dramatically over the past two decades.[6] With the Net, perhaps this audience will never acquire the habit of reading a print version of a newspaper.

Inherent Advantages

Despite all this, the future for traditional news media organizations is, surprisingly quite bright. The above gloomy assessment rests on the false assumption that the Internet is actually a competitor with the traditional news media. In and of itself, it is not. Rather, it is a tool, much like a printing press or a microphone or a coaxial cable. The information posted on the Net is prepared and delivered by individuals or groups or governments. The news media are no more competitors with technology in the Internet age than they have been in the past. Those who employ technology, however, can be such competitors.

Even though upstart news delivery organizations will attempt to exploit the transformation to Internet delivery, they face an uphill battle. In fact, news organizations possess inherent advantages in placing their own information onto the Web, just as they do now on newsprint or over airwaves. These advantages will allow them to retain their distinctive role as news sources, even via the Internet.

One enormous advantage is that they already possess the requisite newsgathering apparatus. Newcomers would have to duplicate that structure in order to acquire the global surveillance major news organizations possess. In order to establish that worldwide reach, they would have to establish bureaus in areas where traditional media currently exist. To cover American politics, they would need correspondents at the Congress, the White House, the legal beat, and other issue areas. While news organizations are capable of sending journalists where fast-breaking news occurs, new media players would find that competition difficult to match. They might have to rely on contact with a local citizen who may offer on-scene reports.

Occasionally, such newcomers will break new stories, as the Drudge Report on American Online did in January 1998 with the Monica Lewinsky story. However, these occurrences are and will remain rarities because these supposed news sites depend on stories coming to them rather than engaging in active newsgathering.

Moreover, they face another problem: reliability. News organizations bring to the Internet a status of long-term recognition as reliable news providers, both nationally and locally. In the competition for customers, that reputation will greatly benefit a *New York Times* or even a regional daily newspaper over unknown newcomers.

Fortunately, for traditional media, the American news consumer has become accustomed to the existence of some standards of news presentation. The established traditional news organizations are staffed by trained journalists, and thus they hold a distinct appeal to the public seeking legitimate information. Newcomers may be attempting to use Internet correspondents in far-flung areas as reporters, but they will lack the public recognition as professional journalists. The journalistic reliance on official reliable sources will stand the news organizations in good stead as they transfer to the Net.

In the past, such standards have been lacking on the Internet. A photo purportedly of a dying Princess Diana trapped in an overturned car on August 30, 1997, was posted on the Web for several days before it was acknowledged as a fake.[7] In April 1997, after an Air Force jet disappeared in the mountains of Colorado, militia groups flooded Internet newsgroups with stories about the pilot stashing the plane and using it to bomb federal facilities on April 19.[8] Conspiracy theories have abounded about government possession of UFOs, Heaven's Gate, and the death of White House aide Vincent Foster.[9]

Now, irresponsibility is common on the Internet because Net content is a hodgepodge of self-published stories and essays.

Anyone can put anything on the Internet and seemingly does. Often, one cannot be sure of the reliability of the information provided. Reliability diminishes exponentially as the information is passed from user to user and e-mail list to e-mail list until it acquires a degree of legitimacy by virtue of its widespread dissemination and constant repetition. Yet, it remains rumor, not fact. However, as mainstream news media move onto the Internet, they transfer with them their journalistic standards. That does not mean all publishers of news will meet such standards. Nor does it mean that even reputable news outlets will not be driven at times by the pressures of a 24-hour clock to disseminate unconfirmed rumors. One example was the Web-posted story from the *Dallas Morning News* that there was an eyewitness to a sexual encounter between President Clinton and Monica Lewinsky.[10]

But traditional news organizations will bring higher standards of news dissemination to the Web than currently exist, primarily through their reputations. One analyst suggests the reputation of a news source will matter in the search for online news:

> In the past, newspapers or the TV news would run stories from their little-known reporters and "bundle" them together under their logo. The identity of the bundler, the newspaper or TV network, gives this information credibility. In cyberspace, bundling of information that is credible, in one place where people know they can go to get the straight scoop, is going to be very important.[11]

Finally, traditional news organizations will enjoy an unmatched advertising advantage. They can use their current format to advertise their Internet product. Increasingly, newspapers and broadcast stations are using their own space or time to lure readers to their Web sites. For example, many newspapers devote permanent space, usually near the front of the paper, to describe the activities of their Web site or to promote specific stories about the site. The *Salt Lake (Utah) Tribune,* for example, uses the bottom quarter of each issue's second page to announce new information on the paper's Web site, and broadcast stations are posting their site address at the bottom of the screen before, during, or after news broadcasts. Newcomers will find it hard to match this free advertising of traditional media sites.

The Internet also may help traditional news media, particularly daily newspapers, win back a now-vanishing audience—young people. Via the Net, media organizations will be able to supply news to this group in a form more compelling than traditional methods.

Realizing these advantages, news organizations are not allowing themselves to become obsolete. Instead, they are experimenting with the Internet to expand their audience and, to an extent, transfer their existing audience from their traditional product to the Internet one.

The Development of
Internet-Based News

The transformation to online news delivery has occurred over a remarkably brief period. In the early 1990s, local newspapers such as the *San Jose Mercury News* became experimental sites for online textual retrieval of newspaper stories. By 1992, *USA Today* had placed abstracts of its stories online, and three years later included the full text.

Those early pilot programs were duplicated by other newspapers, both large and small. Large metropolitan dailies such as the *Dallas Morning News*, the *Houston Chronicle*, and the *San Francisco Chronicle* offered versions of their paper in cyberspace. Even smaller local newspapers, such as the Casper, Wyoming *Star Tribune*, the Syracuse, New York *Herald Journal*, and the Tacoma, Washington *News Tribune* joined the rush to online text retrieval.

Growth in online versions of newspapers has been phenomenal. In 1993, 20 newspapers were online. By early 1996, more than 1000 newspapers had electronic issues, including 175 daily newspapers.[12] One year later, more than 500 dailies were online. Ninety-five of the top 100 circulation newspapers have online versions. [13]

Some news organizations moved more slowly than others, favoring a cautious approach to the Internet. Many began with simple pages merely announcing their existence, monopolizing a desired address, and listing organizational information, such as staff, program schedules, and e-mail addresses. However, over time, a rapidly expanding number of newspapers, newsmagazines, radio news shows, and television news programs have established Web sites.

One example of this movement is the *New York Times*. Their site began with a restricted edition of its print version, with only a few selected stories and photographs included. However, it has now expanded to full text and near full inclusion of at least major articles.

Even the sources of news outlets—the wire services—are now accessible. Both the Associated Press (AP) and Reuters wire service stories are available to many computer network users. Indeed, news on these sites is often more current than daily newspapers, allowing the user to predict what will be printed in the morning paper.

Many standard features of traditional news increasingly are being transferred to the Internet. These include weather forecasts, classified advertisements, and even comics. Display advertising is also appearing. Moreover, this is likely to continue. According to a survey of Webmasters of news media sites, while 43 percent said currently most or all of the news from the traditional version is reproduced on the Web, 64 percent said they estimated that within a year most or all offline content would be placed online (see Methodology).

But other features have been revamped as befits the characteristics of the Net. One example is letters to the editor. The Internet bulletin board, where users can post messages either in reply to items on the site or previous messages, serves a similar purpose. Nearly two of five news organizations surveyed said they had such bulletin boards. But "live" discussions, where users can interact with one another or designated guests, go one step further by facilitating a real-time discussion. They also can perpetuate regular interest in the site beyond following late-breaking news, since users are drawn back again and again to join the discussion. Chat rooms and discussion sessions with featured guests are becoming staples of sites.

Newsmagazines have also moved onto the Web. *Time* debuted online in the fall of 1993, first through America Online. It was an instant success. The site received 126,563 hits in the first three weeks online, and, within the first six months, it had been visited 1.5 million times.[14] *Time* allowed Internet users to read the full text of articles in the current issue. Users could also see the cover and select articles from the sections of the issue, including "Milestones" and "People." *U.S. News & World Report* includes the weekly issue, but also more breaking news, special feature articles, and the magazine's more popular section—"News You Can Use."

Not to be left behind, the major broadcast network news divisions also established Web sites. Initially, these served as advertisements for the network's news programs. But that has since changed. The Web has become a tool for actual news dissemination by the broadcast networks. Fox News offers real time video of news stories presented on air. ABC links to local affiliates to provide local news. NBC joined Microsoft in 1996 to form MSNBC. NBC's expansion to the Net is a model of cooperation between a broadcast network and a computer giant capable of helping the network make the transition to online news delivery. It is also a highly dramatic example of how, rather than being shunted aside, news organizations are determined to continue to be players in the newsreporting business.

The cross-ownership linkage that has long existed between media outlets is more apparent on the Web. Media conglomerates are using sites to advertise their array of media products. For example, *Time* magazine's site features links to *Money, Fortune, Life,* and other properties of Time Warner, Inc.

Many news outlets, such as CNN and *Time,* though under separate ownership, also have joined forces to complement each other. State and local news outlets also have created joint sites. These usually have been jointly owned newspapers, but sometimes even competitors have merged sites. Connecticut Central, a Web consortium of five local newspapers, merges generic news, including features, while retaining the news from each of the towns represented. NewJersey Online, a larger consortium, sorts out news by community and even includes local community discussion groups.

These mergers acknowledge that much of local newspaper content is uniform, but local news is important to the audience. Moreover, given current trends in readership, it is expected that local news users will be more interested in visiting one site, that is, their local newspaper with a combination of local and national news, than national news media sites, such as *USA Today* or NBC News, all of which lack local news.

Radio programs also have their online counterparts. Continuous radio news has become common as an Internet option. National Public Radio provides near real-time audio of its regular daily news programs. ABC radio news offers a 24-hour news service complete with audio clips of latest news. By downloading the appropriate software, a user can choose various segments of the NPR programs and listen *sans* radio.

Many local television and radio stations also began by using their sites as advertisements for news programs. These ranged from program schedules to brief news reports designed as teasers for newsviewing. But some stations have already progressed to online news delivery. Full video is provided for selected stories at some local television stations. Even where video is not provided, some stations offer full text of their news program scripts.

Hard news is not the only type of political information available. Public affairs programming is appearing more frequently. C-SPAN has placed on its home page audio and video of broadcast programs.

Fittingly, new media have found their way onto the Web. Radio talk is available through Internet talk radio sites. The Web sites of nationally syndicated hosts such as Michael Reagan, Alan Colmes, and Ken Hamblin, offer another contact for fans. Many hosts rely on e-mail messages from listeners, in addition to the traditional calls. Other pages, such as the Unofficial Rush Limbaugh home page and the Howard Stern fans home page, have been established not by the hosts, but by devoted fans. The Limbaugh page, for example, features information about the popular host, as well as a review of his famous tie collection and a listing of his "35 undeniable truths." Television talk programs such as *Late Night with David Letterman,* the *Tonight Show,* and *Late Night with Conan O'Brien* can be accessed via computer. Letterman's Web site includes his famous Top Ten Lists. Tabloids, such as the *National Enquirer,* are even available online with excerpts from the printed issue.

The Present and Future of Internet News Delivery

Adapting to the Web

Early online news was only text, resembling teletext and representing a backward step from the heavy graphic-oriented presentations both print and broadcast media outlets had incorporated. That has quickly changed. The introduction of the World Wide Web opened the door for Net newspapers to look more like their print versions. Not only could they display photographs and other graphic material, they could go even further with moving graphics, animation, audio, and video.

At first, news outlets, particularly print, were content to duplicate graphically their hard copy versions onto the Internet. They used their signature mastheads to reassure users that they had actually reached the familiar news outlet; the main page often resembled the front page of the print version. This practice was similar to television's first experimentation with news presentations. Television news had it roots in print journalism and print served as the model. Over time, television news began to utilize still photographs and moving pictures effectively to distance itself from print journalism, and, perhaps surprisingly, even to shape print's presentation of news. When it first emerged as a national newspaper in 1982, *USA Today*, with its heavy graphic emphasis, appeared to be competing more with television than with other newspapers. The new daily's tactic eventually spawned changes in the way other newspapers presented news.

The same is occurring with the Internet. Media organizations are adapting the news presentation to the Internet's characteristics rather than the other way around. The design and layout are becoming more distinctive. Increasingly, newspapers are adjusting to the layout opportunities of the Internet that do not exist in print. Since the Internet is an active medium that requires the user to make choices, interactivity should be a highlight of news media sites. The site of the *Christian Science Monitor,* for example, opens with a menu, not the front page. Even the Net "front page" is not the same as the print version's front page. Going to the front page is only one of several initial options for the *New York Times* Web site visitors, and the information presented does not necessarily duplicate the offline product. According to a survey of Webmasters of news media organizations, 71 percent said their sites include information that does not appear in the offline product (see Methodology).

Gathering News

Adaptation is also underway in the newsroom. The way news is gathered is being modified by the presence of the Web. Internet use in the newsroom is growing. Between 1994 and 1996, use of the Internet by journalists increased by 24 percent. By 1998, 93 percent of news organizations were using the Internet for news gathering.[15] According to this survey of journalists, 51 percent said they had been using the Internet for one to two years, while one-quarter had used it less and one quarter had used it more. Sixty-nine percent said they used the Internet at least several times weekly.

Journalists find the Internet a useful tool for connecting to a mul-

Table 2.1 Journalists' Newsgathering Use
of the Internet

Newsgathering Activity	%
Follow up on hard news stories	33
Gather background data	98
Find sources	86
Communicate with sources	46

titude of news, public affairs, and other political sources.[16] For example, the Internet increases a journalist's mobility. Through an Internet connection, the journalist in the field can be as knowledgeable as the home office. Placement of government and other data online has been a boon for information-seeking journalists. Documentary information, statistical databases, press-related material (press releases, transcripts of briefings, texts of speeches) are all easier to find and will become even more accessible as agencies place increasing amounts of data on the Internet. Ninety-eight percent of journalists reported using the Internet to gather background data for a story (see Table 2.1).

News coverage of electoral campaigns is materially benefited. Without having to return to the office, journalists can check the accuracy of politicians' claims. When following presidential candidates, they can compare their past votes and positions with their current statements. And candidate sites are providing another new source of information for political reporters.

Eighty-six percent of journalists said they used the Internet to find sources. Forty-six percent said they used it to communicate with their sources. One online journalistic information source is the newsgroup. Newsgroups are becoming popular sources for journalists to follow specialized topic discussions.[17] Forty-three percent said they browse through newsgroups. Of those who browsed, nearly half said they did so at least weekly. Journalists have been joining groups and then posting messages seeking information, including interviews, for stories. One journalist posted a message asking for help in covering the Mad Cow epidemic in the United Kingdom. The journalist received a variety of messages, including notice of the existence of a Mad Cow home page.[18]

Internet sites specifically designed to facilitate newsgathering are proliferating.[19] The *American Journalism Review* site, for example, offers an array of journalistic resources, including links to major metropolitan newspapers, wire service stories, and news releases from various organizations. [20] The Reporters' Internet Guide organizes subjects by newsbeat to ease reporters' ability to gather news about their beat area.[21] The Poynter Institute's site gives journalists further tips or contacts on late-breaking news stories. For example, during the O. J. Simpson civil trial, the site offered journalists transcripts of the trial, texts of major news coverage, and other documents from the case. Thirty-eight percent of the journalists surveyed said they use such sites.

However, acceptance of the Internet has not been universal among news professionals. One critic of increasing journalistic reliance on the Net suggested that the old interview style should not be replaced. "As technology makes it easier to compile information from computer screens, it could become less appealing for some reporters to foray out into the public, and talk to people face to face."[22] Moreover, use of the Internet for newsgathering brings its own set of ethical dilemmas. For example, should the audience be informed that a piece of information was obtained from the Internet or that an interview took place "online" instead of in person? Should e-mail posts be considered "public information?" If so, does an individual who posts a message on a Usenet group have the expectation that his or her statements could end up in a news story? Would such an expectation inhibit newsgroup debate?

Journalists plainly are divided on these questions. Forty-seven percent said they do state in the news story that the information was obtained online. But 44 percent said they do not, while another 9 percent said they do sometimes. Of those who conducted online interviews, most said they rarely or "never" mention in the story that the interview was so conducted. A plurality (46 percent) of the journalists said they felt that Usenet postings are not public and therefore cannot be quoted without obtaining permission from the individual. But a majority said that they believed such postings were public (37 percent) or were at least some of the time (17 percent). The journalistic community is clearly split over how to treat these postings.

Still another dilemma for journalists is the reliability of Internet sources. News organizations are expected to depend on credible

Table 2.2 Journalists' Use of Information from Websites of Organizations on Their Journalistic Beat

	Press Releases	Documents	Speech Texts	E-Mail Addresses	Data
Frequently	3	23	6	24	21
Sometimes	65	69	22	47	62
Rarely	24	9	50	6	6
Never	9	—	22	24	12
Total	101*	101	100	101	100

*Rounding error.

sources. But, as discussed earlier, the Internet provides access to a plethora of unreliable sources or sources whose identities are not always clear. The example discussed in the introduction of Pierre Salinger's use of an Internet communication demonstrates the problems for journalists in verifying information obtained through the Internet.

As a result, journalists are becoming more wary of what they read and who they cite from the Internet. (Three-fourths said they felt Web information was somewhat reliable, while only 15 percent felt it was "highly reliable" for newsgathering. Moreover, half said that, before publication, they always confirm offline the information they read online, while another 38 percent said they sometimes confirm. Another 2 percent said they don't use the information at all.) Like the public, journalists will turn more to known sources— government agencies, public officials, traditional interest groups, and elite media organizations. Seventy-five percent of the journalists reported that the organizations they cover have Web sites, and 77 percent of those journalists said they use these Web sites to survey the activities of the organization. And 91 percent of those who used the Internet to cover the organizations on their beat said they use documents posted by the organizations on their Web sites, with 68 percent reporting that, at least some of the time, they use press releases these organizations post on the Net (see Table 2.2).

News organizations, rather than being left behind in the rush for use of the Internet, are leading the way. The Web potentially is a highly useful tool for newsgathering, which journalists increasingly will discover. It is also reshaping news dissemination as news organizations are placing their products on the Web and encouraging users to turn to them rather than to new, alternative information sources.

Structuring News

Traditional news organizations' sites have become more than locations for their own news reports. They have been transformed into megasites, offering a gateway to a wide range of other sites. News media sites are becoming one-stop sites for locating current events and public affairs information on the Web. For example, the *New York Times* offers a list of political sites from political parties to interest groups organized by topic. The site even includes other media sites, although not other daily print media sites.

Such a megasite is designed to become the launching point for readers searching for political information. Users may go elsewhere for more, particularly specialized, information, but the media site will be the source for doing so.

It is logical that news media sites would fill this role. Internet users know the content of news sites will change regularly, usually daily but sometimes more often, and that these sites discuss a wide range of topics of general interest to the user. Links from there to various other Web locations become a follow-up to a general story.

The development of news media megasites is undoubtedly a response to the disorganized state of the Web. News organizations are attempting to provide the structure that, particularly, newer users seek and that will be critical if the Internet is to reach further into the populace. Of course, such structure places the news organizations in the most advantageous position. Their sites will be the most visited. They will offer the largest audience for advertisers. And they will develop audience reliance designed to offset the short-term negative effects of movement to a fee-based service.

Customizing News

As discussed at the beginning of the chapter, news organizations are already customizing the news presentation for their consumers. News organizations are also benefiting from a new development called "push technology" or "intelligent agents."[23] This new Internet tool gathers customized information and then "pushes" those news sources selected by the user onto the screen, thereby automatically presenting them to the user when they log onto the Net. The user no longer must surf or browse for them, or even go to selected bookmarks. Push technology is much like the newspaper being delivered to your doorstep.

At first glance, push technology may appear to hurt traditional media on the Net, but in fact it is an advantage for them. For example, one such push technology product, Pointcast, can be customized by the user to receive various news sources. But the choices include such well-known traditional media sources as *Time,* CNN, the *Boston Globe,* or local newspapers. The emphasis is on news organizations the user is already familiar with, that is, the traditional media.

Traditional media are directly supporting this trend by offering the option to users of receiving regular, even daily, e-mail messages listing news stories in areas of interest to them. Imbedded with links, the e-mail message allows the reader to simply click on a link to read that story. MSNBC is just one example of a news organization allowing users to choose which types of news they want to receive.

The customization of news offers a high degree of control for the user. The reader can shun news stories about topics of little interest to them. While readers of newspapers and newsmagazines already engage in such avoidance, it is currently a more difficult task. Over time, and in response to consumer preference, newspapers have placed news by topics in various sections of the paper to ease the task of finding news of interest to the individual, be it entertainment, sports, local news, and so no. The Web versions of newspapers are separating out news sections already. Customized news simply accelerates that trend.

However, there is a down side to this process. The cost for the user may be increased specialization at the expense of general information. For example, it will be harder for a news consumer to stumble upon a story that is important but not within that individual's range of usual interests as expressed by the customized news presentation. Such serendipity is now common for television viewers or radio listeners, where there is no user control of the news presentation (only control over its reception), and it is at least occasional for the newspaper reader as the eye glances over the page on the way to some other type of story.

What does this mean? It could create a news audience knowing less about broader subjects and having less and less in common with each other. General consumer interest news means a broad array of knowledge transferred to much the same population. That will be reduced.

Such customized news does not bode well for political news. Currently, many people may hear such news on a local news broadcast on their way to finding out more important things, in their view, such as sports or the weather, or they may see it on the front page of a newspaper while heading for other sections. With customized news, however, such inadvertent exposure may be a thing of the past. It is possible that what little political news many citizens receive now will be reduced even further.

Challenges and Opportunities

News organizations' embrace of the Net has not meant an easy transition within the newsroom. The Internet has challenged news organizations' long-cherished notions about news delivery. During the twentieth century, discrete categories of news products had evolved—broadcast and print, radio and television, daily newspaper and general interest weekly newsmagazine. Admittedly, the conglomerates owning these entities crossed boundaries. But the consumer saw separate and distinct types of news products meeting a variety of needs.

Plainly, the Internet has already confused these distinctions. It has the ability to mix broadcast and print, audio and video, and daily, weekly, and monthly publications. Weekly newsmagazines, like *U.S. News & World Report* or *Time,* can offer daily updates, while daily media can update their broadcasts several times a day. Television networks and individual stations can offer text versions. Newspapers and newsmagazines can employ audio or even video to tell stories. That jumble of media forms on the Internet has produced one unifying trend—more rapid and frequent news dissemination. This trend toward continuous news delivery is not new. CNN first altered broadcast news transmission schedules with its 24-hour news service, forcing the major networks to choose between entertainment programs or late-breaking news in order to compete as news providers.

Broadcast is not the only affected party. Print media have found that weekly or even daily versions seem archaic in an age of news on demand. Yet in the past these organizations have not been organized to deliver news in that manner. They will be expected to do so in the future.

The Internet places great demands on the news media by reorganizing the timing of the news delivery process. For the user, the Internet, like 24-hour broadcast news stations, offers the opportunity of constant updating. For the news organization, the Internet's contribution is the challenge of 24-hour newsupdating. Fifty percent of the Webmasters said their sites are updated at least several times daily. Traditionally, news media outlets have been governed by publication schedules or broadcast program schedule holes provided for news programs. Broadcast networks like CNN and news services will find that challenge of constant updating easier to meet. But print media will not.

However, print media will be able to produce their news product much more cheaply. The very act of publication on the Web is simpler and less expensive than computerized typesetting and publishing. Not surprisingly, all of the surveyed Webmasters predicted that the amount of content on their site would expand during the next two years, rather than remain the same or decrease.

Another challenge for news organizations is that of specialized information. Due to the general consumer nature of news media outlets, specialized information is a particularly difficult challenge for news organizations. Since the Internet places more control in the hands of the user, the news presentation will have to emphasize choice and specialization. However, since news organizations are limited in the amount of specialized news possible, due to their traditional general consumer orientation, they will need to expand their offerings. And although they often devote large amounts of resources to studying what audiences want and how to deliver it, news organizations are limited by the nature of their audience to a general news presentation.

Still another problem for news organizations is the priority of news products. Should the Web support the traditional news product? The idea that new technology merely serves as advertising for existing ones has historical roots. That is how newspapers saw early radio, for example. But each technology comes into its own and is seen as valuable in its own right as those already in existence.

This challenge is one that has already divided newsrooms.

Which product should get the late-breaking news? For the time being, the traditional version has been granted priority. Most managing editors still prefer reserving their late breaking news for the print version.[24] Yet, news can be placed on the Web when it is available, not when there is a next edition of the paper.

Despite the traditional preference for the offline version, the Web is gradually winning the battle. Most Webmasters say they are not prohibited from being the first with the news. And of those who say they are embargoed, most believe such an embargo will be lifted in the near future.

Traditional media have moved slowly to incorporate this new mode of disseminating news. Web versions initially consisted of teasers for the hard copy. Newspapers and newsmagazines, particularly, have saved their best stories for the print version.[25] Editors are concerned that with the Web as the platform for late-breaking news, they will no longer be able to scoop their competition. Competitors would be able to adjust the print or, in the case of radio or television news, the broadcast version, to reflect that scoop revealed on the Internet.

The priority dilemma is integrated with another dilemma, which is the problem of profit. The vast majority of traditional media still focus their attention on the traditional version because it is their bread and butter. It is the traditional version, the daily print issue or the evening news broadcast, which produces the revenue necessary to stay in business. Even though 71 percent of the surveyed media sites included display advertising, only one-third were financially self-supporting.

If the traditional product is the moneymaker, then the Web news cannot interfere with the news organization's attempt to build an audience for that product. Hence, news cannot be delivered first on the Web site, where it will overshadow the traditional product.

But news organizations increasingly are seeing that such protection of the traditional product to the exclusion of the Web version will not work. People do not want advertising from the Web; they want information. As a result, they may change their information retrieval habits to get more information from the Web and less from other sources. This will be particularly true if Web TV achieves widespread public acceptance.

Both the priority and the profit problems will diminish as use of the Internet for news consumption increases. More and more users will come to expect late-breaking news through the Net, see that it is not being delivered by some media, and punish (through avoidance) those news sources that refuse to provide it. In turn, however, there will be costs for such a service. Subscribers to print versions of newspapers already incur such costs and may be willing to meet such costs in the future.

Media outlets did not expect to turn a profit at first, but instead saw their relationship with online access services as a low-cost means for experimenting.[26] But as the news delivery function increases and impacts the offline circulation, costs will have to be recovered. Moreover, about one in three newspapers already are turning a profit on their online versions, while about one-quarter expect to do so within the next four years.[27]

Paid circulation for Internet products met with initial resistance from consumers. The *Wall Street Journal* was one of the early services to charge. The constituency, primarily business users, made that action more likely to succeed. But in return users received full value with complete newspaper text.[28] Many media organizations began by offering free services, but some, like the *Wall Street Journal*, have moved to a fee structure for nonsubscribers to the hard copy edition. Others have charged, not for the current issue, but for access to the newspaper's online story archives. This was true of 21 percent of the media organizations surveyed. In the future, fees will be required both for full text as well as other services.

Online versions of traditional media will offer real financial advantages. The cost of delivering news via the Web is potentially far less than for print versions. Capital costs are much lower compared with existing expenses for printing and circulation, and while labor costs in the newsroom may not be cut, staff in production and circulation could be drastically reduced.

These issues present a crisis for traditional news organizations, but one that ultimately will be resolved with a common solution. Increasingly, they are (and yet will be) viewing the Web site as another format for news dissemination and not merely as a teaser for the existing product.

Inexorably, however, despite the challenges of the Web, media organizations are moving toward usage of the Net to actually convey news, that is, provide their regular news services via the Internet. This development does not replace the news product's other forms;

rather, it is treated as a supplemental but equally legitimate news delivery form.

The Traditional News Media Audience

Will the audience now turn to the traditional news media's online product? Existing evidence suggests that is exactly what users will do. For example, during a San Francisco newspaper strike in 1993, management and reporters together bypassed the traditional printing process and produced online news products. Daily readership of the online version reached about 100,000. That was a fraction of the estimated 600,00 daily print circulation, but a remarkable figure given the limited number of Internet users in the Bay Area at that time.[29]

Usage of the Internet for news is increasing.[30] Seventy-one percent of Webmasters for news organization sites reported visits to their site had increased significantly in just one year. Seventy-nine percent said their sites receive more than 2000 "hits" per week.

And online users already are turning to the traditional media for their news. Among the most popular sites for online users are traditional media sites such as the *Washington Post*, the *New York Times*, the *Wall Street Journal*, the national broadcast networks, and CNN.[31] During 1996, the most-used political news site was the CNN/*Time* All Politics site.[32] Nearly one in five users sought information from their local news media sites. Far more people accessed these sites than used newer political Internet sites such as Rock the Vote (4 percent) or Citizens '96 (2 percent).[33] Major news organization sites were even more popular for those specifically seeking election news. Fifty percent of those surveyed said they used sites such as CNN, the TV networks, or newspaper sites.[34]

The Internet has not displaced people's traditional print or broadcast media use habits. Rather, it has become a supplement; it is a means for following up on stories first heard or read in traditional media.[35] In the future, it may be the other way around with news first heard on the Web and then followed up by television viewing. Interaction with offline formats is more likely to be a feature of audience use of the Internet, rather than use of the Internet alone.

It is unlikely that news organizations will dramatically increase their circulation figures through the Web. Consumer use of the Internet for news and information still lags behind other uses. According to a Times-Mirror Center survey, users are far more likely to use their modems for work-related communication, research, or e-mail than they are to follow news.[36] News retrieval can be a secondary motive for going online. One survey found that slightly more than a majority of online users said they read news while online, even though they go online initially for other purposes.[37]

Interestingly, since geography will not limit use of media anymore, it is possible that news organizations actually will increase the audience for their news product by reaching an audience far beyond their normal geographical circulation. That audience will be useful in determining Web advertising rates. However, it is doubtful there will be any attempts to cultivate such readers editorially.

Adaption and Dominance

It should be clear that news organizations are not allowing the Web to displace them as news providers. The Internet is not the death knell of the mainstream media.

News organizations are adapting, and thus they are surviving and will even thrive. This development is no different from the one that has occurred with each new technology during this century. Newspapers bought into radio and both newspapers and radio bought television. News media conglomerates have lined up to acquire cable and satellite companies. Now, news organizations are moving onto the Web.

It is true that their sites will constitute a tiny fraction of all the sites available. Yet that will not matter. In a public library, for example, current newspapers, in volume, are a minuscule part of the collection, but they are accessed by library users at a rate far higher than the rest of the print collection. The same will be true with news media offerings online. They will outdistance other types of information sites and become the primary hard news sources online.

They will be advantaged because they offer structure and credibility; structure facilitates the users' access to news and information, and credibility gives the reassurance that the news presented has reliable foundations. Such traits, important for news consumers now, will remain critical in the future.

The Internet has posed a new, but not insurmountable, challenge to the news dissemination process. And news organizations are meeting that challenge. They are one of the existing important players in American politics who will continue to play a similar role in the Internet age.

THREE

Electronic Lobbying

On March 26, 1997, police officers found 39 bodies in a rented southern California mansion, the remains of a joint suicide by a strange religious organization, the Heaven's Gate group. Their mass suicide prompted saturation media coverage of the group's doctrine and practices.

However, when the group's Internet site was found, public concern deepened. Not only were group members bent on killing themselves, but they sought to use the Web to justify their actions and even recruit others. Though the Web has been linked to the wake of other gruesome events—the Oklahoma City bombing, the TWA 800 explosion, the death of Princess Diana—that discovery symbolized the Net's communication potential for new or nontraditional groups.

Other extremist groups have received media attention over their use of the Internet: conspiracy groups trading theories over black helicopters, terrorists describing how to make bombs, or militia groups explaining how individuals can defend themselves against government troops.

Though these groups have received the greatest press attention, other Internet-based groups have also emerged, such as Voters Telecommunication Watch, the Internet Society, and the Electronic Frontier Foundation. With an agenda of promoting new technology, particularly the Internet, and preventing censorship, they have become active lobbyists in the policy-making process.

The emergence of these new groups on a medium that defies structure and invites individual participation could be viewed as the beginning of the end for interest group politics as we know it. One scenario would see these new cyberspace groups, which reach a mass audience electronically and instantaneously, as the new political organizations.[1] Internet users in groups may become a new force unto themselves, highly interested in Internet issues not currently addressed by existing organizations. One representative of an on-line group predicted that many "Internet users will be single-issue voters. We'll help them identify friendly candidates."[2]

Or perhaps political organizations as we know them will fade. Traditional groups will be replaced, not by new groups, but by nothing. Citizens will gather their own political information on the Net, even very specialized information. One political scientist has noted that one of the advantages of groups is to collect information that is not usually readily available to the public. "A good intelligence service is therefore the basis of effective pressure tactics."[3] But perhaps such an advantage will be erased by the Internet. As Anthony Corrado predicts, "voters will be able to decide for themselves what information they consider to be most important."[4] They then will respond spontaneously and independently, identifying the policy makers they need to reach and crafting their own messages based on their own Internet-based research.

The growth of the Internet raises the prospect, then, that the large, traditional groups who dominate American politics will become anachronistic, that is, organizational dinosaurs in the cyberspace age. They will be displaced by new organizations or by citizens who no longer need groups at all. They will become mediators in an era of unmediated communication. When citizens will be able to interact with elected representatives without the necessity of intermediary organizations, what then is the role of interest groups? Why would citizens turn to groups for information or political action when they can do it for and by themselves?

Contributing to their decline could well be the intransigence of the groups themselves. Born of a different age, they may have difficulty coping. Perhaps they will be unable to change their established methods to conform to the imperatives of electronic communication. As a result, their power will be diminished, particularly in the face of new Internet-based associations and the emergence of sudden participation by the populace.

Moreover, they will face more intense competition from groups who, in the past, were easily defeated due to their lack of resources.

Therefore, there will be a power shift with smaller, poorer groups capable of competing more effectively against those more-established and better-funded organizations. This will happen because the former set of groups faces low costs for communication on the Internet. Their lack of resources is not a barrier since they will be able to set up homepages and reach large numbers of people just like the resource-rich groups. The Internet, then, will place groups on a more level playing field. It will devolve power to the other groups and/or to the people directly.

This scenario may sound particularly appealing to those who yearn for power to pass beyond the Washington beltway. But, as I will demonstrate, this scenario is hardly what is occurring. Nor is there much evidence that it will occur in the future. In fact, the evidence, based on a content analysis of sites and a survey of interest groups, suggests traditional groups will flourish in the Internet age (see Methodology).

Traditional groups have been moving onto the Net in large numbers and in rapid fashion. To supplement their nonelectronic communication, groups are establishing their own Web sites and using e-mail to communicate with their respective constituencies. They are indeed adapting their communication tactics to the presence of the Internet, rather than being left behind.

The list of groups coming onto the Net reads like an association directory: the National Audubon Society, the National Organization for Women, the National Rifle Association, National Right to Life, and so on. But it also includes many lesser-known established groups who also lobby but who are not public interest groups and communicate primarily with their own members rather than with the mass public. These groups are now using the Net to promote their specific-issue interests.

Surprisingly, even when the Internet itself is the policy issue under debate, traditional groups weigh in strongly. The fight in Congress over the Internet Decency Act was waged primarily between groups such as the Christian Coalition and the Family Research Council on one side pitted against others such as the ACLU and various media organizations.

Why will traditional groups continue to serve as dominant players, even in an Internet age? The major reason is their willingness to adapt.

Communication and Group Constituencies

Interest groups are rapidly adapting to electronic communication with their constituencies: the mass public, to whom the primary objective is education and persuasion; their own membership, who need to be educated more than persuaded; and a submembership of activists who can be mobilized to political action.[5]

Communication with the public has been a major objective of many interest groups, especially public interest groups.[6] They feel compelled to "go public" in order to achieve their policy objectives. According to David B. Truman, "almost invariably one of the first results of the formal organization of an interest group is its embarking upon a program of propaganda."[7] These groups pursue outside strategies, that is, efforts designed to shape the public agenda and mobilize public opinion in support of their causes. The most likely seekers of public attention and support are those groups who perceive they cannot win policy battles without "going public."

Groups who are successful at inside strategies (i.e. directly lobbying policy makers) feel less need to acquire press and public attention. Groups that have close association with governmental agencies are unlikely to pursue an outside strategy to accomplish a specific policy end, since the inside one can be just as effective at less cost.[8] However, some groups pursuing inside strategies and preferring to remain invisible become drawn into the media glare by opposing groups who do go public. As a result, even these groups must engage in an outside strategy in order to present their version of issues. A prime example is the tobacco industry, which has sought to blunt the negative portrayal of itself in news stories generated by the anti-smoking lobby and successive government administrations' public hostility to their industry positions.

Most groups pursue combinations of inside and outside strategies. Therefore, they must both persuade and mobilize.[9] Persuasion is directed primarily at the general public, from whom groups would like at least vague support for their policy objectives. Mobilization is usually directed at the group membership.

Public interest groups, particularly those without membership, also rely on the general public for mobilization. Groups such as the National Organization for Women, which has a small membership compared with the constituency they claim to represent, need support from others who have no interest in joining the organization but share the group's policy objectives.

The news media serve as a critical link between the group and the mass public. As Jack L. Walker has noted, "Groups seeking to further a cause thrive on controversy and must gain the attention of the mass media in order to convince their patrons of the organization's potency, and also to communicate effectively with their far-flung constituents."[10] Mass media messages are directed to potential supporters and often to organization members as well.[11]

Communication with groups' own membership also has been conducted through internal publications, such as the NRA's *American Rifleman* or the *National Right to Life News*. The organization can use these publications to speak directly to those who are already persuaded of the group's stances, but who may not be well informed about policy issue specifics, the status of those issues in the policy process, or the activity of the group to achieve its goals. They allow somewhat more private communication with members of the group, which cannot be achieved through mass media messages.

The group leadership needs to demonstrate to policy makers that the group's issue positions (and their intensity in support of those positions) is shared by others. According to Charlotte Ryan, a group "use(s) media as a vehicle for mobilizing support. Organizers are usually aiming at several audiences simultaneously: they want to consolidate membership and active supporters; to reach a more general public and move it from disinterest to sympathy; to show their strength to the powerful players involved, be they government or corporate officials; and finally, to win over the mass media as an audience in its own right."[12]

The manifestation of public support usually comes in the form of action by group members (or other group supporters) who express opinions directly to policy makers. Kay Lehman Schlozman and John T. Tierney found 80 percent of groups rely on grassroots lobbying at various times.[13] Groups are particularly interested in engaging their supporters in political activism that communicates widespread and intense public support for the group's position. Direct mail and newsletters targeted at those likely to be activists have characterized many groups' internal communications.[14]

As a caveat it should be noted that the boundaries between these constituencies are not always clear. There is considerable overlap in the make-up of these constituencies and therefore in the messages they receive. Moreover, some groups lacking a large membership (or any membership at all) will rely more heavily on their communication with the general public for education and mobilization.

Nevertheless, for most groups there are three distinct constituencies: the general public, the general membership, and an active submembership. Communication with each determines the group's ability to maintain relationships and achieve policy goals. Examining each of these constituencies separately will help identify the extent to which traditional groups are utilizing the Net to achieve their organizational aims.

Educating the General Public

The Internet today is an open medium, almost by definition. With few exceptions, when people post sites they have no control over who actually sees the site. Groups expect that their Web sites may be read by users ranging from committed members to the merely curious. Groups expect, even hope, that browsers who have no connection with the site will happen upon it and use it. So it becomes an ideal tool for communicating with individuals who have no relationship to the organization.

From the information they post on the Web, most groups view their home pages as public education tools. Obviously, merely telling people what your group is about and what it stands for is basic to this purpose. Not surprisingly, according to a content analysis of interest group Web sites, 94 percent of the sites set up by groups included a description of the group's mission, perhaps assuming that the random visitor would be uninformed about the group's objectives (see Methodology).

The home pages of these groups often featured organization logos, summarizing the organization's view of its mission. The ACLU site verbally explained the ACLU's purposes, but its logo also prominently featured the words "Freedom Network." The PTA's was "Children First."

Most groups also wanted to make clear what their policy interests were. Sixty-seven percent specifically listed the policy issues their group addresses. Planned Parenthood, like others, listed its issues, such as pro-choice advocacy and family planning, at the top of its main page. The ACLU main page includes a prominent listing of issues on which the ACLU takes a stand.

Another indication of policy stances was the existence of links to other like-minded organizations, with 69 percent of groups linked to other groups. For example, the National Postal Mail Handlers Union site links to the AFL-CIO, and Catholics United for Life links to other pro-life organizations as well as Catholic groups.

Seventy-six percent of sites included reports the group had published on topics relevant to group interests. Many included electronic versions or abstracts of the group's offline publications. The National Organization for Women Web site included articles from the organization's monthly newsletter and the AFL-CIO site included labor news drawn from its regular publications. Others offered regular news briefs on relevant issues. Fairness and Accuracy in Reporting included clips from its weekly radio series on media bias. Or some provided information emanating originally from other sources. The main page of the Action on Smoking and Health included reports from other groups such as the American Cancer Society and the Advisory Committee on Tobacco Policy and Public Health.

Some groups rely on independent news media accounts to convey the significance of their topic. Action on Smoking and Health links to a number of current news items on smoking-related topics. And some emphasize already existing public support for their positions by posting public opinion data. The League of Conservation Voters site included a section reporting polling results, demonstrating broad public support for the group's positions on environmental issues. Still others effectively personalize their persuasion messages in order to attract user interest and support. The National Coalition for the Homeless posted the story of one family's descent into homelessness from the family's own e-mail messages, complete with photographs of the family.

Since the Internet today is much like a bulletin board in terms of lack of control over who actually reads the message, many groups sought to elicit more information about "the public" visiting their sites. Thirteen percent had guest books where visitors were requested to provide information about themselves.

Yet another means of obtaining data on users is to offer them free information. During the legislative debate over partial-birth abortion, National Right to Life, for instance, offered a free packet on partial-birth abortion if visitors gave the organization their name and address.

In summary, the Web is a significant new tool in group communication with the public. It offers the opportunity to communicate with an interested general public, and to do so with greater depth than the groups could through news releases-turned-stories.

Press Relations

A minuscule but significant subsection of the general public is the press. But, as indicated in the previous chapter, journalists are becoming more consistent users of the Internet in order to cover their respective beats. Therefore, traditional groups can expect that visits from reporters will be frequent and serious.

Some groups placed special emphasis in their sites on serving the needs of journalists covering the group. Twenty-two percent of interest group sites included a press section designed for journalistic usage. Texts of news releases, press advisories, and online press kits about the organization characterized these sections.

Membership Recruitment

New member recruitment is a critical activity for most groups. Not surprisingly, many organizations also use their site to recruit new membership. Seventy-one percent of sites included a solicitation for membership recruitment. For many groups, addresses of local or state chapters are included to encourage direct contact with more proximate regional headquarters. Becoming a member of many groups is easier than ever. Casual viewers of sites can join the organization through membership applications the user can print and mail through regular mail. Forty-eight percent of sites included such online membership forms. The ACLU, for example, includes an online membership application complete with a method of online payment.

Some sites even seek not only members, but also organizers. For example, the AFL-CIO site includes instructions on how to organize a union or become a union organizer.

Communicating with Members

Potentially the Web affects three major types of activities related to member communication. One is information retrieval. The gathering and compiling of information is necessary for the second function, which is the dissemination of information. Third, is decision making within the group. Let's examine each of these in turn and see what the Web's impact has been on the way these groups communicate with their members.

Information Retrieval

Major beneficiaries of the Internet's information dissemination capabilities have been interest groups actively following legislation. This benefit not only applies to the group's dissemination of information to its members, which will be discussed below, but also to the group's *retrieval* of information essential to participation in lobbying.

Since the collection of information is essential to the task of acting as a player in the policy-making process, groups devote large amounts of resources to following legislative activity, that is, tracking bills through the legislative process. Some of the data gathered is private (such as estimates of the direction of forthcoming congressional votes and presidential decision making) or proprietary (public opinion surveys, content analyses, and other internal reports), but much of it is public: government agency statistics, texts of bills, or committee hearing schedules.

Information is a prime benefit for group membership. Groups like the United Mineworkers offer updates on black lung disease or miner benefits programs. The National Governors' Association keeps its members informed of developments in federalism and innovations in state government.

But for groups without members, or public interest groups, information is designed for a broader dissemination. Common Cause, for example, tracks campaign finance revenue and expenditures, thus entitling this public interest group to a major share of news coverage of campaign finance policy. Without such information, these groups would possess no special significance in the policy debate.

Information retrieval is a function where the Internet has made a significant difference. The research costs for interest groups have dropped with free electronic information services such as *Thomas*. Groups can search for the current status of bills, preview committee schedules, peruse committee prints, or retrieve other congressional information within minutes. One scholar has summed up the effect on congressional behavior: "The computerization of data and its ready accessibility render the terms 'obscure paragraph' and 'hidden provisions' obsolete."[15] Groups will be able to find information more readily and more thoroughly. This development has not been lost on policy makers who might not want that information made available, as will be discussed in chapter 5.

Information Dissemination

Those groups with members (the vast majority) usually are in regular communication with members through a variety of mass mailings—newsletters, magazines, and direct mail. The Internet obviously can achieve those results at much lower costs.

Indeed, various groups, and even coalitions of groups such as the National Coalition Against Censorship, the American Arts Alliance, and the United States Industry Coalition, have established their own Web sites as regular information sources for their members or other interested individuals.[16] The Internet has not replaced the group's offline efforts; rather it has supplemented them. It has become another point of contact between interest groups and their related constituencies.

The Internet is a mechanism for communicating information the group already transmits offline, such as the group's activity as an intermediary for the membership, specialized information the member would not find elsewhere (or at least not easily), and the activities of other group members.

The Internet site is an important reinforcement mechanism for members. Content is used to reassure members of the group's active status on their behalf. Many highlight their own efforts and subsequent success in policy influence. Common accomplishments mentioned included presenting testimony before congressional hearings, promoting the group's cause in speeches to various audiences, repeating favorable news media stories or editorials, and describing positive actions by Congress, the executive branch, or the judiciary as a result of their efforts. Twenty-seven percent of the groups posted information on their past legislative activity.

Some sites also describe what other members of the group are doing both nationally and, often, across the states as well. Fifteen percent of the sites described activities of state or local chapters of the group. Some encouraged visitors to provide input about their own activities. For example, NARAL (National Abortion Rights Action League) invited users to submit information about right-wing activities in their communities.

The Internet is being used to sell the groups' offline publications. The National Rifle Association site allows people to electronically order its offline publication, *The American Guardian*. But others are actually reproducing their regular newsletters online. Fifty-five percent of the sites include organization newsletters, magazines, or other regular publications. The information is similar to the non-electronic news that groups send to members. The National Organization for Women Web site includes articles from the organization's monthly newsletter and the AFL-CIO site includes labor news drawn from its regular publications.

But many sites also include more lengthy reports. Seventy-six percent published online reports on topics of interest to group members or other interested persons. Through such Web sites, organizations can convey more lengthy and detailed information at much less cost than through direct mail. For example, the League of Conservation Voters offered online its "Green Guide," an extensive report on members of Congress and environmental issues.

Groups display information the average person, even the active member, would find difficult to compile or even locate themselves. The National Rifle Association site, for example, includes a state-by-state description of firearms laws. The ACLU site includes texts of judicial decisions related to civil liberties issues.

One problem for groups seeking to use the Internet to communicate specifically with their own members is the fact that the Internet, for the most part, is not a private medium. The distribution problem of the Internet, which is an advantage in terms of reach, but a disadvantage in terms of control over readership, means that internal communication for groups is more difficult to achieve. Groups can use their sites to communicate with their own members, but they also must consider that any other interested person can receive the same information quite readily, including those who are working against the group's interests. Moreover, groups again face the "free rider" problem. If the group provides free information to all, then what is the value of acquiring membership in the organization?

Understandably, some groups wish to communicate exclusively with their own members as they do in direct mailings or newsletters. As a result, some have established sections designed for internal communications with members. Ten percent of the sites analyzed had secret site pages accessible only with a password. The American Institute of Architects reserved access to online information databases for their members only. The National Postal Mail Handlers Union site was one of the more exclusive with one-third of the links from the main page accessible only by password. The U.S. Chamber of Commerce was even more restrictive, placing off-limits to visitors almost all political information the group had placed on its site. The National PTA offers its members exclusive access to on-line legislative news, chat rooms, and an electronic PTA publication.

The small number of groups using such private sections may be a result of the perception that the group has something to hide. Or it may be a trend that just has not caught on yet. Groups with less visible sites, perhaps visited primarily by their own members, may be more inclined to limit access without the perception of exclusiveness.

The future will likely bring group sites featuring a combination of public and restricted links. The trend may be toward basic messages about the group and some news that will be offered to all, along with links to other organizations and an invitation to join. But more in-depth reports, online publications, and access to other databases will be restricted to group members or subscribers willing to pay for the information without joining. This strategy conveys the message that the site is worth visiting for nonmembers, but membership would be beneficial to gain even more information.

Members find the group still provides information the individual would find it difficult to obtain and compile, even from the Internet. Individuals can still conduct such research themselves at great cost in terms of time and money. But why devote that time and money when the information is readily available on the group's site? Moreover, as more and more Internet information is handled on a fee basis, the benefits of group membership will become increasingly apparent to the member seeking such specialized information.

Internal Decision Making

One thing missing from the communication with members on most group sites, either public interest or otherwise, was a solicitation for input. Sites did not include requests for opinions from members (at least in the public sections) on group policy, such as which issues the organization ought to address, what positions the group should take, or how battles over policy should be waged. Most groups had e-mail addresses, but the Internet was not used to solicit opinion on specific issues. Given the fact that such solicitation, and subsequent aggregation, becomes remarkably simple with the Internet, one might expect the presence of such opportunities for input.

Yet, such solicitations pose a serious problem for group leadership by encouraging members, not leaders, to take control of the group's agenda. Members could determine the group's issue priorities, and even positions, more easily through the Internet, thus reducing the power of the leadership.

Such input also could attract others outside the organization. Moreover, a general call for opinions could attract many nongroup members who have little commitment to the organization. Even worse, it could well be swamped by opponents of the group's positions.

In response, groups could limit opinion expression forums to members-only sections. Groups could sort out member opinion, especially by use of a password. But public interest groups without members would not be able to use that tactic.

Group leadership, especially for public interest groups, may feel any such solicitation would generate a response that would be inherently unrepresentative of the general public or even the group membership, since it would likely attract only the most active subsample of the group membership or its supporters. Moreover, soliciting opinion in that way runs risks for the leadership. The result could be a group leadership bound by the members' agendas. Groups are not likely to do so since it would offer the membership more power and the leadership less.

Even among groups with membership, such opinion solicitation, beyond a vague invitation to make general comments via e-mail, will not be a staple of Internet sites. Group leadership would have no incentive to incorporate it in the future.

Lobbying Government

But has the Internet affected the basic political activity of groups, that is, lobbying for their interests? One would certainly expect so. Since grassroots lobbying is defined as "any means by which a group generates public pressure on those in government," the Internet can be considered such a means, in fact one with inherent advantages over more traditional forms.[17] Mobilizing the grassroots would seem to be much easier and less expensive via the Web. Because groups now can send messages to large numbers of recipients simultaneously, via the Internet, they avoid the cost of hand-dialed fax transmissions. As a result, groups have cut the costs of labor for faxing or postal fees.

Moreover, hypothetically e-mail transmission can achieve nearly instantaneous results in terms of both reach and response. Individuals on group mailing lists can be reached within minutes. In turn, the group can stimulate near-automatic response to policy maker action. Contacted individuals can do in minutes what used to take days before the creation of the World Wide Web. "Politics is about timing, and being able to send messages quickly on the Internet is an important resource," explained the head of one public interest group.[18]

Anecdotes exist of groups using the Net in this way. In opposing a bill that would have limited lobbying by federally funded public interest groups, a coalition of such groups sent their members bulletins as frequently as twice daily.[19] The Children's Defense Fund sent a press release out via e-mail subscription lists, urging recipients to lobby the president to oppose changes in Medicaid proposed by the 104th Congress. The organization included the e-mail address of the White House to facilitate e-mail lobbying by supporters. It also urged recipients of the message to send the organization their e-mail number to send them flyers to distribute.

But are many groups doing so? Let's answer this question by separating lobbying into two parts—mobilization-specific information and actual mobilization.

Mobilization-Specific Information

This may seem a repetition of what has been discussed above, but there is a difference. Unlike information such as group activities or legislative successes, this news is geared toward effective grassroots participation. Effective grassroots participation, however, requires more specific knowledge regarding pending policy actions and those who undertake them. This information includes background on policy options, particularly bills under consideration, specific pending policy maker actions, and information about which policy makers to contact and how to do so.[20]

Groups have long provided such information offline through newsletters and direct mail appeals. But many now provide that information online. Thirty-seven percent of groups included information on current pending legislation relevant to the group's interests. The United Mine Workers site, for example, posted the full text of bills under consideration. Handgun Control also told the user whether the organization supported or opposed the bill.

Some focused on state-by-state policy actions. The Council on State Governments site included "Issue Alerts," providing brief descriptions of events related to federalism and state government issues. NARAL's site included predictions of the outcome of pending legislation in various states.

Another imperative is knowing who should be contacted. The local member of Congress is the most likely (and effective) target of grassroots lobbying. But since other members with specific committee jurisdictions also affect group interests, they become objects of grassroots lobbying campaigns. Therefore, it becomes essential for activists to know how members of Congress voted on issues of interest to them. Such publication also is designed to alert the policy maker that constituents have access to his or her record on issues of importance to them.[21]

Despite its importance, however, only 16 percent of sites had information about how members of Congress had voted. That dearth is most likely attributable to the cost of creating such databases. Not surprisingly then, those with databases included the larger groups, such as the National Rifle Association, the American Civil Liberties Union, and the American Conservative Union, with the more high profile and probably more visited sites, as well as greater resources.

Finally, since it is necessary to know how to contact relevant policy makers, many groups provided online policy maker contact information. For example, Planned Parenthood, like many other group sites, included a search facility allowing the user to find their member of Congress and receive the respective member's e-mail and Web site addresses. Others, such as the United Mine Workers, merely linked to other sites with lists of members or search facilities.

Mobilization Vehicle

Group sites were used as mobilization tools both for offline as well as online grassroots lobbying. Some sites advertised opportunities for members to lobby in traditional ways. Two-thirds of group sites used the Web to inform members of upcoming group events. However, less than half of those groups used the site to explicitly urge members to participate in group events, probably due to the lack of geographical boundaries of the Net. Exceptions were groups engaging in activities where a significant number of Internet site visitors might be able to participate. Fairness and Accuracy in Reporting, for instance, urged supporters to join the group's picket lines around major newspapers such as the *Washington Post* and the *Los Angeles Times* on specific dates in several cities around the nation.

Some group sites gave advice on how to become involved. The National Coalition for the Homeless offered tips on how to write or call members of Congress or federal bureaucrats. Action on Smoking and Health advised supporters on how to submit their testimony for congressional hearings.

Others were more vague in their promotion of offline activity. Thirteen percent urged members to write to policy makers offline. Often words such as "action needed" or "act now" were displayed in bold letters to stimulate users to offline activity, much as they appear in direct mail pieces. The Amnesty International site featured its "write a letter, save a life," implying that your action (or inaction) would mean life or death to another human being.

One tactic for encouraging mobilization has been to actually facilitate it. In recent years groups have sought to mobilize the grassroots by reducing the effort individuals must undertake in order to participate. They have developed handy postcards the member need only detach from a newsletter, magazine, or direct mail piece. Some groups have even urged members to give permission for their names to be used on telegrams and other mailings to members of Congress without having to continue to obtain the individual's permission or await their own action.[22]

Here is where the Internet comes in as a technological boon. It aids groups both in identifying activists and in soliciting their rapid participation in grassroots lobbying campaigns. Many of the groups are utilizing the Net in just that way.

First, there is the prerequisite of having specific people to mobilize. This usually has consisted of the most active submembership of the group or lists of individuals who are probable supporters of the group's interests.

Groups are incorporating Usenet groups and chat rooms into their mobilization strategies. Such groups instantly reach people with interests the group shares. The proliferation of Usenet groups with narrow, specialized interests aids interest groups in identifying and mobilizing supporters. By posting messages on a variety of Usenet groups, the Taxpayer Assets Project, a Nader public interest group, successfully killed a provision of the Paperwork Reduction Act, which would have limited public access to government documents.[23]

Many groups are creating their own more specialized electronic mailing lists. By joining an e-mail distribution list, the individual is promised regular communications of group news and alerts for mobilization. Such a subscription assists supporters by providing them with information they don't have to hunt for, even on the group's Web site. The group's benefit is the existence of a mailing list of activists who can be mobilized in the group's behalf. This tool gives the group the opportunity to get its message out to supporters quickly, particularly in a legislative crisis situation.

The group hopes individuals on its e-mail distribution list will take immediate action, when called to do so, by sending e-mail or fax messages to policy makers. This is especially true when the group actually embeds e-mail or Web site links to policy makers in the message itself.

Eighteen percent of the sites included solicitations to join their respective e-mail distribution lists. NARAL even had several e-mail distribution lists available depending on the interests of the individual.

The distribution list solicitations promised the user exclusive information on policy issues. The American Conservative Union

(ACU) InfoNet, for example, includes "confidential memos, published commentaries and essays by ACU's leaders, news releases, letters to Congress on key legislation, and other materials" designed to "help you stay on top of what's new and significant in conservative politics."

The titles of these distribution lists often seem designed to stimulate immediate participation. The Feminist Majority Foundation termed its distribution list the "Feminist Alert Network," which offers regular updates on the group's activity. For The People for the American Way, it was "Action Line," which unlike the others, required a fee for enrollment.

But some groups seek to facilitate user participation even further. Fourteen percent of the groups provided their own online form for sending comments to policy makers. Users needed only to fill in the message box and click on the "send" button to register their opinion with the policy maker.

Other organizations, such as the Feminist Majority Foundation, went one step further and provided an actual message to be sent. The sender needed only to fill in personal message header information and then designate which policy makers she or he wished the message sent to. The group had already checked all of the boxes of relevant policy makers allowing the sender to do as little as merely clicking on the "send" box in order to send an e-mail or fax message to groups of members of Congress.

NARAL also had a similar facility for sending e-mail to media organizations. The pro-choice group site offered a page of talking points for the user to include in such mail. Users also could read a sample letter to the editor on current issues, such as legislation on the late-term abortion ban. The user, then, could copy the sample letter into the message box and mail it directly to the media organization, rather than take the time to compose their own.

The American Conservative Union included a section titled "Latest Political Outrage," which targets one or more members of Congress taking positions the group opposes. After explaining the ACU's perspective on the policy maker's action, the group urges site visitors to send e-mail to the legislator and conveniently offers an e-mail link on the same page. The usual targets were Republicans who the group felt had taken liberal stances and might be susceptible to pressure from its supporters.

One measure of the growth of this usage is the emergence of a new industry supplying this service. New companies are forming to provide online grassroots lobbying forms for various groups. And groups such as the Christian Coalition, the League of Women Voters, and the National Funeral Directors Association are signing up for these services.[24]

E-mail was not the only online activity groups encouraged. The ACU also offered supporters an opportunity to sign an online petition to repeal the 16th amendment. People for the American Way included a voter registration form as well as an application for an absentee ballot.

Electronic Mobilizing Effects

But does all of this make any difference? There is evidence that electronic mobilization does facilitate grassroots activity. E-mail received by members of Congress has mushroomed as groups have begun to flood their e-mail systems. During the 105th Congress's debate over Internet censorship, one U.S. senator's office reported that they received more e-mail messages than phone calls or faxes.[25] It is true this was an Internet issue, and therefore likely to draw out Internet users, but other issues will likely receive similar treatment in the future.

The fact that members are receiving much more mass e-mail, much of it potentially generated by groups, than ever before, is attributable to the ease with which groups can mobilize their members through a combination of Internet and e-mail. Once a distribution list has been created, groups or individuals mobilized by groups can send messages just as easily to all members of Congress as they can to one. Consequently, the volume of e-mail in congressional offices has skyrocketed. Much of this can be attributed to the practice of sending widely distributed mail, better known as "spamming." Many groups have long sought a means for alerting their active members to immediate action and then achieving that quick response. E-mail distribution lists offer both ease and rapidity of communication and reaction.

But are these efforts influential? Maybe or maybe not. While unique at first, interest groups' e-mail lobbying efforts have acquired the same status as bulk mailing of forms or post cards. Members of Congress soon begin to discount their role. Their reaction to e-mail may be similar to that of Representative Tom

Campbell: "When it came out it was great. . . And then I began to get unsolicited e-mails, then the majority are unsolicited, then the majority are blast to a hundred people. And so it becomes less and less useful."[26]

At least 50 percent of the incoming e-mail to half of congressional offices consists of generic messages sent to all members of Congress. One staff member admitted that "we hate the mass mails," referring to junk e-mail or "spamming" that has become more common. Another congressional staffer opined that "the e-mail address for the Congressman has to be one of the biggest wastes of taxpayers dollars—the whole thing is a real headache for staff and of no value to the actual constituents."[27]

The Resource Gap

The competition among groups in American politics is often intense but rarely equal. Groups have formed in competition with each other, but they are not guaranteed equal voices or shares in power. As E. E. Schattschneider has noted, "the flaw in the pluralist heaven is that the heavenly chorus sings with a strong upper-class accent." [28]

Most press and public notice as well as policy maker attention is centered on groups who possess substantial resources. The AFL-CIO, the Teamsters, and the United Auto Workers are major players in labor policy. The Sierra Club, the Wilderness Fund, and the National Audubon Society weigh in on environmental matters.

However, size is not necessarily a prerequisite for influence. Groups, such as Greenpeace, can be small, yet influential within their own policy area. When a group possesses both size and intensity, such as the National Rifle Association, it can become quite a force to be reckoned with.[29]

The possession of these resources offers these groups a significant edge over other, poorer groups in the competition for the Internet user. These poorer groups, many of whom are in direct competition on specific legislation (or at least competitors for public resources) with the more powerful groups, lack the resources to be effective players. Groups such as the National Coalition for the Homeless are poorly funded compared with other more high-profile groups.

But shouldn't the Internet change all that? If the Internet is a

Table 3.1 Web Sites by Group Wealth

	Annual Budget		
	Up to 1 Million	1–5 Million	Over 5 Million
Site	50%	56%	85%
No site	50	44	15
Total	100	100	100

Note: See Methodology for explanation.

populist medium, it should be evident in the relationships among groups. With the help of the Internet, it might be assumed that resource-poor groups should be able to narrow the resource gap between themselves and rich groups. Given the relatively low capital costs for communication (essentially hardware and a modem), why shouldn't these smaller groups be able to compete as effectively as the larger ones in affecting public opinion and, ultimately, policy? If this did occur, the Internet would become an equalizing medium between groups and increase the likelihood that the imbalance in group roles would be corrected.

However, the Internet has not had that effect. Resource-rich groups still enjoy a substantial edge. One advantage, of course, is simply being on the Net in the first place. Rich groups will have sites while poor groups may not be able to allocate the resources to establish sites. Poor groups are hard pressed to afford the staff to establish and then maintain Internet sites. Nor do they have the income to pay external contractors.

This difference is dramatically demonstrated in Table 3.1. It shows that 50 percent of groups taking in less than $1 million a year and 56 percent of groups making between $1 and 5 million annually had Web sites. In contrast, 85 percent of those with budgets over 5 million had created sites.

Beyond merely possessing a site, groups differed significantly on the extent of the site. Well-to-do groups were more likely to have sites that were more content-filled, with an attractive layout, and sprinkled with technical innovations. Even if they can do so, the site appeal for poorer groups is likely to be less due to limited resources. For example, the sites with searches of policy makers and specialized information databases are those from more well-off groups. The extent of that information varies depending on the group. The

League of Conservation Voters, for example, has its famous score-card of members' votes on several environmental issues, while Catholics United for Life, a shoestring anti-abortion group, simply lists those members of Congress who had voted against the partial abortion ban. The World Wildlife Fund provides zip code searches so users can find and contact their member of Congress, while the National Organization for the Reform of Marijuana Laws includes merely a list of legislators. Wealthy groups generally can update their sites more frequently, at least weekly and often daily. The National Coalition for the Homeless site, in contrast, was updated only occasionally. More well-to-do groups are more likely to have interactive elements and multimedia features.

The Internet does not level the playing field among groups. Even online, resource-rich groups still have the advantage.

Conclusion

The vision of an Internet age with the public suddenly becoming their own advocates *sans* groups or, at the least, the competition among groups achieving more parity is a lively one in speculation, but hardly matches reality.

Traditional interest groups have found the Internet to be a useful tool for disseminating information to both their members and the general public, maintaining contact with their membership, recruiting new members (or at least reaching a sympathetic audience), and mobilizing their constituencies for political action. They have utilized the advantages of the Internet in order to lower the costs of monitoring politics, organizing group members and other interested individuals, and reaching more individuals who are like-minded but anonymous to the organization.[30]

Power has not shifted to an amorphous group called "the People." They have not challenged groups. Nor is there any indication that common, ordinary citizens will suddenly rise up and take the place of established groups, even in the Internet age.

Among citizens, the actual beneficiaries are the traditional activists who have at their disposal a new, powerful tool for expressing their opinions. These activists will rely on the traditional sites with which they are familiar (those established by the groups to which they already belong). These sites will remain important because they collect information efficiently and rapidly for individuals laboring under time constraints, and they offer a vehicle for uniting their voices with other like-minded activists at times when many others are similarly engaged in grassroots lobbying for the same cause. That is what groups are for, and activists know that.

Nor has the balance of power within groups moved toward the members. Policy making within the group is still within the purview of the leadership. Even in an age when groups could rapidly poll their own members to determine group direction, there are strong disincentives for them to do so.

Nor has power shifted among groups. The technology that will allow people to customize the news they receive and the sites they access (as discussed in the previous chapter) will benefit the established, resource-rich groups. Individuals who choose to view various sites will naturally turn to those sites of groups to which they already belong or sympathize with. The structure increasingly imposed on the Internet will result in maintenance of the status quo—the role of groups as we have known it.

Resource-rich groups still enjoy significant advantages over resource-poor groups: These include advertising more heavily in order to alert Internet users to their presence, developing more technically advanced sites, and offering a greater wealth of relevant content.

Nor are any of these expected power shuffles probable in the future. Traditional groups plainly have adapted and are continuing to adapt to the cyberspace age. This survival mechanism has long characterized successful groups. "The most successful organized interests," predicts Allan J. Cigler and Burdett A. Loomis, "will respond effectively both to internal demands and external circumstances."[31] The threat and challenge of the Internet has motivated groups to adapt this new communication tool for their own purposes.

This will occur not because there will be no change in the way groups operate. The changes instigated by the Web have been dramatic for groups in areas such as information retrieval, information dissemination, and grassroots mobilization. But that is quite distinct from a revolution in power structure, which has not occurred, and which, given the adaption that has already transpired, is unlikely to occur in the future.

FOUR

The Virtual Campaign

At the end of his first presidential debate with Bill Clinton, 1996 GOP presidential candidate Bob Dole did something no other candidate has ever done in the history of presidential debates; he announced the address for his World Wide Web home page and encouraged voters to visit the site. For the GOP presidential candidate, the invitation was a subtle reassurance that he was futuristic and not too old to be president. But, more important for electoral politics, Dole's announcement was a symbol of the Internet's expanding role in the American electoral process.

Dole's act was only one sign that 1996 was an important milestone for the Internet as an election information tool. Election-related sites multiplied throughout the year, representing parties, interest groups, the media, and voter educational organizations.

Political parties developed their own sites—at the national, state, and local levels. The two national major party sites offered users dynamic graphics, clips of speeches and/or advertisements, as well as the texts of press releases, convention speeches, and other news of party events.

Their state affiliates also created separate Web sites. These sites informed voters of their party's candidates in the state, usually through links to home pages of candidates. But they also served internal purposes. They were designed to unify and mobilize party supporters. The Louisiana Democratic Party site featured a chat group and offered assistance on how to obtain an absentee ballot. The Colorado Republican Party site told users, likely those who were already activists, about upcoming party activities.

Even local party organizations provided their own online messages. The Arlington County Republicans featured information on active candidates in the county for whom users could volunteer. Near the end of the campaign, the Grand Prairie Democrats' site listed polling places to encourage local Democrats to vote.

National minor party sites flourished. The Reform Party offered a site where voters could learn about the party's principles, news, and activities. Other parties did similarly, such as the Natural Law Party, the Libertarian Party, and the U.S. Taxpayers Party. Some minor parties even sponsored state or local sites as well. The site for the Green Party of Brooklyn, for example, explained what the Green Party stood for and listed upcoming campaign-related events.

Interest groups even created election-related Web pages. The large national groups featured information about the presidential and congressional campaigns. There was also the very local. The site for the Ballston-Virginia Square Community Association in Arlington, Virginia, for example, informed its members about school board candidates for upcoming elections.

Media sites geared to interest in the election also appeared. Newspapers such as the *Washington Post,* the *Charlotte (N.C.) Observer,* and the *Houston Chronicle* offered online local voters' guides. Other media sites gave voters varied campaign information such as candidate links, poll results, analyses of the campaign, and new campaign ads. These sites included, for example, PoliticsNow (a site created by the *National Journal*) and AllPolitics, maintained by CNN and *Time.*

Educational groups also incorporated the Web in their citizen education efforts. Project Vote Smart's extensive site provided information about state election laws and procedures and links to candidates' home pages. It also published results of questionnaires it had sent to all candidates for state and federal office.

It was the candidate sites, however, that represented the most significant change in 1996. The proliferation of candidate sites confirmed that the Internet had become a tool for candidate communication and voter information. Candidates for all offices were hard pressed not to have some exposure to the Web as a potential communication mechanism. *Campaigns and Elections,* a publication for the elections industry, carried a series of articles about candidate use of the Web.[1] Newspaper stories proliferated about candidate use of the Web to reach voters. At the end of the campaign, the *Wall Street Journal* even published lists of the best and the worst sites. Web addresses appeared in campaign literature, media advertisements, and even on billboards and lawn signs.

The first use of the Internet in a presidential campaign was not in 1996, but in 1992. That year the Clinton-Gore campaign placed campaign-related information on the Internet such as full texts of speeches, advertisements, and position papers, as well as biographical information about the candidates. But Internet use was far smaller then, and there was little notice from journalists or the public, few of whom would have been connected at the time.

Early in the 1996 presidential campaign, however, it became obvious that the Internet would be a component of electoral campaigns. Lamar Alexander was the first to utilize the Internet for campaigning when during the primaries he participated in interactive online sessions with users. Subsequently, a bevy of other candidates such as President Clinton, Senate Majority Leader Bob Dole, Representative Bob Dornan, Senator Arlen Specter, talk show host Alan Keyes, and Senator Richard Lugar created their own campaign home pages. Supporters of potential candidates even created home pages to stimulate interest in a prospective campaign. Colin Powell was the subject of a Web site before he announced he would not be running.

Supporters and opponents of candidates developed their own Web sites. The latter received more press attention and perhaps user notice as well. Bob Dole, Bill Clinton, and Pat Buchanan, among others, were the targets of attack sites. These sites appeared, at first glance, to be the candidate's official site, but a closer look revealed the parody. One such site parodied the Pat Buchanan campaign in 1996. The site's main page design paralleled the official Buchanan site, except for the addition of the Nazi flag in the background.[2]

Presidential candidates were hardly alone in turning to the Web as a voter communication tool. Other candidates responded both to a rapidly expanding online usership and the expectation that at least some users were interested in utilizing the Net to follow the campaign. Candidates in races from Congress to local judge established sites: A.J. "Stan" Musial, Jr., a primary candidate for judge in Hillsborough County, Florida, set up a one-page Web site. Others at the local level included Todd Schmitz, running for Wisconsin State Assembly; Brett Ladd, a District Attorney candidate in Fulton County, Georgia; and Bennett Rutledge, a candidate for the Fairfax County (Virginia) School Board.

More and more people were going online in 1996 for political purposes. According to a Voter News Service exit poll, 26 percent of voters in 1996 said they were regular users of the Internet. Younger voters (under 30) were the most likely of any age group to be on-

Table 4.1 Major Party Candidates with Web Sites
by Type of Candidate

Party	Candidate Type		
	Incumbent	Challenger	Open Seat
Democrat	44%	59%	50%
Republican	56	41	50
Total	100	100	100
	N = 373	N = 116	N = 32

line.[3] According to a Pew Center study, the percentage of people going online for presidential election news moved up to 5 percent in 1996, while 10 percent of voters got election news from the Internet.[4] Among online users, 22 percent said they went online to read news about the 1996 election.[5]

Communicating with Internet users might appear to be more productive than door-to-door canvassing because those using the Web are more likely to vote. In 1996, over two-thirds of Internet users said they would vote. In fact, the proportion of intended voters was even higher among people who used the Internet for political information.[6]

Candidates were responding to these changes. Yet, it is difficult to know exactly how many candidates posted Web sites. A search of three Web candidate lists of congressional candidates immediately following the November general election found 521 congressional candidates with Web sites (see Methodology). Incumbent members of Congress were profiled in 373 or 72 percent of those sites (see Table 4.1). One hundred and sixteen challengers had Web sites, which constituted 22 percent of all candidate Web sites. Open seat candidates constituted the rest. Most incumbents used their official site. Ninety-three percent of the incumbent Web sites were official sites. Many members of Congress who had set up Web sites in the 103rd and 104th Congresses moved easily into campaign sites, particularly since they were constrained by the rules of Congress on the official sites. Representative Peter Torkildson of Massachusetts told his staff he wanted to include in his campaign Web site items he couldn't put in the official one, such as a more expansive personal biography, political speeches, press releases, and issue statements.

The Predicted Electoral Role
of the Internet

Given the interactive nature of the Web, it would be expected that campaign Web sites would be interactive, allowing candidates and voters to engage in a two-way dialogue. This could be accomplished by e-mail, where voters and candidates would exchange correspondence. Such interactivity would also enable voters to learn from other voters, so the interaction would not only be between candidate and voter, but also among voters. This could be achieved through bulletin boards or even candidate-established "chat" rooms or town halls where candidates are available live to respond to voters' queries. One model would be Pat Buchanan's home page which included a bulletin board, allowing users to post messages to be read by other users.

If such individual-oriented campaigning occurred via the Internet, it would signal a return to a campaign style from the pretelevision days. Mass media-oriented campaigns have largely replaced retail campaigning. What interaction occurs is designed for the television cameras, not really for the individuals actually present. This is the case not only for presidential campaigns (with the exception of early primaries such as the Iowa caucus and the New Hampshire primary), but also for many statewide campaigns, especially in larger states. It would mark a reversal in campaign development, particularly at the state and national levels.

Another expected effect of Internet-based candidate communication should be more extensive issue discussion. As voters are able to interact with candidates, candidates would respond with answers related to the issues of concern to voters. That interaction should produce candidate statements addressing specific issue positions. Since candidate Web pages are able to address specific topics at length, the imperatives of soundbites would not be an excuse for superficial issue treatment by candidates. As a result, one would expect a high level of issue content on Web sites.

A seeming beneficiary of Internet-based campaigning would be the resource-poor candidate. Since, theoretically, access to all candidates' sites by the user is on an equal footing, and the cost for posting a home page is minimal, the Internet would appear to have the potential of serving as an equalizing medium for all candidates, both major and minor parties, both well known and obscure.[7]

For example, candidates for third and minor parties rarely have the resources to wage viable campaigns for federal or state elective office (Ross Perot excepting). Minor parties may view Web site creation as an opportunity to make inroads into the domination of the two major parties and place all candidates on a more level playing field. Libertarians, who seem to have a representation among Internet users far beyond their proportion of the general population, would apparently have the best chances of taking advantage of the Internet to reach potential supporters. It has even been suggested that, with the aid of the Internet, the playing field will be leveled to such an extent that "in the future the political system may no longer be dominated by the Democratic and Republican parties."[8]

As a result of this leveling of the playing field, the voter should receive a wider array of viable choices of candidates, parties, and ideologies. Though candidates other than those from the two major parties have long appeared on ballots, voters now will be able to know who these other candidates are before casting a ballot. Given the low cost, coupled with potential high exposure, one should see as high a proportion of sites from lesser-known or obscure or resource-poor candidates as the well-off and well-known candidates.

The Actual Role

Now, by looking at a sample of 100 candidate Web sites, let's look at whether or not these effects occurred (see Methodology). Did Web sites accomplish these developments, or make significant progress toward them, in 1996?

If interactivity is measured by e-mail alone, most candidates attempted interactivity. Seventy-five percent of sites included an option for sending an e-mail message to the campaign. Through their sites, candidates invited public response, typically as an option on the main menu such as "Contact _____ " or "Send a message to _____."

Obviously, candidates were most interested in mail from their own constituents. One candidate's site included the caveat: "We want your input, especially if you reside in the Eighth District of Ohio."

Candidates found, however, that many of the messages they received were from nonconstituents. Why would a nonconstituent write to a candidate for whom they could not vote? Some nonconstituents wrote to comment on the Web site, praising the candidate for putting it up, but also often recommending additions or changes. Others were drawn to candidates who they had found on the Web (perhaps through interest group links) and who they agreed with on key issues. One Democratic candidate for Congress in Texas, who was pro-life on abortion, received e-mail from pro-life Democrats around the nation who were following her campaign.[9]

If candidates had screened e-mail messages in order to concentrate on constituents, they would have avoided the problem of going through nonconstituent mail. But most did not; only 12 percent of the candidate sites requested that the e-mail sender identify himself or herself before sending a message.

Such screening was not necessary in 1996 due to the dearth of e-mail messages. Most candidates contacted reported receiving few e-mail messages through the site anyway. Yet, that may not be true in the future as Internet usage increases. Candidates will want to give priority in replying to their own constituents.

If interactivity is gauged instead by the voters being able to hear from one another, as well as the candidate, then that also occurred rarely in 1996. Only three of the sites featured bulletin boards where e-mail messages from visitors were posted on the site.

Only two candidates took further steps toward interactivity. Representative Tom Campbell, in his reelection campaign, introduced an electronic town hall, where users could send him e-mail messages which he then posted and publicly answered. The site included a commitment that he would respond to e-mail within 48 hours. The other candidate, Ken Poston, a congressional candidate from Georgia, featured a virtual reality town hall, where the candidate appeared once a month to take questions from participants who created avatars for themselves and interacted with each other as well as the candidate. The peculiarities of the Internet were still new to Poston. "You'd be sitting there discussing policy with a giant tuna," said Poston. "The message on the screen would be 'Giant Tuna wants to know your position on such and such policy.'"[10]

Interactivity was attempted by most candidates, but the response attracted less voters within their constituency than they had expected, and more of a different variety of voter: Internet surfers who were interested in political sites. If interactivity is measured by live interaction through chat rooms or virtual town halls, such interactivity almost never existed.

The extent to which candidates promoted interactivity was either an e-mail address, or more frequently, an actual link to a message box where voters could write a message. Admittedly, this level of interactivity allows the public to respond, but it lacks the public nature of such interaction. The extent to which the candidate responds (whether he or she responds at all) is private. With the exception of Campbell, candidates did not promise to respond within a certain time period.

Candidates usually did not invite specific replies to issue positions or to campaign events. Candidate appeals for e-mail consisted of general solicitations for input. If users wanted to view the e-mail link as an opportunity for expression of views on specific positions of the candidate, it was at the initiative of the user, since the site rarely mentioned it.

Moreover, e-mail links are rather sterile, much like a postal letter. A "chat" room or virtual town meeting demonstrates the candidate is there (or perhaps someone else writing on their behalf); one is communicating with an actual live individual and getting an instantaneous response.

The perception of interactivity candidates created in 1996 gave the illusion of interactivity, that is, the candidate wants your input. Yet, it gave the candidate complete control over how or whether she or he responded. It left the interaction, if it actually occurred, private. It also did not allow users to interact with each other.

Such control makes sense in a campaign. Otherwise, the candidate ends up responding publicly to others' agenda, particularly others who may not be in the district, or even so, not necessarily representative of constituent concerns. It should not be surprising that in a medium where control has the potential of slipping away quickly, candidates would want to maintain restrictions on how their site is used.

For most candidates, the discussion of issues on sites was not any more extensive than a campaign brochure. This was despite the fact that the Internet nearly abolished space limitations. Eighty-seven percent of candidates discussed their own issue positions, but such a review usually did not constitute most of the content of the site. The Internet primarily acted as a personal image advertising tool, incorporating the candidates' biography, a solicitation for help from potential activists, and the perception of interactivity with the candidate.

Surprisingly, candidates did not use their Web sites to discuss the Internet itself. Only 8 percent mentioned issues related to the Internet. They may have not held positions on Internet issues or they may have assumed most Internet users were more interested in other issues.

Was the playing field leveled through the Internet? Some candidates seemed to hope it would be. For example, long-shot candidates for president established home pages during 1996. Republican contenders Representative Bob Dornan, Senator Richard Lugar, and talk show host Alan Keyes, all likely losers, had their Web sites listed alongside those for Dole, Buchanan, and Alexander. Home pages, including biographical information as well as platform positions, organization addresses, and press releases from their campaigns, were created by dark horse candidates (and unlikelies) such as Charles Doty, a Tulsa, Oklahoma minister running for the Republican nomination; Charles Collins, a Florida rancher also running as a Republican; and William Winn, an independent from Mesa, Arizona. Minor party candidates also set up sites. Many candidates up and down the ballot for the Libertarian, Reform, Green, and Natural Law parties had sites during 1996.

The Internet, then, apparently equalizes the playing field in one sense since sites for these lesser-known candidates do exist. And, theoretically, once on the Web they are equal in terms of access. Armed with an address, any site can be as easily accessed by a user as any other.

But is that enough? No.

Resource-rich candidates were still advantaged. Incumbents usually the most well-endowed candidates in congressional races, could rely on their own official government sites.

Challengers, on the other hand, were forced to create (and pay for) their own sites, thus devoting usually scarce resources to match the incumbent's free Web publicity. Challengers did have more freedom with their sites. They could be blatantly political, while incumbents were limited by rules of the U.S. House or Senate on the campaign usage of their site. In fact, technically, the official sites were not campaign sites at all. Yet, they often substituted for such.

Some incumbents in 1996 created separate campaign sites in order to avoid the official constraints imposed by the House or the

Senate on official member Web sites. South Carolina Senator Strom Thurmond's campaign, for instance, had its own well-developed Web site, perhaps to dispel the idea that Thurmond, like Dole, was out of touch with the technological age. Thurmond's campaign site featured his party ties, polling results during the campaign, and a solicitation to contribute to the campaign. All of these features were prohibited from Thurmond's official site.

This is a trend that will mushroom in the future. Incumbents will create Internet sites explicitly for campaigning. In fact, many of the winners in 1996 kept their campaign sites opened and used them as political sites through 1997 and then again as campaign sites in 1998. They will be joined by other incumbents in the future who will not want to be limited by House or Senate rules of official sites.

As a result, incumbents will be even further advantaged. Not only will they have an official government site advertising themselves, but they also will own a political site that will be in effect throughout their term and not just during the electoral campaign.

Resource-poor candidates remained unequal in other ways as well. They were still disadvantaged by advertising, voter interest, and site appeal. Advertising their home pages is a major problem for candidates seeking to attract visitors in the midst of a chaotic and constantly ballooning World Wide Web. Challengers in 1996 often had to depend on links from organizations that cover politics. Web sites such as PoliticsNow, for example, linked to sites of several lesser-known presidential candidates, including contenders for the major party nominations, minor party candidates, and independents. Other candidates were at least given space to advertise their names, addresses, and party affiliations, if any. Since these sites have established well-recognized and advertised home pages, and are willing to offer links to less-established candidates, the challenger can get some publicity.

News media coverage of sites favored the well-known candidates, which excluded minor party candidates. One Libertarian candidate complained that the news media wrote articles about the Web sites of the major parties but would not mention those of Libertarian candidates.[11] One Webmaster found that journalists would "look at [the web site] and see if they could get some more information for their article (about candidates), but they wouldn't advertise it in the paper."[12]

The incumbents' official government sites, on the other hand, were free advertisements for the member. And they were more likely to be found and seen by voters, since they were linked to other official government sites and voters were more likely to know an incumbent by name and conduct a search.

Another advantage for established candidates is voter interest. Voters' likely approach to the Internet as reinforcement dictates focusing on the sites of candidates with whom they think they would agree. The two major party candidates will attract more users seeking such reinforcement, though supporters of other parties may visit their respective sites more frequently due to the need for stronger reinforcement.[13] Candidates such as Bob Dole or Pat Buchanan, who already have broad name recognition, are going to attract more users than other candidates who are less well known or supported.

For the most part, voters are not going to gravitate to sites of parties or candidates they have never heard of, do not agree with, and assume will not win. Why should they do so?

Site appeal attracts users in the first place but also maintains their interest. The differences between rich and poor candidates can be stark. Resource-rich candidates can devote part of their vast resources to a well-developed Internet site and still retain sufficient funds for other activities. Meanwhile, resource-poor candidates must choose to have a simple site or no site at all.

For example, Chris Cannon of Utah, who eventually spent $2 million dollars on his congressional campaign, developed a site with extensive features, including a specific listing of position differences with his opponent and a calendar of candidate events which groups could use to request the candidate's appearance. His opponent, Bill Orton, who raised only $697,000, did not have a site at all, figuring that the site would be a waste of the campaign's limited resources. Cannon defeated Orton, even though the latter was the incumbent.

In 1996, those candidates who were resource-poor did not want to "waste" resources on a technology that attracted relatively few users. They needed to husband their resources for more proven techniques of reaching voters.

Will the choice be easier in the future? No, it will become harder. Resource-poor candidates will know they need something. The Internet will become more of a staple in campaigning, but it will not necessarily become a less-expensive one. In fact, with the growing presence of multimedia, the gap in site appeal between rich and poor candidates is more prone to widen, not shrink.

Candidates who are truly resource-poor will not be establishing Web sites. Only those who are poorer than their opponents (but not actually poor) may fit in this category of constructing sites and attempting to compete on the Web. But even they will be confronted with the realities of finances as greater resources bring more features attractive to users.

The Functions of Candidate Web Sites

The failure of the Web to achieve the populist ideals attributed to it does not mean the Web does not play a role in campaigns. Bluntly, that role is to serve the candidates, the very people who create the Web sites in the first place. Since the sites belong to them, it is logical to assume the candidates would use their resources to promote themselves.

The main goal of viable candidates is to win. Other candidates run to prepare for anticipated success in the future or to achieve publicity for other purposes such as ideology or amusement. The Web should be seen as viable candidates see it, that is, as one of the tools available to achieve victory.

So, our attention should be directed to how *candidates* used the Web to affect the electoral outcome. Using 1996 as our case, we need to explore what functions these sites perform for candidates. Trent and Friedenberg contend that "communication is the means by which the campaign begins, proceeds, and concludes," while Goldenberg and Traugott posit that "conveying campaign messages to win votes is the central activity of political campaigns."[14] Since communication is so vital to a campaign, and candidates and voters are turning to the Internet to transmit and receive information, the Internet must be studied as a communication tool.

The existence of the Internet not only offers candidates another avenue for reaching voters, but is, in some respects, advantageous over offline communication forms. One such form is news releases. Though many smaller newspapers and radio stations use candidate news releases practically verbatim, other larger ones do not. The candidate can attempt to influence production but cannot control it. With the Web, the candidate can govern the production of the message. Web site layout and content are completely within the dictates of the candidate.

This control is important for a candidate. Obviously, the candidate Web site exists in a competitive world. Yet, unlike news accounts, the information the candidate transmits over the site is of the candidate's choosing. Hence, while visiting a candidate's site, the user is being exposed to the candidate's message unfiltered by other forces.

However, the Web plainly is less useful than, say, direct mail or newsletters because unlike those communications forms, the campaign lacks control over Internet distribution.[15] Yet, the distribution problem is not as acute as with news releases, since Internet political site users, at least to this point, are more likely to be politically interested and actual voters. Given the demographics of Internet users, combined with those of politically active individuals, distribution can be assumed to be more narrowly focused to those who are middle to high income and fairly well educated—seemingly a model audience of potential voters.[16]

Another lure for the Web in 1996, and certainly still to be true in the future, was the limited cost of establishing Web sites. For some candidates, the cost was nothing. Volunteers offered to establish and maintain sites on their behalf. Even for those candidates who paid, costs usually did not exceed $10,000 and were far less for simple sites with relatively few pages. Maintenance was not expensive either, usually no more than one or two thousand dollars, but often much less.

Web site creation and maintenance for candidates is a new cottage industry.[17] This is true not only in certain known high-tech areas, such as the Silicon Valley in California, the area around Microsoft in Seattle,and the Research Triangle in North Carolina, but also throughout the entire country.

What does the Internet do for campaigns seeking to communicate with voters? What are the communication functions these web sites perform for candidates in an electoral campaign? Six functions of Internet sites can be identified for campaign communication: candidate symbol, information dissemination, opinion gauge, reinforcement of vote choice and GOTV (Get Out The Vote), volunteer ID and fundraising, and interactivity. How does the Internet perform these functions?

Candidate Symbol

Clearly, candidate Web pages are created to communicate to voters. But in 1996 many of those for whom the message was intended would never access the Internet themselves. The message was not any specific information the candidate may have placed on the site, but a general message that the candidate was utilizing this new technology to communicate with voters. One Webmaster admitted that "most voters are not using the Internet. We used the existence of the pages to show that (the candidate) was in touch with current trends."[18]

Some campaigns assumed voters expected them to have a Web site. "I think having a Website these days is like having a mailbox," explained one campaign aide. "You gotta have one. You can argue about how important it is. But its just seen as a greens fee that you have to pay."[19] Others were prompted by voters who urged them to establish one.

The Web site became a symbol of the candidate in the minds of voters. The site connoted awareness of the future and an ability to adapt to new innovations. It symbolized the candidate was current with the times, even futuristic in approach. Candidates and their Webmasters saw Web site launches, particularly, complete with press releases and press conferences, as the first and best opportunity to convey that symbolic message. Bob Dole's Web site announcement during the presidential debate was one such effort. The point of Dole's statement was not so much the site itself as it was Dole's need to reassure voters that he had one. (Interestingly, Dole was not as fully adapted to the Internet as he pretended. He misspoke the address leaving out a crucial period, which is a cardinal sin for Net users. He also described his home page to a *New York Times* reporter as "my whatchamacalit.")[20]

The symbolism was seen as critical for certain groups of voters. Among some constituencies, failure to have a Web site in 1996 would be viewed as an inability to adjust to the future. The symbolism of the Web site was most important not only for regular Internet users, but also for particular groups of voters, such as college students, many of whom have access to the Internet through their universities. For example, congressional candidate Julia Carson sought to reach college-age people in order to blunt her primary opponent's contacts with the local College Democrats organization.[21]

Some sites were created only as necessary responses to opponent's sites. Candidates borrowed not only the idea of a Web site, but they probably also stole the ideas for specific features. One candidate contended that one of her opponents incorporated a poll on his site only after her site had created a successful one.[22]

The design of the Web site was also intended to shape the users' image of the candidate as a person. Webmasters sought to overcome the sterile nature of the computer screen through graphics, layout, and overall structure, offering a warm and attractive portrait of the candidate. Joe Rogers' Webmaster sought to reflect Rogers' light-hearted personality. For example, in part, the site parodied Mr. Rogers' Neighborhood.[23] Julia Carson's site included flowers on various pages. The decoration received favorable comments from site visitors and, according to the campaign, contributed to her "ladylike" image.[24]

Information Dissemination

Information dissemination is a critical component of campaign communication; one might argue it is the core.[25] It includes both candidate name recognition and familiarity.[26] It also means conveying image as well as issue information, and including facts about the opponent in order to weaken voter predispositions toward the opponent or reinforce already existing negative predispositions.

Like other forms of campaign communication, Web sites concentrated on two types of information—positive information about the candidate and negative information about the opponent. A third type of information was about the candidate's ideology. This was found primarily among minor party candidates, particularly the Libertarians.

The Candidate   Not unlike other communication vehicles, the priority message on Web sites seemed to be image information about the candidate—personal biographies, photos with the family or constituents. Candidate sites usually opened with a menu of options for the user, such as a biography, issue positions, press releases, volunteer opportunities, links, and so on. A common feature of Web sites was the inclusion of biographies of the candidates. Eighty-seven percent of the candidate sites included a biography, usually similar to the kind printed on brochures and flyers. A few also included photos of the candidate and the family.

The personal sections about the candidates often read like campaign brochures, which, in many cases, was exactly their source, although one candidate turned the order around. Julia Carson's congressional campaign printed the Web site main page and laid it out in a brochure, which became the primary door-to-door handout during the last month of the campaign.[27]

But many candidates also used their site for more substantive information dissemination, such as position papers, descriptions of their records, and goals if elected or reelected to office. Candidate Web sites certainly were not devoid of issue content. Eighty percent of the candidate sites analyzed included issue positions of the candidate. At times these positions were extensively described through separate links connecting to lengthy statements. One example was William Pascrell, Democratic candidate for Congress from New Jersey, whose site featured "Bill on the Issues." Each issue—health care, entitlement programs, education—linked to a page or more of discussion by the candidate about that issue area.

Candidates also were not shy about identifying themselves with a political party. Of those who belonged to a party, 96 percent so identified themselves. But by another measure, the partisan affiliation was less important. Only 39 percent of candidates linked to a partisan site, such as the home page of their national, state, or local party organization. All of the Libertarians, however, did so.

Some sites included speeches or press releases announcing their candidacy. This was common also because many candidates did not take the time to update their sites, and the announcement was fresh material at the time the site was created.

Realizing that users may view the site information as mere propaganda, some candidates featured material from more objective sources. For example, 11 percent of the sites mentioned newspaper endorsements of the candidate, and some included the texts of such editorials. Some even inserted news media stories about the candidate and the campaign. Fourteen candidate sites included endorsements from other politicians. Some included poll results showing them, not surprisingly, ahead or at least gaining.

Some of the campaign Web sites advertised the candidate's schedule in order to alert supporters to the candidate's appearances and opportunities to help out. Twenty of the sites analyzed included a calendar of upcoming candidate events. The purpose, according to one Webmaster, was to "have a recourse for volunteers to know where they can find out what they can do."[28] One even included a function on the calendar to allow groups to send an e-mail message requesting the candidate appear at a function, although it was rarely used.[29]

Six of the candidates even offered campaign finance information about themselves. (The FEC could require candidates who take matching funds and who use the Internet to supply such information about themselves or at least include links to the FEC, where the voter could obtain the information.)

Another aspect of candidate information was the nature of affiliations emphasized on the candidate's site. Including hot links to other sites is a favorite way to enhance the attractiveness of a site. It offers ease for the user in moving among like-minded sites and avoids lengthy bookmark lists. Hot links offered the candidates an opportunity to readily demonstrate their ideological and partisan leanings. Some Republican candidates linked not only to the national or state party organizations, but also to ideological groups such as the Heritage Foundation, a right-wing organization, or to the Cato Institute, a libertarian think tank.

Yet, hot links were also risky. The content of the site's links could hurt the candidate if users had a negative connotation of a group's site. One conservative candidate's site, for example, featured links with Operation Rescue and its radical pro-life operations. This connection was noted on talk radio interviews the candidate participated in and she was labeled a radical.[30] Only 22 percent of the Web sites included links to interest groups. This included the four Libertarian candidates who all linked to libertarian groups, such as the Cato Institute. Only one in five candidates included links from news organizations, local or state attractions, or governmental bodies such as Thomas or the White House. Some links touted the state or community. These included links to local government, tourism, or educational institutions within the constituency. A comprehensive list of sites or hot links to political megasites was more safe for the candidate than a shorter list of specifically designated sites reflecting the preferences of the candidate.

Forty-eight percent of the candidates did not link to any other site. The failure to link sometimes was the result of neglect of the site administrators after its initial creation, but in some cases it was strategic. One Webmaster admitted he chose not to include any links not so much to avoid negative associations, but to prevent users from prematurely leaving the site.[31]

Related to linking is the inclusion of mentions of group endorsements. Twenty-five percent of the Web sites mentioned groups from whom the candidate had received an endorsement. The relatively low number of such endorsements on home pages may be due to the lack of group endorsements. Or, more likely, most candidates may have been reluctant to use such information when they were unsure who was viewing it.

It should come as no surprise that the material candidates placed on their sites about themselves was wholly positive. Yet, coverage of their opponents was not so positive.

The Opponent   Fifty-three percent of the sites mentioned the opponent(s) in the race. This number may even be inflated, since most of these candidates were challengers or contenders for open seats. Incumbent sites were less likely to mention opponents since it would give the challenger unnecessary publicity. While 58 percent of the challengers mentioned their opponents, only 25 percent of the incumbents did so.

Internet sites would seem to be an ideal opportunity for candidates to specify their issue positions and to offer a contrast with opponents, thus providing useful issue information for voters. But most candidates did not do so. While a bare majority mentioned opponents, only 39 percent offered any criticism of other candidates which may have alerted voters to the differences between the candidates. Even fewer, 27 percent, explicitly mentioned any issue position of an opponent that would then serve as a contrast with the candidate's positions.

Challengers, particularly, would appear to want to communicate information about their opponents that will reduce the opponents' electoral support or prevent its occurrence in the first place. Web sites, with their seemingly limitless text possibilities, offer candidates the opportunity to paint a portrait of the opponent without direct challenge.

One example is Bill Pascrell's attack on the incumbent:

> The Republicans in Washington have talked a good game, but as the saying goes, "actions speak louder than words." Bill Martini gutted Medicare, voted to cut school lunches, to reduce Head Start for

preschoolers and to cut student loans for college by 10 billion dollars. While I was co-sponsoring a progressive policy in New Jersey to keep our minimum wage at a level where it encouraged work, Bill Martini repeatedly flip-flopped in Congress. He also raised taxes on those making less than $28,000 a year by voting to cut the Earned Income Tax Credit, a program praised by Ronald Reagan. These programs are critical to the hard-working families of the Eighth District. Bill Martini has failed these families.

Congressional candidate Chris Cannon's Web site listed 446 differences between himself and his opponent.[32] Cannon was unable to get the news media to cover more than a few of these differences in media coverage. Many were minor in nature. But Cannon's site could and did document in detail those differences for the interested user.

Cannon found what other candidates did as well, that is, that they could say much more about their opponents on the Internet than in other settings. One even posted the interest group ratings of his opponent, the incumbent. Many of those criticisms were personal, not issue-related. Only half of those who criticized their opponents mentioned the opponent's issue positions. For example, Julia Carson's congressional campaign in Indiana, which avoided "going negative" generally, did go negative on the Web. A "Newt" page documented the relationship between Carson's Republican opponent and House Speaker Newt Gingrich, thus tying the opponent to an unpopular national politician.

Another example of a personal attack was Jeffrey Kitchen's Web site:

> On a very personal level I am deeply offended by do nothing politicians such as the incumbent from our district, John A. Boehner. Mr. Boehner represents the very worst in American Politics, and represents the people of Ohio's 8th district, not at all.

One drawback with criticizing an opponent on the candidate's Web site is the inability of the candidate to disassociate himself or herself from the attack. Negative campaigning on the Web, unlike negative advertising elsewhere, is clearly tied to a candidate making the charges since it is, after all, their Web site. Candidates are unsure how much negative campaigning should be pursued on the Web. Are Internet users more likely than other types of voters to feel the Web should be a positive tool?

However, another type of site can serve that role. Backers of candidates who create their own sites can be a source of vigorous criticism of the opponents without any responsibility by the candidate. These sites also proliferated in the 1996 campaign and played that role.

Most of the sites studied relied on positive messages—the candidates' background and issue positions—rather than negative messages. Negative messages usually did not appear on the main page and usually were not clearly identified as a link; the user could find them only after looking. Even comparative messages were not frequent, nor were responses to the opponent.[33] The absence of response messages suggests the Internet still has not achieved the level of interaction common now in candidate advertising on television. Nor did the Internet itself become an issue in campaigns, except on rare occasions.

The open nature of Internet sites invited opponents to keep watch on each other. Candidates and Webmasters related that they would frequently visit opponent's sites to collect opposition research. However, such visits can be almost as transparent as walking through the door. Some Webmasters tracked whether their opponents were frequenting their site and wondered whether recurrent visitors, as evidenced by host names, included more than just supporters.

The lack of control over the distribution of the message plagued campaigns. Some candidates were afraid that going negative would backfire on them. One campaign staffer said that the campaign "would never put anything up there that we wouldn't put on CNN."[34] One candidate refused to discuss issue positions on his site for fear of use by his opponent in negative advertisements."[35]

Candidates also worried that opponents would not only use the information but play tricks in other ways, such as by pretending to be supporters in order to be placed on the e-mail distribution list and learn about campaign activities. The e-mail function, due to its relative anonymity, worried some Webmasters as a tool for potential mischief: "You can't ever tell who you are handing it to," one campaign staffer complained. "If you're out there and somebody says they're going to help you, you can look in their eyes and tell if they're going to be on your side or not. But, on e-mail you can't do that."[36]

Collecting information about the opponent became easier with the Internet. Sites were also used to collect opposition research.

With easy access to legislative information, challengers could easily document useful ammunition such as incumbents' votes on issues, bills sponsored and cosponsored, and activity on committees.

Ideology   A few candidates emphasized ideology, not themselves. These were primarily Libertarians who used their sites to introduce site visitors to Libertarian philosophy through statements of Libertarian platform planks, links to Libertarian sites, invitations to take what is called "The World's Smallest Political Quiz" (which is weighted toward libertarian ideas), and solicitations to join the Libertarian Party. But Reform Party candidates also placed some emphasis on party positions. Such minor party candidates, perhaps realizing their likely electoral defeats, promoted ideological conversion, rather than electoral victory.

Opinion Gauge

Candidates seemed to fall into two categories: One group employed the site for advertising themselves much like a paid advertisement or brochure, while the other group viewed the Internet as a participatory forum as well. They conducted nonscientific surveys and allowed visitors to the site to post their own comments. The former group, however, was by far the larger of the two. Only one of 10 candidate Web sites analyzed included an opinion poll for users to register their opinions.

Opinion polls allowed the candidate (and when the results were posted, the users as well) to see how visitors to the site who participated felt on various issues. But candidates who used polls usually kept the results to themselves. Only two of the sites analyzed also included poll results.

Approaches to the polls varied. Those using polls commonly posted questions on several issues and then allowed the user to click on boxes to express their views. Ed Munster, candidate for Congress from Connecticut, polled users on issues of general interest such as a flat tax, but only featured one issue at a time. Such a tactic offered a nearly automatic updating option since a new issue could be added regularly, thus attracting the user back again and again with the opportunity to vote on another issue.

Online polls were attractive to many users because they were allowed to express opinions anonymously. For example, the site of

Michael Robinson, candidate for Congress from Colorado, attracted 2000 participants in his online opinion survey.

However, as a gauge of constituent opinion, the polls were seriously flawed. Few candidates identified whether participants were constituents. Most of the users voting in Robinson's poll did not even live in his district.[37] Moreover, Robinson's survey included his own view and then allowed participants to vote whether or not they agreed with him. The result was the posting of survey results that showed a large number of participants disagreeing with his position on some issues. For example, by the end of the campaign, 49 percent said they disagreed with his position on gay rights. That practice enhanced voters' attitudes that their votes would be counted and displayed, even if they ran counter to Robinson's views, but it could not have been useful in demonstrating the appeal of Robinson's issue stances when so many survey respondents were seen in disagreement. Essentially, Robinson was offering free advertising to those who disagreed with him. Candidates, then, would be expected to be wary of publicizing poll results if they vary from their own positions on issues.

Voter Reinforcement and GOTV

Campaigns use a variety of methods to assess voter opinions, such as commissioning surveys, holding focus groups, mailing questionnaires, querying selected close associates such as party leaders or other political activists, or merely talking with voters while engaging in personal campaigning.[38] The purpose is to identify supporters in order to reinforce the intent to support.

But voters who have already made a vote choice before election day occurs also must be reinforced in their decision and encouraged to appear at the polls. The messages to this group are far different than those to voters who are still undecided. Newsletters, direct mail, and phone banks are usually employed to communicate the reinforcement and GOTV message.

The Internet was used as a tool for such identification in 1996. Candidates searched for interested voters, volunteers, and even donors through the Net.

Mailing List Creation   The Internet allows users to browse through sites seemingly anonymously. (In reality, users *can* be identified, at least generally.) Yet, some candidates realized that of the visitors coming to their site, there may be supporters who would be willing to establish a continuous relationship with the campaign.

Candidates for offices from national to local invited users to join e-mail distribution lists to obtain messages throughout the campaign. In the Dole campaign, the user could join an e-mail subscription list that would make available to him or her periodic reports on the progress of the campaign. Seven percent of the candidates in the content analysis also included e-mail distribution list options.

The e-mail list became a supporter action network. Periodically messages were sent to users on the list about candidate appearances, press endorsements of the candidate, or statements the candidate delivered to the press. Colorado congressional candidate Joe Rogers sent out periodic "Action for Mr. Rogers Neighborhood" messages to his e-mail list. The messages featured announcements of upcoming campaign stops and media appearances, and newspaper and political endorsements.

GOTV   Immediately before the election, the e-mail distribution list became a GOTV list. Representative Tom Campbell: "Right before the election, 48 hours before the election, I e-mailed everybody who allowed me to, to remind them to vote."[39] However, the e-mail distribution lists in 1996 were not an effective GOTV tool because they were not as popular with Internet users as candidates had hoped. Few people actually signed up for the lists. Candidates reported typically less than 100 names on their list. Apparently, the vast majority of visitors preferred to remain anonymous.

Only 6 percent of the candidate sites offered voting information, such as how to register to vote or find the location of a polling place. Such information will likely appear in the future since placing such information is not difficult and will be viewed by candidates as potentially increasing turnout.

Volunteer ID and Fundraising

A common feature of candidate Web site main pages was the "how you can help" link. This was the invitation to become an activist in the campaign. On Lamar Alexander's home page, users could find a list of local organizers in their area they could contact in order to volunteer. On most of the sites volunteers were asked to complete and electronically submit a form to the campaign specifying what they could do, such as post a yard sign, staff a phone bank, distribute literature, or host a fundraiser. Sixty percent of the candidate sites analyzed included solicitations for volunteers. It is surprising there were not more. But candidates reported that the invitations attracted few volunteers. It is difficult to know whether this failure was due to a small Internet population or the reality that volunteers, when they exist, find campaigns through other, offline means—family, friends, coworkers, clubs, and other organizations.

Volunteering from the Internet returns us to the question of whether online activity actually spurs participation. This is another piece of anecdotal evidence from the candidates that the answer is "no."

Fundraising   Jesse Unruh coined the phrase: "Money is the mother's milk of politics."[40] Most candidates, especially challengers, are desperate for cash. And they spend inordinate amounts of time trying to find it.

In 1996, many of them realized that since the Internet could reach thousands of people, it could also be useful as a fundraising tool. Forty-six percent of candidates included solicitations for contributions on the Web site. Interestingly, most incumbents and almost all open seat candidates did so, while most challengers did not.

The most primitive method was inviting the prospective donor to contact the campaign through telephone or regular mail address, which was usually provided. A somewhat more sophisticated method was clicking on a box and then sending in an e-mail message allowing the campaign to contact the potential contributor to make an offline contribution. A few candidates went further, providing boxes with specific dollar amounts, which the user then printed out and sent back with a check. Some encouraged faxing the form, with a check following.

Noticeably lacking were credit card transfers online, which would seem to lend itself to easy Web donations. However, Internet security for financial transactions is still problematic in the minds of many users, as discussed earlier. Moreover, since campaigns for federal office in 1996 were prohibited from accepting credit card donations, they could not take credit card numbers online.

This is one aspect where incumbents who rely on their official sites are disadvantaged, since no such solicitations can be made. But in 1996, the advantage for challengers was slight. According to the candidates, giving over the Internet was extremely light. Even the Clinton campaign site brought in only an estimated $10,000 through such donations.[41]

Though 1996 was not a successful year for Internet contributions, the future for donor solicitations by candidates may be different. The costs for solicitations are minimal—space on a Web site—and, more important, candidates will still need the money. Since Internet donating is in its infancy, it should not be surprising that few Americans took advantage of it.

But even as Internet usage grows, such giving still may lag well behind other forms. Many givers want something in return for their support—a table (or at least a seat) at a candidate dinner, a photograph with a famous politician, or perhaps a night in the Lincoln Bedroom. Few candidates (and none of those whose sites were analyzed or those who were interviewed) offered anything in return on the Internet. One exception was Bob Dole's campaign, which included an online donation form and also offered a free "Dole for President" mousepad for those giving at least $25.

The Limitations of the Web as Electoral Communication Tool

In 1996, the problems and limitations of the Web became apparent for both candidates and the voters they sought to reach, meaning the politically interested who use the Web for candidate information. Information dissemination was the most common function apparent on the Web. Campaign brochures, complete with biographies, some issue positions, and, occasionally, photographs of the candidate were placed onto the Web.

Other features of campaigns were not replicated on the Web as much. Very few candidates utilized the Web as an opinion gauge. A minority used the Web to reinforce vote choice or GOTV. Volunteer ID and fundraising also were minimal.

The explanations may stem from the experimental nature of the Internet in 1996. Many candidates wanted to be "on the Net," but gave little thought as to how to utilize this medium effectively. They relied on the Web as a duplication of existing campaign literature, rather than employing its own unique characteristics effectively.

The Internet turned out not to be an effective tool for identifying supporters, even for such limited activity as receiving e-mail notices. Visitors to sites were far more interested in perusing than joining. Though many candidates, particularly the major party candidates, received thousands of spectators, they located few willing to participate in their campaign, except perhaps through voting. Most candidates failed to integrate the Web and other campaign communication tools. However, most felt their sites had not been advertised enough to lure users.

One explanation for the discrepancy between the number of visitors to the site and the number who actually volunteered is the number of nonconstituent visitors. Again, since few candidates even identified those who sent them e-mail, it is hard to know how many of the visitors were constituents. But it is not illogical to assume that the politically interested Web surfers, no matter where they were located, were browsing through candidate lists and checking out candidates across the nation as an armchair sport.

This conclusion may be disappointing to those who saw the Internet as a motivating weapon. However, it is the expectation that may be false, that is, that the introduction of the Net, especially with an abundance of political information, would act as a stimulant on voters. It assumes, wrongly, that new technology alone can produce better citizens.

Another fallacy was the expectation that placing a site on the Web would lead to hordes of site visitors, particularly among constituents. It is doubtful many Internet users even knew that candidates within their area had home pages.

Again, finding ways to advertise the Web site is a challenge for many candidates. In 1996, some candidates made the roll-out of their sites major news announcements for the press. For example, one held a ceremony at a local Internet cafe and invited press to come, although none did.[42] Others issued press releases alerting the press to the address of the site. Some newspapers did publish stories on candidate Internet sites, usually focusing on the major party candidates, but press coverage usually did not match what candidates needed to broadly advertise. Some candidates placed the address on letterhead, brochures, newspaper advertising, and billboards. One congressional candidate put the address on his bumper stickers.[43] However, for many, the decision to advertise, if it came at all, usually occurred late in the campaign after literature had been printed.

Though the use of search engines for advertising is common, some candidates tried to alert politically interested Internet users to the site's existence by posting messages on Usenet groups. Others did little advertising, allowing word-of-mouth to spread the news. Still others did virtually nothing to advertise.

Failure to advertise reinforced the conclusion that candidates considered their sites experimental—a frill that would be explored if there was time. There was a low commitment to devote resources to advertising it.

Another problem with a candidate's use of the Web was that e-mail from site visitors often remained unanswered for long periods of time. Unlike regular mail senders, e-mail senders expect quick turnaround. However, some campaigns either were unaware of the rules of e-mail etiquette or were too preoccupied with other tasks. This decision to devote minimal resources to Web site e-mail is understandable, given the experimental nature of the Web and the lack of confidence in its ability to reach large numbers of voters.

Still another difficulty was keeping up with the imperatives of the Internet, such as its dynamism. Unlike brochures, Web sites are not printed once and then distributed. Yet, many candidates treated them as such. In 1996, many candidates posted Web pages early in their candidacy and then left them dormant. As a result, some users likely went to the site periodically at first and then, after realizing it wasn't changing, left and never returned. Sites not maintained quickly became stagnant and useless.

Users expect Web sites to be continually updated, and candidates' sites are no exception. A Web site that never (or only infrequently changes) will be visited once or twice and then abandoned. Voters will lose interest in a campaign site unless they believe something new has been added. And the candidate will have lost an opportunity to engage in regular communication with the voter up to election day. In fact, given the continuous activity of a campaign, these sites should be even more active than most.

In most cases, candidates do engage in activity that could be represented on the Web. Responding to events is a staple activity of active campaigns. Press releases, announcements of speeches, rallies, and other events are standard campaign activities that could be reflected on the Web. In fact, most campaigns, especially those in an electorally competitive district, seek to remain in the public eye.

Yet, that activity must be transferred to the Web. Candidates should not view the Web site as a campaign brochure, but like a newspaper, where constant updating is understood to be critical. Just as a newspaper without recent news would quickly be dropped, a Web site without frequent new information is like a billboard that, after the first few glances, can easily be ignored.

One campaign site included a section titled "Latest Campaign News and Press Releases," designed to alert users to new developments on the Web: "If [users] take a look at it and find something new, they're going to want to go back tomorrow or perhaps next week," explains one campaign Web site designer. "If they don't find something new, . . . not only are they discouraged, they feel that the candidate, or at least the Web site, wasted their time and resources by implying that there should be something."[44]

In 1996, while many campaigns realized the necessity of updating, that did not mean they engaged in it. The task was seen as overwhelming. Weekly updating, which would be the minimum expectation of users, was beyond the ability of many campaigns. Several factors combined to make this true.

Webmasters tended to be volunteers, often using their own equipment. Campaign staff, and even candidates, were hard-pressed to devote time to the Internet in light of so many other activities identified traditionally as successful. Candidates who were sure losers did not have the resources to devote in the first place.

Other factors included the lack of qualified staff, the crush of events, the lack of feedback, and the determination that other means of reaching voters are more productive. Since most staff in 1996 either did not understand or use the Web, or saw it as merely a sideline, Webmasters and staff did not cooperate enough with each other to maintain sites. According to one Webmaster, the campaign staff would provide him with press releases "which were perhaps 5, 10 days out of date."[45]

The most profound problem for campaign use of the Internet, however, was the question of whether communication was actually occurring. Anecdotal evidence suggested political site visitors actually were present. One indication was the massive jamming of Internet election-related sites on election night. Obviously, the system was not prepared for the volume of users seeking online election results information as discussed in chapter 1.[46]

But were the voters there during the campaign? One in four online election news seekers visited candidate Web sites in 1996.[47] The extent of usage in various states or districts is still unknown. The candidates interviewed said they had no idea how much the Internet was used by voters in their respective constituencies. Certain districts in California, such as the Silicon Valley area represented by Tom Campbell, would be expected to include a greater number of Internet users than the national average due to the existence of a computer-literate constituency. Others, such as Ken Poston's district in rural northern Georgia, are not known as high-tech areas with widespread interest in the Internet.

Candidates could not point to extensive usage of their own sites since usership was still too small to accomplish that. One measure they used was the number of visitors to sites. Many candidates did not keep track. Those who did were unsure how to count. Some counted the number of hits, although that figure included all pages downloaded. For a candidate site with 10 pages, that meant 10 hits. The Webmaster for the Democratic gubernatorial candidate in New Hampshire reported 50,000 hits. Others counted "accesses" or the number of times the home page was hit.[48] Representative Tom Campbell's site had 8,000 accesses during the campaign. Given the location of Campbell's district in the Silicon Valley, however, the number may be higher than normal.

Visits to sites grew as the campaign progressed, but still less than might have been envisioned. The site for Julia Carson, a successful Democratic congressional candidate in Indiana, was accessed, on average, five times per day in the primaries, ten times per day throughout the summer, and twenty times per day during the fall campaign.[49] A minor party candidate for U.S. Senate in Massachusetts received 25 hits a day by the end of the campaign.[50]

It is not clear how many visitors were constituents. Candidates who received national attention or the attention of specific interest groups may have been visited more often. Though such attention may increase the number of site visitors, it is questionable whether it is very helpful on election day.

Another gauge of voter interest in candidate sites is the e-mail that users sent from the Web site. But most candidates contacted reported receiving few e-mail messages through the site. Unfortunately for the process of candidate communication with voters, many of these visits, however, were by Internet users outside the district or the state. Again, some of these outsiders may have been attracted to the candidate's issue positions, probably advertised in group publications or links from group sites.

Information on candidates has long been available to voters, even outside the traditional news media. Now, voters can access such information more conveniently and more effectively. In a matter of minutes, in the privacy of their own homes, voters can determine the issue positions of candidates and even their records. But will they do so?

The Future

Two scholars concluded after 1996 that, though the Internet "has not fully arrived as a means of campaign communication, it certainly has a foot in the door."[51] I believe that "foot in the door" will become a full entrance into the operation of electoral campaigns. One industry analyst has opined that "the Internet will be decisive in who's elected president in the year 2000. Its impact on politics will be significant; more people will be more involved in the process and far better informed."[52]

Whether more people will be participating is doubtful, but those who do are likely to be better informed. Unfortunately, for those who view the Internet as a populist tool, site visitors and participants will already be the politically active who are seeking more and more information, especially during electoral campaigns.

What will the Web mean for candidates in the future? Candidate Web sites were still somewhat of a novelty in 1996. This will change. Like television campaign commercials, first aired in the 1950s, sites will move beyond the novelty stage to acceptance and then to a stage of intense competition. Sites will have to become more graphic (assuming the barriers of hardware are overcome), more interactive, and also more useful, that is, something beyond mere text or images.

Political Internet site "surfers" will expect candidates to post sites as a minimum. (Some candidates reported that in 1996 avid Internet users even threatened not to vote for a candidate if they did not have a Web site.) By 1998, the expectation grew stronger. In order to appear viable, candidates in the future will need to place sites on the Web just as they need to raise minimum amounts of money and run television spots. The absence of an Internet site, given the relative lack of expense and the proliferation of sites by so many candidates, may be taken as an indication the candidate has something to hide or is not technologically competent, or just is not viable.

But voters who frequent the Internet for political information will want more than mere sites. They will expect specific information about the candidate, not just images. They will expect the candidate to address their specific interests, be it crime, abortion, or tax cuts. Voters will know the candidate will not be able to claim the information cannot be communicated because of space limitations or the filter of the news media.

Interactivity

One demand of Internet users will be for site interactivity. In response, there will be more movement toward interactivity. But the question is, what type of interactivity? Will users interact with each other, as was true with some sites, or will they interact primarily with the candidate?

Since the bottom line of serious campaigns is electoral victory, the campaign must assess how much an innovation contributes to that objective. Virtual town halls are hi-tech, but the candidate may find that while they are interesting meeting places for users, such site innovations contribute nothing to the campaign. Moreover, bulletin boards can be taken over by individuals who dominate the conversation. If bulletin boards are used, moderators would be needed to assure the messages are not damaging.

In 1996, few serious candidates had time to be able to reply to e-mail messages, though such messages often were shared with the candidate. That allocation of time seemed nearly worthless, given the number of voters to reach and the small number who sent e-mail. It was even more pointless for e-mail senders who were not even constituents, many of whom could not be effectively sorted out.

If e-mail to candidates becomes a frequent activity, it does not mean that candidates will devote time to direct replies. Members of Congress, and candidates for state or federal office, do not have time to reply personally to the volumes of mail they receive. Instead, those functions will fall to staff, as they do now.

The Internet will not change that. For 1996 and beyond, voters will begin to get form e-mail replies, probably tied to the questions raised in their correspondence, much as they would if they sent a regular mail letter.

Updating

Internet users also will demand regular maintenance. A Web site that never (or only infrequently changes) will be visited once or twice and then abandoned. Voters will not return unless they believe something new has been added. Candidates increasingly will have to lure voters with uses and gratifications, such as the opportunity to communicate with the candidate and express opinions, acquire desired issue information not readily available through other sources, and be mobilized to action. Chris Cannon, a congressional candidate in Utah, updated his site weekly with new differences between his opponent and himself.[53]

Campaigns will change as they realize what users want. Once users have been lured, they will return to the Web site as long as it is viewed as useful to their search for political information. Otherwise, they will go elsewhere, perhaps to the opponent.

The growth of Internet users will produce a rethinking about resource allocation during a campaign. As the Net is viewed as a successful method for displaying campaign information to large numbers of voters, the resources will be devoted. More staff will be allocated for updating.

The commitment to updating also will grow as candidates and staff realize the opportunity for continued interaction. Repeated visitors can be strengthened in their commitment to the candidate.

Minor Party Coverage

Attracting visitors will be a major problem for minor party candidates and major party candidates who are barely viable. Visits to the sites of minor party candidates apparently were less frequent than they had hoped. While it is true that long-shot major party and minor party candidate sites will receive more hits in future campaigns than in 1996 (as will many sites as Internet use grows), their share vis-à-vis other major party candidate sites is not likely to grow.

In order to attract visitors, minor party candidates will need offline resources to advertise their sites, such as billboards, television or print advertisements, or widely distributed brochures. And, if past record is any guide, they will not have them.

One hope is news media coverage, which offers access to a wide audience of actual constituents (which is why candidates will still devote most of their resources there for a long time to come). News media coverage of Web sites has the potential of leveling the playing field in terms of advertising.

However, news media organizations have felt no compunction to give minor party candidates equal news coverage in the past. Their Web sites are no different. In 1996, minor party candidates such as the Libertarians or the Reform Party were the most likely to complain that when news media stories described candidate Web sites, theirs were ignored.

Structuring Internet Use

Another change in the future will affect access to candidate sites. As was discussed earlier, the increased number of sites and the growing volume of traffic is now, and yet will be, contributing to the creation of a more comprehensive structure on the Web. The effect will be positive for the traditional two major parties and their candidates. But it will be negative for the rest. Customized structures of sites will become more common. Bookmarks will be replaced by more structured easy access to sites, even involving automatic delivery of certain sites when a user logs on (see chapter 2).

Such structure will allow individuals to create their own world of sites reflecting personal interests, which includes political leanings. Voters actually could acquire *less* exposure to other parties and candidates, not more, than they do now through traditional media. This would occur because the regularly accessed political sites the individual chooses will reflect the individual's political views, and the stories retrieved from traditional media sites will likely also reflect the individual's political preferences. Stories about other candidates and parties can be more easily ignored on media sites than through traditional media broadcast and print forms. Inadvertent exposure to other views, through broadcast news or perusing a daily newspaper eventually will become less frequent, thus narrowing the range of views to which the individual is exposed.

Future Effects on Campaign Participants

However, a few candidates in 1996 demonstrated how the Internet could be used. That usage of the Internet as more than an electronic brochure by some candidates suggests that 2000 will be a year of far more experimentation based on the experiences of these innovators in 1996. The Internet served merely as a supplemental tool for campaign communication in 1996 and was directed explicitly at a very small constituency, but implicitly at a much larger one.

The press will be more consistent users in the future. Some site features were established with the expectation that special users for the campaign sites would be journalists. Candidate sites had special sections called the "Press Gallery," where journalists could get the latest information on campaign announcements, the candidate's issue statements and whereabouts, or press releases from the campaign. Pat Buchanan's site, for example, contained a special section for the press that included a calendar of upcoming media events. As chapter 3 demonstrated, journalists are utilizing the Internet at an increasing rate that will undoubtedly continue as campaigns view press outreach as a critical Web site function.

Another group of watchers will be political action committees assessing which candidates are viable. PACs will use the Internet to identify potential recipients of PAC funds. Such usage will further separate resource-rich and resource-poor candidates, since site appeal will become a factor for financial support.

Responding to events is a staple activity of active campaigns. Press releases, announcements of speeches, rallies, and other events are standard features of viable candidates. Campaigns seek to remain in the public eye in order to continue to affect voter attitudes. Yet, that activity must also be transferred to the Web.

Will the voters become more important? Candidates will be expected to respond to voters via e-mail. Candidates will create more opportunities for interaction with voters. Interactivity will be the rage for campaign sites. But that will not necessarily shift power. Because, in turn, candidates will have made available to them more ways to pitch their messages to voters. Web sites are advertisements. Far more people hear the candidate's message than speak to the candidate. Even fewer get to use the candidate's forum, the Web site, to speak to others.

Will Web television alter that relationship? Not likely. Web television presentations by candidates will still be advertisements. Candidates need to get their messages out to voters. Web sites give them that control, perhaps to a greater extent than they have had on many other mechanisms of mass communication, with the exception of paid advertising.

There will be more movement toward interactivity. But the question is, what type of interactivity? Will users interact with each other, as was true with a few sites, or will they interact with the candidate? Will users be able to send messages and receive responses from candidates or will they be limited to posting messages on a bulletin board? Will users be able to express opinions to candidates in some systematic way? As David Lytel, the creator of the White House Web site and a site for Democrats, states: "I don't think the Net is especially suited for communications between candidates and voters."[54]

It is likely the growth of Internet users will produce a rethinking. As the Net is viewed as a successful method for displaying campaign information to large numbers of voters, the resources will be devoted. And the commitment to updating will grow as candidates and staff realize the opportunity for continued interaction. Repeated visitors can be strengthened in their commitment to the candidate.

Clearly candidates have adopted the Internet. And many more of them will do so in the future, both major and minor party candidates, both the viable and the not so viable. But there will be a difference. The latter in both cases will have a presence, although a smaller percentage than in the former category. And they will remain disadvantaged.

The main beneficiaries among the electorate will be the politically interested. They will have more information on candidates and campaigns. Yet the rest of the electorate, and those in the nonelectorate, may not benefit at all, since they will visit such sites infrequently, if ever.

Among candidates, online benefits will accrue primary to the same players who have benefited offline in the past. And such benefits have nothing to do with the Internet. They stem from party af-filiation, organization, candidate background, and money. This new technology will not revolutionize who gets elected. It will change the way campaigns are run. Candidate communication via the Internet will be a staple. But that will not alter the balance of power in favor of candidates and parties who fail to attract voter support now.

www.gov

Direct democracy has no place for mediating institutions. The ancient Athenians gathered to listen, debate, and decide policy for the city-state. In a more modern setting, New England town meetings feature common residents of small communities gathering in town halls, fire stations, or school auditoriums to vote directly on town policies and expenditures.

Yet, this kind of democracy has faced insurmountable obstacles when applied to large communities. How can the citizens of a major metropolitan area, much less the United States as a whole, gather together to discuss and vote on policy? That was considered impossible, apparently, until now.

The Internet has been billed as a medium capable of linking together Americans to achieve that direct democracy long sought after in a large society. The Internet can connect Americans to each other electronically and facilitate a mass decision-making process culminating in a national electronic vote. One proponent has predicted that "Congressmen will tend to operate more like Lord Burke's once disdained 'weather vane,' than as a distant and independent body with a mind of its own."[1]

For proponents of direct democracy (or at least more responsiveness to public will), the Internet has come not a moment too soon. They believe unrepresentative elected officials and unaccountable judges and bureaucrats have wasted time squabbling among themselves, corrupted the public trust, and thwarted public will, all of which has dramatically demonstrated the need for public involvement.

As a consequence of the Internet, it is predicted that mediating institutions in the process of translating public will into public policy will be forced to step aside, or at the very least, act clearly under the thumb of the public. These institutions, such as the president, Congress, the bureaucracy, the judicial branch, and state and local governments, will possess less autonomy to make independent decisions, since public opinion will be readily known through electronic votes, either binding or, at the least, strongly advisory.

Will this vision of the future actually occur? Will the Internet replace these mediating institutions with direct public decision making, or at the least, plebiscitary votes directly pointed at policy makers and ignored only at the policy maker's peril?

The answer is a resounding "no." In fact, instead of being displaced by the Internet, politicians will utilize it to maintain and reinforce existing power. They already have been, and yet will be, engaged in an accommodation process designed to employ the Internet as a tool for pursuing the same objectives they have sought through other public communication mechanisms. And they will succeed in doing so.

These objectives include personal reelection, general public approval, and specific public support for policy agendas. The Internet has the potential of helping them achieve those objectives, perhaps to an even greater extent than was true before the Internet came along.

This chapter will illustrate the ways in which elected officials and other policy makers in national, state, and local governmental institutions already have turned the Internet to their advantage in order to pursue these objectives. And it will predict how the Internet will be utilized in the future, making it unlikely that mediating institutions will become obsolete even as Internet usage grows. We begin with a discussion of how the two houses of Congress and their individual members are adapting to the Internet to accomplish those objectives.

Congress

When Newt Gingrich became speaker of the U.S. House of Representatives in January 1995, he outlined his vision of a technological future for the House, promising that "every amendment, every conference report," would be online and accessible to the country.[2] Speaking to the members, Speaker Gingrich promised that a bill would be placed online before it is voted on, ensuring that members can see the text of a bill before they are required to assent to it.[3] Since then, the House of Representatives has accelerated toward that future in its online offerings, although not necessarily smoothly.

This movement actually was initiated in the 103rd Congress when Representative Charlie Rose of North Carolina was appointed by the House leadership to create and supervise a House gopher. A primitive start by today's standards, the gopher included listings of members along with committee memberships and party leadership lists. A few House documents were included in the gopher. At the same time, an experimental group of members obtained e-mail addresses.

The Senate took tentative steps in the same direction. A handful of senators, such as Republican James Jeffords of Vermont and Democrat Edward Kennedy of Massachusetts, established e-mail addresses and individual gopher sites.

But in 1995, the House took major strides toward using the Internet as a tool for disseminating political information. The U.S. House of Representatives Web site became an electronic library literally at users' fingertips. The House uploaded all texts of bills, resolutions, and amendments introduced on the House floor. As a result, Internet users can now read the texts of newly introduced bills. The user overwhelmed by legalese can access prepared descriptions of the bills. The House of Representatives' Web site describes current floor proceedings, including a minute-by-minute summary of floor action. For the actual content of the debate and action, the user can retrieve the *Congressional Record* online.

The Senate also moved onto the Web with information similar to the House site. The Senate, however, was the first to set up individual member Web sites for each senator. Each page had a picture of the senator and a few pieces of information. If the senator had an e-mail address, there was a "mail to:" link which allowed constituents to contact him or her. There was a listing of hypertext links to the various committees of which the senator is a member, and the address and phone number of the D.C. office is listed. There was a brief biography as well, drawn from the member's listing in the "The Congressional Directory." The last pieces of information were the party affiliation and which state the senator represents. But the generic sites were gradually replaced as senators established their own distinctive sites. The House subsequently provided the same generic sites, which were even more basic, and also temporary, as members designed their own.

Congressional sites today offer users the opportunity to link not only to individual members, but also to committee sites. Committee actions, including hearings and markups, are described. Transcripts of committee hearings also can be accessed.

Congressional Organization

Much of what the Congress provides on the Web is directed at the external user and is legislative in orientation. Congressional party organizations have created their own separate Web pages designed primarily (and sometimes exclusively) for internal use. These party organization sites usually feature public relations material such as photographs of smiling party leaders and general statements of party philosophy. But they also contain substantive legislative information. The House Republican Conference site contains information about legislative research and the current business of the House. Users can find and use the weekly *Legislative Digest,* as well as a daily agenda for Congress.[4]

But party sites are for more than public relations or even public information. They are a tool for internal communication. Some sites (and sections of other sites) are off-limits to all but members of Congress. The House Republican Conference, for example, has created a "member services" section of its Web site that is out of the reach of average Internet users. This area requires a password to be accessed. It contains postings of form letters for constituents that can be downloaded and used by all party offices, a "discussion center" where party members can chat about current issues, links to conservative groups, and internal publications (like press releases, position papers, and research reports).

The Republican party leadership went one step further and created private pages that are not even linked to public pages, thus making it difficult, if not impossible for the general user to find. This intranet has become a leadership training tool for the new freshman class of the Congress.

Committees also possess their own home pages, usually with a main page featuring a photograph of the chair and/or a listing of committee members. The home page of the House Committee on Government Reform and Oversight, for example, informs users of pending committee meetings and action. It also lists the committee's legislative accomplishments, including a summary of recent bills passed by the committee and subsequent action by the full House, the Senate, conference committees, and the president.

The minority party members of some committees also have created their own Web pages. Their creation has caused partisan conflict, as these sites usually contain negative commentary on the actions of the majority party. As a result, the majority party decided those pages can be accessed only through the committee Web pages. That decision limits the reach of these sites and guarantees users will get the majority party's perspective first.

The Senate's site has been the laggard of the two chambers in Internet development, probably reflecting the Senate's greater caution toward change. But Senate party leadership, committees, and subcommittees have formed Web pages as well.

Obviously, access to congressional information is not limited to the official Web sites of the two houses. Other sites, such as C-SPAN, Congressional Quarterly, *Roll Call,* and CapWeb, all independent sites, offer substantial legislative information. Through the nonofficial sites, an Internet user can find additional information on members. This may include data the member may not be anxious to reveal, such as ratings of the members of Congress by various interest groups or political action committee money contributed to their electoral campaigns. However, neither the House nor the Senate links to these nongovernmental sites, decreasing the likelihood of hearing a version of congressional activity different than what the members seek to portray.

Virtual Constituent Communication

The real change, however, has not been at the institutional level, but at the level of individual members communicating with constituents. The mid-1990s launched the e-mail revolution. E-mail has become the equivalent of free rural delivery of the early twentieth century; it is a bandwagon that is so popular that millions of Americans are signing onto online services just to keep in touch with family, friends, and associates across the country and around the globe.

As discussed above, in 1993, Congress also began experimenting with external e-mail communications. Then in 1995, both houses rushed toward e-mail. The House assigned e-mail addresses to all members, while most senators also received them (although not all actually used them). Public e-mail contact with members of Congress increased as well.

Constituents began to send e-mail about a wide range of issues. Early on, special Internet lobbying efforts were devoted to Internet-related legislation.[5] The first such Internet-lobbying target was the Communications Decency Act in the 104th Congress, which directly affected Internet speech. The proposed law spurred large volumes of mail from e-mail users, though it passed nevertheless.

However, the volume of e-mail soon transcended Internet-related matters. Now, members see an enormous influx of e-mail messages, a trend that has only increased. Currently, given the limitations on staff, members lack the capability to answer hundreds of new mail messages pouring into their offices. Moreover, they don't want to have to answer mail from large numbers of people outside their own districts. Yet, that is precisely where much of the e-mail originates from.

Even constituents may become a problem for congressional offices, given the greater ease of communication. "What's happening is that with the new software programs today," explains Representative Sam Gejdenson of Connecticut, "16,000 kids at a college can send me a letter with a push of a button. I don't have the ability to go through all of that."[6]

A single constituent can deluge or disrupt the e-mail system of a member. According to one congressional e-mail system analyst, "Congressional offices are already so stretched out, and their people are so stressed out. There's the fear that this will take those offices to a whole new level of dealing with the constituent computer hacker."[7]

There is also concern about whether this flood of e-mail actually affects member decision making. There is the fear that public reaction via e-mail is too quick in a representative democracy. One journalist sees the new style of letter writing (via electronics) as potentially less temperate. "Most of us have either sent or received an electronic jolt that would have benefitted from the cooling-down period afforded by the traditional drawer-yanking search for an envelope and fumble for a stamp."[8] The time period between initial reaction and expression of that reaction to a public official has been significantly reduced.

However, the fear that e-mail senders will be more vitriolic because they take less time to ponder the consequences of their messages is not borne out in congressional e-mail, according to a survey of congressional offices (see Methodology). While slightly more offices surveyed concluded that the tone of e-mail was more negative than positive (24 percent versus 19 percent), 57 percent felt there was no difference in mood between e-mail and regular mail.

Despite the technical problems and theoretical dilemmas, e-mail has been embraced by Congress. In the survey of congressional offices, only 2 percent of members surveyed did not have an e-mail address. After the initial test in 1993, office e-mail use spread quickly. Within two years, 67 percent of members' offices had established e-mail for external use. Moreover, e-mail has become a daily routine of congressional offices. Eighty-four percent of congressional offices said they checked for e-mail at least daily.

It should be noted in passing that office e-mail use and personal use by the member are different. Members themselves are slow to use e-mail. Only 27 percent of members who responded said they personally use e-mail. E-mail, like regular mail, is being read by staff members and then, depending on the office, shown to the member. And electronic mail is shown to most members the same way they read regular mail, that is, through hard copy of e-mail messages. Some members want to see all the mail from constituents. Others, however, want only snippets. Still others only read e-mail messages from people they personally know.

Even though members personally are slow to "get online," many of their constituents are not. The volume of e-mail is growing. A majority of members' offices said they received 175 or more e-mail messages a week. One-third said they collected 300 or more a week. In a one-year period, three-fourths of congressional offices said their e-mail volume had increased. The most common estimate of growth was between 25 and 50 percent.

The magnitude of the task of replying is demonstrated in the investment of labor. Ninety percent of the offices said they read e-mail messages manually. While a majority (56 percent) sort their e-mail by topic or issue, only 18 percent conducted some kind of computer keyword search on e-mail to sort it more efficiently. In the vast majority of cases, office staff must cull through the messages manually in order to identify the subjects requested and then reply by regular mail.

It may come as a surprise that e-mail is not usually answered by e-mail. Congressional offices have not made the adjustment to replying by e-mail. After years of fine-tuning regular mail replies, Capitol Hill offices are reluctant to convert to another system. Seventy-five percent said only e-mail from constituents is handled for reply in the regular mail system. The rest usually goes unanswered or receives a form reply stating that the office does not answer e-mail from nonconstituents.

However, e-mail is not designed for regular mail reply. The problem with regular mail replies is that e-mail correspondents rarely provide their regular mail addresses with their messages. Again and again, members' offices complain that they cannot respond in their normal manner to e-mail correspondents. They often will send a form reply via e-mail requesting the sender's regular mail address.

Fifty-nine percent of offices said they respond to all incoming e-mail messages with an automatic "canned" e-mail response. The response usually merely acknowledges the receipt of the message, thanks the sender for the letter, and informs the sender that a regular mail reply will be forthcoming.

A major problem with e-mail for members is the nonconstituent issue. Nearly all of the offices estimated that half or more of their e-mail comes from nonconstituents. Replying to all of this mail would strain their resources to the breaking point. Yet, 89 percent said they found it difficult to sort constituent and nonconstituent messages. Obviously, this would be a problem, particularly if the majority of messages are coming from nonconstituents. Fifty-six percent said they do not reply to e-mail from nonconstituents.

One member requests the sender include their zip code in the message. Then, when the member gets the message, the words "not constituent" appear if the zip code does not match those within the district.[9] Such programs will proliferate through Congress as a way to screen out nonconstituent e-mail.

The frustration of currently handling a majority of e-mail messages not even from constituents leads to unhappiness with e-mail, particularly e-mail sent as part of a broad sweep of congressional offices. Half the members' offices reported at least 50 percent of their incoming e-mail consists of generic messages sent to all members of Congress. One staff member, referring to junk e-mail or "spamming" that has become more common, admitted that "we hate the mass mails." Once an e-mail correspondent has established a distribution list of selected groups of members, or even the whole Congress, it is just as easy to send to 500 members as it is to send to one. This tactic can be used by a lone individual who wants to be heard or by interest groups who view this as an easy way to send a press release. another congressional staffer opined that "the e-mail address for the Congressman has to be one of the biggest wastes of taxpayers dollars—the whole thing is a real headache for staff and of no value to the actual constituents."

One difference noted by congressional offices between regular mail and e-mail was the timeliness of messages. E-mail writers can respond to events nearly instantaneously, a press conference just concluded, a vote just taken, or even a C-SPAN hearing they are currently watching. In turn, e-mail etiquette carries an expectation of more rapid responses than with regular mail. Since they know e-mail can be received quickly, they often expect a speedy reply.

However, not unlike senders of regular mail, e-mail correspondents tend to be "pen pals" with members of Congress. One staffer concluded that "you get the same people always e-mailing because it's free." Such frequent correspondents may be discounted, but their mail must still be sorted.

Online Homestyle

The online presence of individual members has now progressed far beyond e-mail addresses. Members of Congress now have individually distinctive home pages complete with background information and committee assignments, as well as a listing of legislation either sponsored or cosponsored by the member.

Why do members have such pages? To what uses are they put?

These questions are even more relevant given the importance of constituency relations and the individual members' development of certain homestyles, which is their way of relating with the local constituency in their respective states or districts.[10] Political scientist David Mayhew concluded that members of Congress engage in three categories of reelection-related activities: advertising, position taking, and credit claiming. They advertise themselves as well as their constituencies. They take positions that will be interpreted by the constituency as reflective of their interests. And they claim credit for legislative activity which helps the constituency.[11] Political scientist Diana Evans Yiannakis found that members' communications (newsletters, press releases) are a "function of the political circumstances in which members find themselves." She adjusted Mayhew's categories to address the types of credit claiming (particularized) and position taking (national) that members engage in. She concluded that members from poor districts are more likely to engage in particularized credit claiming while members from more affluent districts more safely take on national issue positions. Also, ideologically driven members gravitate toward issue positions while senior members tend toward particularized credit claiming.[12]

While "homestyle" has been conducted through the news media (such as interviews, press conferences, and press releases) as well as personal contact, the Internet raises the possibility for another vehicle for homestyle. At first glance, the Internet may not be the appropriate vehicle for communicating homestyle. Members' Web sites are not exactly "in the district" since they actually occupy cyberspace, nor is it really possible for a member to tailor their Web site exclusively to the constituency since anyone anywhere can see it.

However, in another sense the Internet seems the perfect vehicle for member communication to their districts. The member can be in the district without actually being there. The member can communicate messages without having to rely on local news media, party organizations, or even his or her own staff. Moreover, the message communicated is an unfiltered one.

Yet, it is still valid to ask the extent to which members' home pages reflect this homestyle. They may assume that three types of constituencies will constitute frequent users of their site: Constituents; Other Members; and Interest Groups, particularly those who share the member's issue priorities. Let's concentrate first on constituents because the members of that group have the greatest effect on the member's reelection prospects and, therefore, the ability to remain important to the other groups as well.

From a content analysis of congressional Web sites, it was obvious that members use their sites for these purposes (see Methodology). Members employ the Web as a vehicle to advertise themselves. Nearly all placed on their sites personal narrative biographies, often emphasizing their roots among their constituents as well as their past legislative accomplishments (see Table 5. 1). Representative J.D. Hayworth (R-AZ)'s stresses that "J.D. goes home almost every weekend to his Arizona district, meeting with constituents and spending time with his family." Another example is Congressman Sam Gejdenson (D-CT), whose biography calls him "a

Table 5.1 Item Features of Member
Advertising on Members' Web Sites

	House	Senate
Biography	92.8%	91.0%
Press releases	74.7	65.0
Legislation sponsored	46.4	40.0
Legislation cosponsored	36.1	38.0
Floor speech	26.5	47.0
Recent legislation	30.7	1.0
Status of legislation	28.9	2.0
Newsletter	24.7	8.0

passionate advocate for children, senior citizens, and working families," and continues that "Gejdenson has fought to make education more available and affordable, expand and enhance retirement security, protect the environment for future generations to enjoy, and create jobs and economic opportunity here at home by promoting American-made goods and services in new markets overseas."

Members sometimes discuss their families. The Web biography of Representative Richard Armey (R-TX) relates that Armey and his wife "attend Lewisville Bible Church. They have five children. Armey is an avid bass fisherman and believes in the restorative powers of fishing, where he can put aside the pressures of work and spend time with his wife and children." The biography is accompanied by a photograph of Armey kissing a fish. One of the few openly gay members of Congress, Representative Barney Frank (D-MA) mentions on his site that he lives with his gay partner.

The Web, then, is a vehicle for helping representatives to convey a less formal portrait of themselves, particularly one that conforms to the expectations of the district. In other words, they communicate homestyle.

Another function of members' Web sites is advertising their willingness to hear from constituents. According to the content analysis, 93 percent of House members and 95 percent of Senators informed visitors about how the member could be contacted in Washington. Two-thirds of both House and Senate members also listed regular mail addresses and phone numbers for their offices in the district or state. More than three-fourths of members of Congress included an e-mail link to the member (see Table 5.2).

Table 5.2 Ways to Contact the Member
Provided on Member Sites

	House	Senate
Washington office address	92.8%	95.0%
E-mail link	71.7	76.0
District office address	63.3	68.0

In advertising themselves, members described their work in their chamber as well as their affiliations. Eighty-four percent of senators linked to the committees they sat on, while 58 percent of representatives did (see Table 5.3). Many connected electronically to the sites of their chamber's party organizations, such as the House Republican Conference, or the Senate Democratic Caucus. Senators were more likely than House members to make the link. Thirty-four percent of senators linked to their party site, while only 17 percent of House members did.

Equally interesting was who or what members did not link to. They were not interested in linking to each other. Only 20 percent of the Senate and only 9 percent of the House members included links to their own state delegations to Congress. This suggests they have little incentive to advertise other members of Congress, even from their own states or parties. Also, lacking were links to interest groups. Only 14 percent of the sites of representatives and senators were so linked.

Members don't just advertise themselves; they also advertise their constituents. Some opened their site with images of their constituency. For example, the site for Representative Neil Abercrombie (D-HI) opens with a picturesque scene of Hawaii. Most House members and about half of the senators linked to local or state govern-

Table 5.3 Percentage of Member Sites with Links
to Other Congressional Sites

Other Congressional Sites	House	Senate
Committees	58%	84%
Caucuses	13	4
Party sites	17	34
State delegations	9	20
Thomas	70	48

Table 5.4 Constituency Advertising—
Percentage with Links to Constituency Web
Sites

	House	Senate
State/local government	82.5%	54.0%
State/local education	67.5	47.0
State/local tourism	37.3	36.0
State/local—other	68.1	59.0

ment or educational sites. About one-third of each linked to tourism sites within the district (see Table 5.4).

Most members have transferred already existing press operations to the Web. For example, 75 percent of House members and 65 percent of senators included texts of press releases they had sent to the press.

Yet, most members of Congress did not discuss legislation, even legislation they had sponsored or cosponsored. Also, most avoided discussing policy issues. Perhaps this tactic was designed to avoid trouble with the chamber rules on Web sites. But it also conforms to aspects of homestyle by placing emphasis on the safest aspects of a member's relationship with the constituency, that is, the member as an accessible representative touting the virtues of the home constituency in the halls of the Capitol.

More surprisingly, and not according with expectations of homestyle, was the dearth of discussion about casework. Only 21 percent of representatives and 2 percent of senators linked to bureaucratic agencies to facilitate casework. That will likely be the growth area for congressional Web sites. Such linking reinforces the safe image of the member as facilitator of constituent service.

Members do make themselves available as sources of government Internet links. Seventy percent of the House sites and 48 percent of the Senate sites linked to *Thomas,* the Library of Congress server, and 54 percent of the House sites and 49 percent of the Senate sites linked to the White House.

Congress is often slow to take advantage of new technology because of the accompanying dilemmas such technology brings. Though members have moved onto the Web and have adopted the Web to their homestyles, their use of the Web brings its own problems, such as how to get the word out about their Internet sites without incurring constituent wrath. They are concerned that advertising their Web sites will be construed as a violation of taxpayer money. Since the sites so often slavishly praise the member and serve his or her interests, such concern is well founded.

Of the offices who responded to the survey, a majority did not include their home page address on stationary, as part of e-mail replies, or in bulk mailings to the district (such as constituency newsletters). Fifty-one percent said they did not advertise the home page address anywhere offline.

Like constituency mailings, press releases, and speeches on C-SPAN, the Internet provides yet another venue for favorable attention to the member. Members are not going to offer negative information about themselves on their own sites. Nor are constituents apt to find negative information about the vast majority of members in many other places without more searching than most people care to engage in. Theoretically, the constituent could conduct her or his own research. Political activists are finding the Internet an invaluable tool for such research, but few constituents will go to such lengths. Therefore, rather than reallocating power away from the elected member of Congress, the Internet is far more likely to reinforce it.

Of course, other sites, particularly the electoral opponent's, will offer a contrasting view of the incumbent, as was discussed in the preceding chapter. But not unlike other offline advantages, the member's site will be continuous while the opponent's usually will exist only during the election year and probably not even during all of that. Moreover, incumbents will be able to advertise their site more readily than their opponents, via newsletters, stationary, and links to the House or the Senate's main Web site. Opponents, on the other hand, must pay for advertising their Web site addresses out of their own pockets. Party or interest group links may help.

Making Legislation

What effect does all of this have on the legislative process? Probably none. That statement may seem amazing given predictions that the Internet would institute direct democracy or, at the least, cause representative democracy to become more of a mirror of public will. But the Internet has little effect now and it is unlikely to have more effect in the future. In fact, as indicated in chapter 3, members may even discount e-mail communication. What changes do occur in the legislative process are likely to be procedural rather than substantive. For example, committees could hold virtual hearings, thus reducing the need for witnesses to travel to testify.[13]

Members do not use Web sites in order to facilitate the public role in the legislative process. Information that would aid the constituent in affecting the legislative process is noticeably lacking. Few sites offer member-initiated information on recent legislation. According to the content analysis, few members provided constituents with their own news about the status of legislation, particularly bills related to their own constituency interest. Congress has adapted the Internet for serving the institution's purposes— publicizing itself and enhancing internal communication. Individual members also have adapted the Internet as a tool for primarily communicating their own respective homestyles.

As indicated in the ways in which members of Congress are adapting to the Net, the Internet has not lived up to its promise as a forum for public expression to elected officials. In fact, while publicly encouraging e-mail, members are becoming increasingly disenchanted with it. If the most idealistic members originally envisioned e-mail as the impetus for intelligent communication with constituents, they have seen e-mail deteriorate into a mass mailing tool for political activists. Not surprisingly then, members have done little to use their sites to assist political participation, such as mobilization or even public education. Instead, they have used it to do what they do with other communications tools in other, offline settings, that is, advertise themselves.

The White House

Though personally not a computer user, Bill Clinton has presided over the first presidential administration to use public e-mail and the Internet. Various administrations have long used internal e-mail, but since 1993, the White House, and many government agencies, have begun to offer e-mail as another communication link for the general public.

Early in its first term, the Clinton White House created a new position: White House Director for E-Mail and Electronic Publishing.

President Clinton wanted an e-mail system for the public to contact the White House and an Internet site offering a plethora of information on the administration's activities.

Once the two systems were established, the administration widely advertised both to the public and invited public response. They were not disappointed; in fact, they were overwhelmed. By the summer of 1993, the White House was receiving about 800 e-mail messages per day.[14] At first, the White House was unprepared for the deluge. It had no system of handling the influx of e-mail messages it had created. Messages were merely stacked up on the floor and left unanswered.

The White House's system has become more sophisticated over time. E-mail sent through the White House's Web site now appears on a standard form and can be easily categorized. Senders are asked to identify the type of letter they are dispatching with options such as seeking assistance from the White House, extending a speaking invitation, or expressing agreement or disagreement with a White House position, along with information about their policy topic and their own status or affiliations (such as veteran, student, civil servant, or senior citizen). This sorting allows the White House to organize the reading of the mail and forwarding to the appropriate departments.[15]

Sorting is critical due to the volume of e-mail received. By 1997, President Clinton was receiving an average of 1800 messages daily, but has received as many as 5500 in a day. Vice President Gore was sent an average of 300 e-mail messages each day, while Mrs. Clinton garnered an average of 125.[16]

The White House also has pioneered an executive presence on the Internet. The Bush administration never established such a presence, while the Clinton administration carried over its Internet interest from the 1992 campaign, when a Clinton gopher site offered texts of speeches, campaign advertisements, and press releases.

The White House gopher site opened in January 1993. It has since expanded to a colorful multimedia presentation stuffed with information disseminated from the White House. The merely curious can take a virtual tour of the White House, read recent White House press releases, or browse through a special section for children. Users who want to know more about the First Family are treated to a scrapbook of pictures of the Clintons engaged in various activities from Hillary with school children to the president playing the saxophone. The presidential cat, Socks, even provides an audio of a "meow." Users also can hear an audio message from the president welcoming them to the historic structure. The tour includes the featured rooms of the usual tour as well as a peek at the Oval Office.

For the more policy-oriented, the White House site offers access to presidential announcements, transcripts of daily press briefings, and the texts of major documents such as the annual budget, proposed administration bills, and major agreements and treaties (i.e., NAFTA and GATT). In addition, the White House links to executive agencies, helping users find where they need to go to get government information quickly through the Net.

The site quickly became highly popular with Internet users. By 1995, in one six-month period, it attracted more than one million users.[17] A year later, the site was being hit approximately 900,000 times a month.[18]

The existence of a White House site raises questions about how it should be used. Should one expect that the Internet will lead an administration to listen more intently to public will? Referring to the White House's Internet presence, media analysts Edwin Diamond and Robert A. Silverman conclude that "the promise of access was fulfilled, but with little relationship to democratic governance."[19]

The Clinton administration, not unlike any other administration would, has settled that question in its favor. It has been pro-active, not in soliciting public opinion in the presidential decision-making stage, but in using the Internet for the administration's purposes: selling its policies, claiming successes, and offering its services as an ombudsman. With its many site visitors, the administration is able to expose the public not only to the historic nature of the White House, but also to its role as an ombudsman for citizens needing help sorting through the complex maze of federal bureaucratic agencies.

Executive Agencies

That complex bureaucratic maze also has been duplicated on the Web. Most agencies have established sites on the Internet, including all the cabinet level departments and many of the bureaus within those departments. But again, those Internet users with expectations that such information is designed to enhance their participation will be disappointed. Site information falls in four broad categories: agency mission description, mission activity, consumer information, and interactivity.

Mission Description

The initial forays into cyberspace by agencies focused on existing basic agency descriptions. Mission statements, program descriptions, brief messages from the director or department secretary, and lists of contacts (usually regular mail and telephone) were included. The sites were similar in their inclusion of information such as addresses and phone numbers. Some included past speeches and congressional testimony by the secretary or director.

Even agency sites still containing information primarily in this category have more attractive appearances. The movement to the Web has enlivened sites with more appealing graphics. For example, the Department of Interior features photographs of American landscapes. But the function is still the same—use the opportunity of the user's visit to educate him or her on what the agency is designed to do.

Mission Activity

The next stage of cyberspace activity was inclusion of ongoing mission activity, such as product warnings by the Consumer Product Safety Commission or new safety features on U.S. currency implemented by the Treasury Department. Most agencies have moved to this stage, offering regular updating of information about their activities. These often take the form of the latest agency press releases or reports issued by the department. They duplicate the official information the agency delivers to the press corps through its public information officers.

But it is specific audiences to which much of this information is directed. The Veterans Administration offers updates on veterans benefits. The Defense Department gives information about how to purchase equipment from the department. Housing and Urban Development (HUD) offers notices of property for sale. Some of this online information is even denied to the general public. For example, the National Science Foundation offers confidential communications to researchers on the status of their grant proposals.

Consumer Information

Federal agencies are shifting toward offering more consumer information. This may reflect the lack of user interest in the agency's mission statement, but high interest in specific assistance the agency can provide. Some of this information duplicates what agencies publish in printed brochures. For example, the Federal Emergency Management Agency (FEMA) gives tips on what to do during a natural disaster, and the Small Business Administration offers suggestions on whether to start a small business. The Federal Communications Commission (FCC) advises consumers about telephone toll fraud or how to file a complaint to the FCC. And those planning international travel can tap the State Department's site to read the latest foreign travel advisories or weather reports from the National Weather Service.

Some of the material offered is general information and not necessarily consumer-oriented. The Central Intelligence Agency offers views of declassified satellite imagery, political reports on other nations, and the sale of CIA maps and atlases. Users can search the latest CIA World Factbook. The FBI offers information on the latest crime statistics.

The most visually entertaining site belongs to NASA. Users can follow the space shuttle in flight through real-time data images from NASA's television cameras or a 3-D tracking display. Or, with video capability, the user can see an animated video of the shuttle in flight or watch daily video clips transmitted from inside the shuttle.

NASA's information reflects a commitment to use the Internet for educational purposes. In response to a specific directive by President Clinton, federal agencies have developed "for kids" sections on their sites or devoted site space to activities designed for classroom use.[20] The Environmental Protection Agency site is a place where teachers and students can play games related to conservation and environment protection and conduct science projects. The Smithsonian's "Especially for Kids" page offers a virtual tour of exhibits most attractive to children. Even the CIA has a page for kids interested in spy work.

Other sites, however, represent information demanded by consumers or interest groups about the industry over which the agency has jurisdiction. Examples include the Federal Aviation Administration's publication of airline safety records and the Federal Election Commission's offerings of candidate receipts and spending.

Some sites offer information related to consumer interaction with the agency itself. The Internal Revenue Service educates users on how to file an electronic income tax form and even offers copies of forms. The Education Department offers instruction on applying for grants or contracts. A Personal Earnings and Benefit Estimate Statement can be obtained from the Social Security Administration. The Peace Corps provides information about how to become involved in a Peace Corps project or even become a volunteer.

Agencies are linking themselves to other sources of information on the topics under their jurisdiction, providing the user with a one-stop source for information on toxic waste, campaign finance, or homelessness. By doing so they serve constituent interests and organize information in such a way that preserves their role as an information source.

Interactivity

However, the next step in the progression of the Internet, that is, interactivity, is still missing from federal agency sites. Nearly every site volunteers agency e-mail addresses or, in many cases, even displays forms that users can complete to transmit e-mail messages. And specialized e-mail posts are appearing. For example, users can lodge e-mail complaints of fraud, waste, or abuse to the Inspector General of the Department of Housing and Urban Development.

Citizens are given the impression that they are important to the agency's mission. But that interactivity has not been used to affect the agency decision-making process. For instance, many e-mail posts go directly to the site's Webmaster, not to a policy official. And some agencies even explicitly limit e-mail queries to technical questions related to the Web site.

Few agencies include e-mail addresses of specific policy officials, even by title. In some cases, e-mail addresses are available online but not readily apparent to the user. In these cases, the user must conduct a search to obtain the e-mail address of a particular employee. But first the user must know the name of the employee.

Yet, forums for public input could be established. Electronic public hearings could be held. Citizens who visit the site could be asked to comment on specific policy options under consideration.

That has not happened, nor is it likely to. Certainly, it would offer the Internet user the opportunity to respond to the information presented on the site, and it would greatly facilitate such input. Individual citizens would not need to go to public hearings or write letters, activities that require much more time than a response through e-mail.

Yet agencies have no incentive to offer such opportunities. Do they want to hear from the general public that much? Do they want to have that input? Even if agencies established such opportunities, the forums would not be purely populist. Mediation would still appear; in fact, it would be imperative to the site. However, the result is a filtering of public input. For example, when Vice President Al Gore visited a CompuServe chat room, approximately 900 people tried to join the conversation, but only 10 were able to put a question to the vice president.[21] Who determines those who are successful and those who are not? It is not the users who do so, but the mechanisms which filter public input.

Moreover, even if federal agencies created such opportunities, would the members of the general public participating be different from those responding now? The most likely scenario is that interest groups would coordinate e-mail campaigns mobilizing their own members to respond, a situation similar to offline public involvement.

Judiciary

The federal judicial branch actually was one of the first branches with information online. Admittedly, it was not the judiciary actually sponsoring a site, but, thanks to the Lexis service and later Westlaw, legal data, such as court opinions, has been online since the 1970s. Initially available to a small number of law firms and legal scholars, these legal data bases are widespread and have even been replaced, to some extent, by the wealth of judicial information available publicly on the Web.

The Supreme Court has been reluctant to establish a Web site, but the Court's products, are readily available online. For a secretive, tradition-bound institution, the U.S. Supreme Court itself has moved quickly to place its own documentary material in electronic form for online retrieval. In 1990, the Court initiated Project Hermes, a venture designed to place Supreme Court documents (opinions, briefs, cert petitions) online for public access. Project Hermes was an early, pre-World Wide Web site on politically oriented gophers and even community bulletin boards. Opinions are now available online and even accessible through e-mail subscriptions on decision day.

Since the Court allowed scholars access to its audio tape collection of oral arguments, audio clips of the arguments have been appearing on the Internet. Even fairly recent opinions have appeared. This means the voices of the justices are being heard for the first time for many Americans, since these individuals endured public televised confirmation hearings at the time of their respective nominations.

It is extremely unlikely the justices will take the next steps, including allowing live audio (much less video) broadcasts of oral arguments via the Internet. Even though the justices could exercise more control over the broadcast on the Internet, they could not control subsequent use by those who download the broadcasts. By cutting and pasting, the justices could be made to sound silly or voice sentiments they don't share. Also, broadcast networks might use clips in news broadcasts, thus circumventing the Court's avoidance of such exposure. The justices reluctantly will approach participating in chat rooms, even on legal matters.

Overall, the Court will move into the Internet age with the greatest caution of any institution in order not to jeopardize its status as the institution least concerned about public opinion. Similar to its approach to media innovations, the Court is adapting in a way that preserves its interests—placing its product before the public, but avoiding any possibility of interactivity, such as e-mail addresses, that might be construed as encouraging public contact and, even worse, outright public lobbying of the justices.

State Government

National government is not the only level of government embracing the Web. State government sites serve several purposes—promotional brochures for the state's tourism industry, general state information sources, advertisements for the governor's record, and links to specific state agencies and local governments.

State Legislatures Online

Like Congress, the various state legislatures have gone online, and individual legislators have created Web sites and encouraged constituents to correspond with them via e-mail. The offerings at sites vary, but certain functions are common across many sites: information about individual representatives, legislative business, the structure of legislative chambers, and the legislative process. And more frequently appearing is the opportunity for citizens to send electronic correspondence to legislators.

Web information about members at the state legislative level is not as extensive as it is for the U.S. Congress. (One exception is California.) Due to low visibility of most state legislators, often constituents do not even know who their state representative or senator is. To address that problem, many legislatures provide maps or zip code searches to help constituents find their own representatives.

In many state legislatures, individual senators and representatives have created their own home pages. Similar to those for members of Congress, these usually include biographies, committee assignments, and e-mail addresses or hot links to e-mail boxes for constituent-legislator communication. Some legislatures have gone even further. Each Arizona legislator's home page also lists all the bills that member has sponsored. Rhode Island's site publishes the full text of press releases issued by individual members.

Many state legislatures have placed legislative business online, including lists of bills introduced, texts of bills and amendments offered, current status of bills under consideration, and the schedules of committee and chamber proceedings. Some include a description of that day's legislative action. In some states, the journals of chambers are available online. Users can also see the text of new laws just passed.

Many state legislatures have sought to make legislative information retrieval user friendly. Realizing that few users know bill numbers, they have included legislative search engines on their sites. Users can conduct searches for texts of bills by subject or keyword, as well as number.

Like Congress, legislature organization information includes party leadership pages, legislative officer lists, committee membership, and so on. Committees of some legislatures have dedicated pages to the committee business, including lists of members, jurisdiction, and legislative agenda. Committee agendas and minutes of meetings are available. Some legislatures publish committee reports online. The members are not the only ones listed in some sites. South Carolina, for example, also lists registered lobbyists and media representatives accredited to the press gallery.

Florida takes a topical approach, allowing the user to examine recent and pending legislative, as well as executive, actions in a specific policy area such as health care or education. Some other states also include citizen's guides, such as general information on how bills become law, the rules under which the legislature operates, and a glossary of legislative terms. Many sites include information on visiting the capitol building or visual tours of the state capitol building and histories of the legislature, the building, or the state. Children's education about the state legislature is accorded a separate section in some legislative sites.

Legislative sites are designed for publicity about the institution and, increasingly, the individual members as well. There are some exceptions. The California Assembly site includes a town hall where users can chat online about legislative activity. E-mail correspondence is growing and will soon become an expected component of a legislator's communication with the district.

Other potential uses include full video of legislative proceedings. The user could choose among live video of floor debate, committee proceedings, or other activities such as member press conferences or speeches. Even taped presentations could be selected. Legislatures will develop the full range of uses of the Internet. Professional legislatures such as California and New York will develop such uses first.

Local governments have not been left behind in the rush to get online. The emphasis of local government sites has been citizen information about services, activities, and policy making. Local metropolitan areas are placing online information about city services, such as regulations on animals, gun permits, and garbage disposal, as well as information about city ordinances. City departments include their own home pages. The home page for the city of Seattle, Washington includes Web pages for a wide range of city services such as homeless shelters, marriage licenses, rat control, and pothole repair. Madison, Wisconsin's Web page describes city bus routes as well as current city job openings. In Cambridge, Massachusetts, readers of the city's Web page can learn of current volunteer opportunities.

Like state government sites, many local government sites offer consumer information. For example, the Domestic Violence Unit of Seattle's Department of Housing and Human Services offers tips on how to handle potential domestic abuse situations.

Local officials are utilizing their government Web pages as a mechanism for publicizing themselves. Many sites include photographs of local elected officials (particularly mayors), as well as biographical information, texts of speeches and policy initiatives, and press releases. Some include audio and/or video clips of messages for Internet users.

Some government sites also offer more than information about public services. They offer the opportunity to become informed about current issues. Many local governments use the Internet to post announcements about meetings, full minutes, and final decisions of governmental bodies. The Taos, New Mexico City Council, for example, posts the agendas of City Council meetings, as well as minutes of past meetings. More and more documents are appearing online, such as city annual reports and budgets and departmental or commission reports. Official election-related information is also appearing. The Los Angeles site informs users of who is running for elected office, and also provides the text of the voters' information pamphlet.

Even tribal governments have gone online. The Oneida Nation of New York's Web site includes facts about tribal government services and tribal news, and also has audio samples of the Oneida language and texts of treaties with the U.S. government.

The text of local government sites' falls into three categories: general information about government activity, specific tools for individual use of government services such as employment or health care, and information useful for facilitating public involvement in state or local policy making.

What has not occurred yet is widespread use of this technology for direct democracy, even at the local level. Granted, encouraging political participation via the Net is still at an early stage. The efforts are tentative. At many sites, local citizens are being educated on the voter registration process. A rapidly growing number of Web sites include e-mail addresses of government officials. Some also even feature surveys, where users can express opinions.

But there has not been more than an experimental reliance on computer networks for expression of public opinion about policy. The Internet could be useful as a tool for informing constituents of pending issues and then soliciting input. However, that development has not yet occurred.

Another proffered role for the Internet is as a means for bringing a local community closer together by uniting it technologically.[22] Local government could be a part of that communitarianism by offering the structure for the technological networking of individuals in the local community.

On the other hand, the Internet may play a detrimental role in bringing a local community together. The Internet, with its access to widespread groups, could well be argued as having the effect of fragmenting local communities by placing their loyalties with far-flung interests. The demise of geographical boundaries, so touted as a boon of the Internet, also can reduce a sense of physical community to isolated individuals tied virtually to other isolated individuals but unconnected to those who are actually physically proximate.

In fact, neither of these scenarios will occur. The Internet is not the panacea for local apathy or loss of community nor is it the curse of atomization. Rather, it is a tool that, to the extent that it effects at all, is most likely to maintain the status quo. Information at the local level will be more readily available, but, again, whether average citizens will be inclined to utilize it is debatable. One exception though is election time.

Local government is the last place where virtual politics would even be necessary. People can physically lobby for their interests. They can make local telephone calls to local elected officials and appointed policy makers. They can visit city or county government office buildings. Their vote can have the greatest impact. Nevertheless, local government is embracing the Internet as much as other levels of government.

The Future of Government and the Internet

Each level or branch of government, or individual agency or member office, is using the Internet to fulfill the same functions carried on offline—primarily touting the accomplishments of the office or individual and/or soliciting public support for policies. All of these activities are carried out at taxpayer's expense. The Internet thus is a public relations rather than a public participation tool.

Given this usage, it is no surprise that government officials have adapted quickly to the Web. Moreover, in the future more public officials will utilize the Web because it allows them unfiltered access to those in their constituencies who use the Net and visit government sites. For public officials who must primarily rely on the press, the Internet is a boon. They have another mechanism for advertising themselves.

This conclusion is disappointing only if there was the expectation of something quite different, say, a new mechanism for enhancing representation or at least the expression of public will. Further evidence that such an expectation will remain in the ideal world, rather than the real one, is the existence of governmental limitations over what material actually appears on the Web. We would expect, in the ideal world, such material would be freely available, particularly information that might be pertinent to public participation.

But, of course, that is not what is happening. Not only are public officials placing on the Net favorable material about themselves, but they are also attempting to restrict access to other bits of information they don't wish the public to have. In a dispute over whether committee reports should be placed online, the chair of a congressional committee said he had the power to determine which committee documents could be placed on the Internet. In another instance, the White House issued a news release in January 1994, attacking a *New Republic* article criticizing the administration's health care reform plan. However, the administration toned down the electronic version before placing it on the Web. As justification, the White House press secretary claimed that the White House could "reserve the right to edit."[23]

Even what is placed on the Web will not necessarily be publicly accessible. Increasingly, government-sponsored sites will exist without public notice or awareness. And passwords will become more common ways to limit access to Internet information, even by government entities.

Indeed, the idea of the Internet—a source for unfiltered information about government—does threaten power. However, public officials have learned how to utilize the Internet so it does no such thing. By using the Internet as a means for self-promotion (exactly as they do with offline constituent communication methods) and restricting public access to material not designed to further that goal, government officials have succeeded in furthering their interests through this new medium as well. And there is no indication they will not continue to do so in the future.

SIX

The Virtual Public

"Governments are only justified to the extent that they uphold individual rights."

"Where's your stash of fertilizer, you anti-government nut case?"

"I don't think mandatory live ammo training at the grade school level would be appropriate to the level of responsibility of most children."

"You better take a high school civics course before you expose your ignorance any more than you already have."

"If you're going to criticize Marx, I suggest you start by reading the texts, in at least a second- or third-hand way, so you know what you're talking about."

"Sheep, the only thing you base your criticism on is what your master the government tells you is true."

"You're being facetious, right?"

So far in this book, the Internet has been described as a communication link between policy makers, the media, or interest groups and the public. Yet, the Internet has produced still another form of political interaction—dialogue among individual citizens. This interaction, via Usenet groups and other bulletin boards, offers a form of virtual association. Hundreds of thousands of messages like those above are posted daily on a multitude of forums. Clearly, an e-mail address and Internet access can offer a window on a world of wide-ranging discussion.

As indicated in the beginning of the first chapter, occasionally this interaction attracts the attention of journalists and politicians as well. As discussed in chapter 3 journalists are tracking the messages of these groups and at times reporting nearly as fact the rumors presented there. Politicians also are taking notice. During the 1996 campaign, for example, the Clinton campaign accused the press of drawing its stories from unreliable newsgroups.[1] And in April 1997, when a U.S. Air Force jet was missing in Colorado, rumors circulated on Usenet groups that the plane would reappear on April 19 and bomb the federal building in Denver where the trial of Timothy McVeigh was occurring. The rumors were groundless, but the Air Force called a news conference to reassure the public that the plane could not have survived the crash. Two years earlier, fearing the Internet's dissemination capability was a terrorist's dream (and the nation's nightmare), the Congress passed an amendment to anti-terrorism legislation, making it illegal to distribute bomb-making material with criminal intent.[2]

What Is Usenet?

What is this new public discussion forum attracting the interest of many computer users as well as even policy makers on occasion? Usenet is a computer conferencing network allowing any user to read and even post messages on an electronic bulletin board. That bulletin board can then be read by any other person who joins (subscribes to) the discussion on that group. Since thousands of Usenet groups exist on a multitude of topics, with varying perspectives on those subjects, the user has opportunities to jump in and out of a dizzying array of conversations on literally thousands of topics.

Usenet began inconspicuously in the late 1970s as a communication mechanism for a group of academics located in Chapel Hill, North Carolina.[3] New versions of Usenet software were introduced in 1982, 1984, and 1987 to handle current and future increases in message traffic.[4] Growth was slow at first by current Internet standards. By 1983, there were slightly over 100 articles posted daily. Five years later, there were approximately 1800 posts daily on Usenet groups.[5]

But use exploded during the 1990s. By 1995, an estimated 180,000 users were posting nearly one million messages daily.[6] Estimates of the number of newsgroups currently range widely, but usually number in the tens of thousands.

Usenet groups cover almost every imaginable type of activity. Relatively few are explicitly political. They discuss parenting, cats, gardening, travel, and a seemingly infinite array of subjects. Usenet groups cover small communities such as towns, universities, and corporations, as well as participants who span the nation and even the globe. Some newsgroups are unique to certain online services, such as AOL or CompuServe, while most are accessible by anyone on the Internet.

Usenet is categorized loosely by subject. Each group is given a prefix such as "alt," "comp," "misc," "talk," and others. These prefixes identify the general discussion subjects of groups. For example, "comp" refers to computer subjects such as *comp.unix*, which is a group discussing the UNIX systems. "Soc" is the designation for groups focusing on social topics such as the environment or feminism.

Political Net Groups

Political groups are most often found under the designations "soc," "talk," "misc," and "alt." Some politically oriented groups are broadly defined, such as *alt.politics.reform* or *alt.politics.constitution* or, even more vague, *alt.current-events.usa* or *talk.politics.misc*. However, most are more specific, particularly those revolving around policy topics, such as guns, the environment, and abortion. These include groups such as *talk.politics.guns, talk.environment*, and *alt.politics.abortion*. Some are centered around current events, such as *alt.current-events.clinton.whitewater*. There are also groups with an intense ideology basis or groups representing the political fringe, such as *alt.politics.radical-left* or *alt.politics.conspiracy*. Others focus on political parties such as *alt.politics.usa.republican* or *alt.politics.usa.democrat*. Still others are individual-oriented, such as *alt.politics.clinton* and *alt.politics.usa.newt-gingrich*.

Each group is designed to attract individuals interested in the subject as described in the title. The titles also often reveal the political bias of the list. And the more specific the title, the narrower the focus of the group and perhaps the more exclusive and partisan the membership. One example is a site titled *alt.impeach.clinton*, which is quite specific and is intended to attract users who want to see President Clinton impeached and removed from office.

Critics of a topic or individual will organize their own Usenet groups, such as *alt.politics.democrat.d*, which includes discussion opposing the Democratic party. Another guide to the group's emphasis is the use of the terms "flame" and "fan." For example, a site titled *alt.fan.g-gordon-liddy* is a group supporting the talk radio host's views, whereas one with the term "flame" indicates an opposing group.

To a great extent, the Usenet community can identify where one stands and what one's interests are by the nature of the lists one subscribes to. For example, the following list (actually taken from a subscriber's list on a Usenet group) would identify a right-wing Republican:

talk.politics.misc	*alt.fan.rush-limbaugh*
alt.politics.libertarian	*alt.politics.guns*
alt.politics.democrats.d	*alt.current-*
alt.politics.usa.republican	*events.clinton.whitewater*

This list of groups, on the other hand, suggests someone on the radical left:

talk.politics.theory	*alt.society.anarchy*
talk.politics.misc	*alt.politics.radical-left*
talk.politics.libertarian	*alt.fan.noam-chomsky*

Granted, anyone can join (or subscribe to) any list regardless of their partisan affiliation or ideological persuasion. And some people will belong to both types of groups simultaneously. One example is the following list of group affiliations of one message poster on a group titled *alt.politics.usa.republican*:

alt.flame.rush-Limbaugh	*alt politics.democrats.d*
alt.politics.usa.republican	*alt.politics.usa.misc*
alt.fan.rush-Limbaugh	*alt.motherjones*
alt.politics.clinton	*alt.politics.correct*
talk.politics.misc	

This poster seems to have a balanced group subscribership. Three of the lists can be seen as more liberal—*alt.flame.rush-Limbaugh, alt.politics.clinton,* and *alt.motherjones*—while three are on the ideological right—*alt.politics.usa.republican, alt.politics.democrats.d,* and *alt.fan.rush-Limbaugh.*

However, those who join group discussions of both sides do so not because they are politically undecided, but because they are aggressive partisans who wish to debate frequently and intensively with those they disagree with. There is an element of "gate-crashing," as these activists attempt to keep a list, even one established primarily by their opponents, from being "owned" by the opposition.

But joining a list, and even posting messages, does not guarantee participation in the debate. According to Margaret L. McLaughlin, new additions to the list may not be welcomed into the community: "The frequent posters may issue a warm welcome, a rebuff, or ignore the newcomer altogether, in effect granting themselves something of an executive privilege or power with respect to entry into the community. In some groups, participation alone does not grant community membership."[7]

Political Discussion

Yet, these groups have been held up as a new and vital means for expressing public opinion on politics and reflecting the public's will. Through these mass electronic communication forums, various Usenet proponents have promised that we will have a new "conversational democracy" where "citizens and political leaders interact in new and exciting ways" and individual citizens will be able to "communicate directly with other citizens locally or throughout the nation."[8] Others have predicted that the Internet and Usenet "present the chance to overcome the obstacles preventing the implementation of direct democracy,"[9] and that "Usenet newsgroups and mailing lists prove that citizens can do their daily jobs and still participate within their daily schedules in discussions that interest them."[10] Usenet is the ultimate democratic forum, it is claimed, because people can participate when it is convenient to them, they can have time to be thoughtful, and everyone gets to participate.[11]

A medium where everyone could participate easily and which would contain thoughtful commentary and information on issues would be ideal for democratic participation. But is this a description of Usenet? One critic has criticized the Net as "cacophony rather than wisdom, a form of expression that follows not parliamentary principles but the Hobbesian law of the boring dinner party: it belongs, that is, to the person who talks loudest, logs on most often."[12] Another critic calls it a "Byzantine amalgamation of fragmented, isolating, solipsistic enclaves of interest based on a collectivity of assent."[13] One journalist declared that "the Net is full of ranters standing on invisible soapboxes, and a great many exchanges essentially come down to: Enough about you. Let's hear from me."[14]

Is Usenet political discussion a guide to the public's mood or is it a babel of voices uttering boring drivel to the already converted? What kind of discussion is going on here and how does it fit with the ideal of democratic participation?

To begin to answer these questions, I conducted a content analysis of three groups—*alt.politics.clinton, alt.politics.usa.constitution,* and *alt.politics.radical-left.* (For a further discussion of this analysis, see Methodology.) Messages posted during a one-week period were coded for each group resulting in the coding of 1666 messages across the three groups.

Posters

My first question was: Who are these people who participate in Usenet political groups? There were 723 distinct individuals posting messages on these three groups during this period of time. However, the discussion was largely carried by a smaller group of regulars who posted often and frequently engaged in the ongoing discussion. These individuals were a distinct minority: only 10 percent of the posters posted five or more times. (Remember that this is over only a one-week period!) This small group would be considered "regulars" in the discussion not only because they posted more than once, but also because they joined a range of conversations. Those 10 percent sent 41 percent of the messages on these three groups.

Since posters are often widely distributed geographically and rarely, if ever, would actually meet personally, Usenet political discussion already allows a high degree of anonymity. However, some Usenet users have sought even more secrecy. Usenet message senders have been criticized for hiding behind a cloak of anonymity—it is hard to identify addresses such as "superspy@worldnet.att.net" or the even more enigmatic "8up@001cu812." Moreover, individuals who subscribe can choose whether or not to include their real names or some other designation.

Of the 723 individuals who posted on these three groups, 24 percent operated under a clear alias. Another 7 percent used names that may or may not have been aliases. Of course, even the presence

Table 6.1 Use of Alias over Name by Frequency
of Posting

Use of Alias	One Post	Two to Four	Five or More
Alias	26.3%	22.2%	18.9%
Name	67.3	68.4	74.3
Unclear	6.4	9.4	6.8
	100.0	100.0	100.0

of an actual discernible name does not necessarily mean it is not an alias. Any name can be created. For example, males sometimes post as females. However, assuming that most names are legitimate, this result would still suggest that at least one-quarter of those who participate on these political Usenet discussions choose not to reveal even their name.

Anonymity on the part of some users became frustrating for other users. Other posters occasionally sought more information about such people. For example, one poster asked another jokingly, "Are you really Dennis Rodman in drag?"

Surprisingly, the most frequent posters were less likely than others to use aliases (see Table 6.1). This may suggest that those who are more regular members of the Usenet community are more prone to shed anonymity in order to engage in a virtual community.

Another issue is whether Usenet political discussion is demographically representative of the electorate. As established in chapter 1, the Internet is a medium appealing more to men than women.[15] Also, men are more likely than women to use the Internet for political information gathering.[16] The same is certainly true for Usenet discussion, at least on these groups. Using name as a gauge (admittedly, with its attendant problems noted above), more than 92 percent of posters who could be identified were male. (One-third of posters could not be identified by gender.) Also, those few females who posted did so less frequently than men. While 41 percent of males posted more than one message, only 26 percent of females did so.

Another measure of representativeness is ideology. One measure of ideology is the nature of the groups posters subscribed to. Of those who subscribed to other groups (in addition to the one they were posting on), the vast majority belonged to groups on the ideo-

Table 6.2 Ideological Direction of Posters Subscribing
to Other Usenet Groups as Measured by Group Ideological Direction

Ideological Direction	Clinton	Constitution	Radical-Left
Predominantly left	25%	3%	18%
Predominantly right	56	81	78
Even number of ideological groups	20	15	4
Total	100	100	100
	(N = 325)	(N = 99)	(N = 253)

*Table excludes posters who did not subscribe to other groups.

logical right. This was true across all groups analyzed (see Table 6.2), which suggests Usenet posters likely are more right-wing ideologically than the general public.

Threads

The discussion on these three groups was wide-ranging with several topics under debate simultaneously. On the Clinton group, topics included Paula Jones, the IRS, homosexuality, and President Clinton and race relations, among many others. On the Constitution group, the discussion included, for example, flag burning, the right to bear arms, militias, and whether the death penalty should be imposed on Timothy McVeigh. Topics for the Radical-Left group involved subjects such as capitalism, socialism, Timothy McVeigh, and David Koresh.

Most posted messages were responses to previous messages, as Table 6.3 demonstrates. However, some posters attempted to start new threads of discussion by initiating a new topic. Often these messages were not replied to. But others became the origination of new discussions. Thread origination was most common within the *alt.politics.usa.constitution* group. The smaller number of messages (232) versus 711 for Radical-Left and 743 for Clinton may be a factor in more threads. But even in the Constitution group, more than two-thirds of the messages followed up on existing threads.

Most people, then, follow along with existing discussions. Agenda-setting was done by a minority of the posters who determined whether a thread would begin. Though anyone could attempt to start a thread, others, probably the small number of regu-

Table 6.3 Select Characteristics of Usenet Messages

Sample Groups	Response to Other Posts	Attack on Poster[a]	Attack on Third Party[b]	Inclusion of Other Materials[c]
Clinton	86.5%	10.6%	7.9%	11.9%
Constitution	68.3	36.7	28.4	9.0
Radical-Left	89.5	61.8	36.9	13.2

[a]Attack on Poster—verbal adverse criticism of a previous poster's ideas, affiliations, background, or personal characteristics.

[b]Attack on Third Party—verbal adverse criticism of the ideas, affiliations, background, or personal characteristics of another individual (such as Bill Clinton or Newt Gingrich) or group (such as conservatives, politicians, or homosexuals).

[c]Other Materials—references to, quotations from, or discussion of materials such as specific books, articles, government reports, speeches, etc.

lars in the group, would determine whether a thread was actually picked up and continued.

Flames

A common complaint of Usenet messages is their vitriolic nature. "Flaming," which was not in our lexicon a decade ago, has become a pejorative term for such verbal attacks on other posters' ideas as well as on them personally.

The degree of negativism varies across groups. The groups differed in the attacks on groups or individuals. The Radical-Left group was the most negative (see Table 6.3). The least vicious was the Clinton group, which was also the most mainstream. The lack of attacks may be due to the group's apparent role as a gathering place for Clinton supporters.

One form of attack targeted the ideas espoused by other posters. One writer termed his opponent's views "pseudo-intellectual flotsam." Another opined that "conservatives have been cloning themselves for years. Ever notice how they repeat the same dumb arguments over and over?" Still another concluded that he did not have "time for such Mickey Mouse drivel."

Some of the criticism centered on the presentation of the argument: "You're long on bluster and short on argument. Provide something less generalized than 'thriving,' 'most new jobs,' 'a great deal of.'"

The attacks in posted messages could be directed at third parties, such as current elected officials (Bill Clinton or Newt Gingrich), organized groups (ACLU, gun lobby), unorganized groups (conservatives, liberals, gays), or institutions (Congress, UN). For example, one writer took on both an institution and an unorganized group: "The EC [European Economic Community] is another economic power block looking for its piece of action at the expense of weaker power blocks. 'One worlders' need to get their heads out of the clouds and look at the world as it really is." Another message from a different poster maligned another group: "No one needs to revel in ignorance. Except, of course, Republicans."

But much of the criticism is reserved for other message posters. Here the Usenet groups varied greatly. Again, the Radical-Left group was the most vicious. More than three fifths of posts included attacks on previous posters. More than one third of the Constitution group posts were similarly attack-oriented. Only the Clinton group avoided much criticism of others who participated in the group (see Table 6.3).

A common feature of this list was the ad hominem attack. Often these attacks questioned the intelligence of the poster:

"Your comment simply illustrates ignorance."

"Of course that's too deep for a shallow person like yourself."

"How can anyone have an intelligent debate with an illiterate?"

"Do you need to be so antagonistic, hostile and just flat out beligerent [*sic*]? I forget who it was—possibly a column in *Newsweek*—who said that the internet has had the dubious honor of turning gutless weanies into mindless bullies. They must have been thinking of you."

"What are you, an idiot?"

"There's no need to force ideas from you, since you probably don't have any."

"It's frightening that they let forms of life like you into college, William."

"You evidently live in a strange parallel universe."

Name calling was a frequent occurrence in these Usenet political discussion posts. Other ideas or groups of individuals are often reduced to simple monikers—"gunloons" or "oneworlders":

"Nor is there much hope of reasoning with the gunloon point of view, is there?   That tired old rube that guns would have prevented this tragedy or that tragedy."

"It never occurs to gunloons that guns had lots to do with making those tragedies possible. Could the Nazis or Bolsheviks have done their work without lots of guns? How about John Hinckley or Lee Harvey Oswald or Colin Fletcher?"

"You jackbootlicking apologist for government mass murder."

"Boy, Jay, you really are a conspiracy nut."

"Bible thumping bigots"

"silly heterosexuals"

"stupid Christians"

"Smearmongers"

"classic hyperconservative"

Some of these attacks become highly personal and accusatory of well-known individuals:

"Milton Friedman and Adam Smith were liars."

"More people have been killed by Ted Kennedy's Oldsmobile than by any of my firearms."

Bill Clinton is probably the most reviled well-known individual on Usenet. Various message posters called him "philander-in-chief," "slick Willie," and "low life dirtbag." One poster claimed Clinton "doesn't have an ethical/moral bone in his body not to mention his pathological lying."

But verbal denunciations also are frequently directed at other participants in the group:

"Racist **** pigs!!!! Go lynch some niggas. I know that's what you want to do."

"Listen to the Idiot Fatman."

"You are lying again, Z. But we expect it by now."

"You are a hateful mean spirited poor excuse for a human being."

"You are a fine example of what I detest."

Occasionally, some group members explicitly tried to close off the discussion by running others off the discussion list.

"[G]o quietly, and do not speak about that which you do not know."

"Go whine somewhere else."

"Are you so arrogant that you believe everything you say should be read by everyone whether they are interested or not?"

Regulars sometimes put down less-frequent posters: One regular admonished another poster "if you hadn't merely butted into the middle of this thread, you would have realized that this thread is bigger than you think." Another reminded a previous poster that "the post you're responding to is over a month old, and you've taken it completely out of context." Still another complained that "people in general who post to the net ought to learn how to read a header."

Usenet exchanges were filled with inflammatory language. Name calling and verbal put-downs were common features. Insults were directed at the object's intelligence or, at times, background, if known.

Below is an exchange showing how three participants interspersed personal attacks throughout their responses to one another:

Mark wrote:
So Jay, above you offered me two challenges, which I answered. Now it's my turn to challenge you and your understanding of basic environmental policy. While I answered two, I'll just ask you for one and I hope you'll attempt to answer this challenge instead of backing out gutlessly as you usually do.

Jay responded:
I was not writing about "basic environmental policy." I was writing about the tragedy of the commons. I don't know what motivates you to change the subject. . . .

Economists have not solved the problem. In fact, I will argue that economists have made it worse by attempting to rationalize it.

There is only ONE theoretical solution to the tragedy; limit the freedom to exploit. But in a political system based on private money, this is impossible. Thus, there is no solution—it's just a matter of time."

Steve responded to Jay's reply:
So there we have it. Jay shows he has no solutions that are practical.

He derides money as a medium of exchange by calling it private money. What other kind of money is there or for that matter why call it private other than to make money a pejorative term to deride a political system based on it. But our political system is not based upon a medium of exchange it is a representative republic under whose constitution certain individual rights are protected including property rights. So Jay once again ducks important questions that Mark put to him. We are still waiting Jay.

Such flaming is not limited to these newsgroups. One study of standards of behavior of Usenet postings on five newsgroups over a three-week period found that 272 individuals were disciplined for various infractions of Usenet conduct.[17]

Evidence

Posters often based their arguments on their own authority. The political discussion usually lacked external evidence that would stimulate further investigation of the topic and allow other posters to test the claimant's assertions. Few posters actually made reference to specific supporting materials such as books, articles, or reports (see Table 6.3). Some posters made vague references to reports and statistics. One wrote, for example, that "there are stats that tell how much each passenger on an airplane is worth." However, since more specific information was not provided, readers could not independently verify the poster's claims.

This lack of supporting evidence became a frequent source of criticism of other posters. One poster responded to a post: "How do you know (many people have an innate instinct to oppose homosexuality or interracial marriage)?" Another asked a previous poster to "provide your backup for stating that the word "people" in the Constitution means the "State." "If you're going to post such allegations, please have the courtesy to provide at least a speck of verifiable evidence."

Usenet as Political Participation Forum

What does this review of Usenet posters and messages tell us about the role of Usenet? It says that Usenet, not unlike other mediums, possesses certain disadvantages as a forum for public discussion of political issues. These include opinion reinforcement, flaming, and unrepresentativeness. Let's take each in turn and examine the problems.

Reinforcement, Not Exchange

As shown above, the Usenet becomes more than anything a forum for reinforcement. Many political newsgroups are established to present a certain argument. Individuals gravitate to groups agreeing with their own views. Moreover, most of the people who posted on the groups subscribed to other like-minded groups, confirming that the objective is reinforcement of views, not actual exchange. Then, if others attempted to engage in actual exchange, the response often is dismissive. Dissenting individuals become frustrated and finally say, as one poster did, "There's no reasoning with these people, is there?" Such behavior inhibits discussion instead of promulgating it.

Usenet proponents would probably respond that the ideal of political debate does not exist elsewhere. That may be correct. But it is not on Usenet either. The Usenet discussion must be viewed for what it is—a means for reinforcing preexisting views rather than a virtual community where people can freely express their differing views with each other and achieve resolution to public policy problems as would be essential in a direct democracy.

Flaming

Too often, even when contrasting views are expressed, there is degeneration to personal attacks, that is, "flaming." Ideas are dismissed as "wacko" or "loony." Groups are stereotyped and the antagonist becomes a "fool," "crazy," or a "mindless bully." Differences on policy issues become reduced to strident, callous remarks: "I am presently pro-life, but I would consider changing my position if the pro-choice people would agree to be aborted retroactively."[18]

There is little accountability for what one says in newsgroup discussions, despite the supposed existence of standards of behavior. Even if enforced by a moderator, the offender can just move on to another group elsewhere. One critic describes the main problems with Usenet group accountability: "People drop in, do their damage, and leave with no accountability, and most discussion degenerates quickly into either obscenity, misinformation, or an outright attack on the person who first asked the question."[19]

Unlike newspaper "letter to the editor" sections or talk radio programs, there is no filter in the public debate. "If you offer an unpopular or impolite opinion in a letter to your local newspaper, they can refuse to print it. If you do the same on a radio talk show, they can refuse to air your call or can cut you off in mid-sentence. But on Usenet, you pretty much determine for yourself what is acceptable and what is not."[20]

As a result, Usenet political discussion tends to favor the loudest and most aggressive individuals. Those who are less aggressive risk vigorous attack and humiliation. Others who might wish to discuss politics in a calmer voice and without bombast exclude themselves from the discussion, thus leaving the field to a minority of noisy partisans.

Unrepresentativeness

Again, Usenet does have the appearance of the most populist element of the Internet, that is, people-to-people political discussion on the important topics of the day. Therefore, it is easy to assume that the participants in this corner of cyberspace should be viewed as reflective of the public at large and their messages as mirrors of public will.

Yet, the appearance belies the reality. First, the frequency of cross-posting means there is a smaller population of Usenet political discussion participants than might be assumed by the number of posts on each site. Fourteen percent of the posters posted messages to at least two of the three groups studied during this one-week period. Message posters frequently send their messages to multiple lists simultaneously, at times with apologies to others who also subscribe to the same lists. This suggests Usenet participation actually represents a narrower group than the number of messages would suggest.

The political forums of Usenet are populated by those who are not necessarily representative of the electorate. Women are underrepresented. People who do not own computers and modems and do not belong to Usenet (and particularly political discussion groups) are not represented at all, and that group constitutes the vast majority of adults in the United States. Therefore, it is hard to argue that Usenet posters are representative of the public at large.

Political Usenet group participants, like Internet users generally, cannot be considered an accurate cross-section of public opinion. They represent individuals who have a hobby different than most Americans, that is political interest and, probably, activism. Whether these activists actually participate in campaigns or parties or even civic causes is unknown. But it is likely they act (or desire to act) as opinion leaders. It is not likely Usenet has attracted people to political discussion who did not discuss politics in other settings. In fact, it may even repel such people. It is more likely they have transferred their medium of discussion (or at least supplemented it) to the Internet.

Usenet groups also include not only activists, but also people who become specialists in their particular subjects. The discussions are not for the average person who is disinterested or uninformed on the subject. The generalist who happened upon the group and interjected a comment is likely to be treated to a barrage of contradicting information accompanied by a strong dose of withering criticism.

Virtual Equals Real Communities?

Welcome to the 21st Century. You are a Netizen (a Net Citizen) and you exist as a citizen of the world thanks to the global connectivity that the Net makes possible. You consider everyone as your compatriot. . . . Virtually, you live next door to every other single Netizen in the world. Geographical separation is replaced by existence in the same virtual space.[21]

Virtual political communities have been trumpeted as opportunities for individuals to become part of geographically limitless communal gatherings. And we will all come together as "compatriots." But are these virtual communities better than real communities?

Actually, there are similarities to real communities, but not in the advertised way. For example, instead of a universal exchange of ideas, group conversation tends to be dominated by people who post frequently. They set the agenda and respond to it. Others participate occasionally or only through looking or "lurking," in the vernacular of Usenet. The number who are passive in the newsgroups is much larger than the number of posts would suggest because many people will read, but not express themselves. These individuals are called "lurkers" by the Net community. But they are much like people in "real" communities who watch political discussions, but do little to voice their opinions.

Given the tumultuous nature of Usenet discussions, these people may feel safer watching the discussion and staying silent than expressing themselves and being criticized for opinions. When newcomers join the discussion, they do so with some trepidation due to fear of rejection or public humiliation. More likely than not, someone will lambast their idea or point of view, and derogatory adjectives may be attached to the ideas or perhaps even to the poster personally.

There is also a similarity in the association with other likeminded persons rather than exposure to conflicting views. People naturally are gravitating to others who share their views in order to reinforce those preset political notions.

The drawbacks discussed above seriously inhibit the promised role of Usenet as a means for public expression and measurement. As a result, this comparison of virtual and real communities shows that Usenet groups have not achieved a nirvana of direct democracy, where all participate equally in a substantive exchange of ideas. Rather, in terms of who participates, they look much like the communities we have already constructed.

Yet, in other respects, Usenet communities are very much different. The tone of the conversation can become very hostile on Usenet. "Netiquette" is a far cry from the more familiar "etiquette," where people are more reluctant to verbally attack another person in their physical presence. Flaming is so much easier online than in person since one is not facing a flesh-and-blood individual, but a bloodless computer screen. Moreover, Usenet communication lacks the other, nonverbal messages communicated through face-to-face communication. The subtle messages of a wink, a nod, or a raised eyebrow offer the message recipient more information to place the verbal message in context. All of that is missing on the Usenet and may contribute to a more hostile environment.

As one Usenet proponent has noted,

> an ironic comment without the benefit of a laughing tone, or a wink, can easily be mistaken for belligerence, perhaps even a personal at-

tack. The odds of misunderstandings like this occurring are increased tenfold by the fact that most of the contact in USENET is between people who have the slightest possible knowledge of each other.[22]

Technological innovations on the Internet could alter that relationship. Text-based Usenet could be displaced by voice communication, and perhaps eventually visual interaction as well. Voice communication already exists, yet is not widespread.

Another difference between real and virtual communities is group stability. Real communities are more stable than newsgroup communities, which tend to be highly amorphous. As one analyst of the Internet concluded, "The newsgroup communities undergo a process of continuous membership evolution having few real counterparts in the life cycles of face-to-face communities."[23]

Still another contrast to most interpersonal political discussions, and certainly mediated conversations, is the multitude of cross-conversations. Topics range depending on the participants, and threads of conversation will seem to die and then be resurrected at some future point. Several conversations can be occurring simultaneously, making it difficult for conversation continuity.

Usenet groups represent chaos because discussion moderators or facilitators designed to stimulate and regulate discussion to encourage representation and maintain direction are plainly absent. That very chaos limits the ability of Usenet groups to function in behalf of all participants. Democratic discussions flourish when a moderator organizes the debate and seeks to regulate how long and often one can speak.

Some groups have turned to moderators to screen messages. In doing so, they can play a filtering role, eliminating chronic offenders or refusing to post messages containing obscenity or other violations of netiquette. However, most political groups lack such structure, and many regulars enjoy their present role and would vigorously oppose the imposition of such order.

The expression of public opinion should be moderated and shaped precisely to avoid the kind of anarchy that characterizes political discourse on these groups. Such intervention should not be designed to inhibit public opinion but to allow views to be expressed, exchanges of information to be made, and effects on policy to result. Any form of filter imposes its own biases. But the absence of any filter also has its own bias. It causes public opinion expression to break down into a babel of voices, with only the loudest achieving some level of recognition.

It is not my argument that Usenet lacks political significance. For those who participate, obviously felt social and political needs are met or they would not subscribe. Usenet subscribership in political newsgroups is a gratification that drives continued logging on to communicate with faceless (sometimes nameless) people across the nation and even the globe. For these people, Usenet is significant as a political force.

Nor is it true that Usenet is relevant only to those who partici-pate. As mentioned at the beginning of this chapter, Usenet postings and conversation threads at times capture the attention of journal-ists, politicians, and the general public. But that does not mean pub-lic policy necessarily is affected. Journalists are the main cause of Usenet's occasional wider audience. But the journalistic incentive is the existence of a good story—Navy missiles blowing up a com-mercial airliner or Vincent Foster suicide theories—not promotion of Usenet as a vehicle for public opinion. In fact, far more often than not Usenet postings have been transformed into news not due to a high level of credibility, but to a high degree of perceived gullibility on the part of the participants.

Nevertheless, the answer to the main question—Is Usenet an ad-equate mechanism for public participation and opinion gauge?—is clearly no. Those who participate in Usenet, particularly those who post, are a small and atypical minority, not a representative cross-section of the American electorate. There is little incentive for oth-ers, "lurkers," who are less vocal, to participate in the discussion. The postings cannot be considered reflective of general public opin-ion. Rather, they reflect the posters who dominate like-minded groups by controlling the agenda, setting the standards for partici-pation, and, in some cases, even attempting to drive off others who differ with them. Moreover, the much-vaunted idea exchange is in actuality a reinforcement of previously held views.

In conclusion, the promise of Usenet is a hollow one. It turns out that even the Internet's most democratic corner is not as demo-cratic as it appears.

SEVEN

The Internet as Participatory Forum

It is easy to forget how new the Internet really is. A Louis Harris poll in April 1994 found that two-thirds of Americans had never heard of the information superhighway.[1] Yet, despite its adolescence, the Internet has acquired a level of permanence. Growth will continue, although probably not at such a rapid rate as in the past half decade. One estimate places Internet access in one-third of all households by the year 2000.[2] Time will tell whether these growth projections are overly optimistic. But the Internet's staying power is assured.

We can make some safe predictions about Internet usage: The most likely Internet users will continue to be the affluent, the most common users of Internet political information will be the already politically interested, and those who will use the Internet for political activity will be primarily those who are already politically active. And that is why the Internet will not lead to the social and political revolution so widely predicted.

Will the Internet achieve the revolutionary tool status predicted for it? Will it upset existing power structures leading the traditional media, existing groups, and even political institutions to be replaced? Will we see the rise of the age of "Internet democracy," a period when the public will suddenly become political activists due to their new capability to acquire information, register opinions, and therefore directly make public policy?

This book has demonstrated that none of that will occur. The reasons are twofold: One, existing dominant players are adapting to the Internet, and two, the Internet is not an adequate tool for public political involvement. Each of these can be examined in turn.

Adaption by Dominant Players

We have seen that existing players in American politics—the media, interest groups, candidates, and policy makers—have adapted to the Internet in order to retain preeminence. This behavior is hardly new, though it may be disappointing to those who predicted something quite different.

This adaption, rather than being opposed by the public, is quite warmly welcomed. As discussed earlier, most Internet users are drawn to the sites of traditional organizations and institutions—media, groups, parties, government—because they offer two critical aspects of the information-gathering process that were missing in the early days of the World Wide Web: organization and reliability.

Organization

The plethora of information on the Web is viewed as a boon to Internet afficionados. But to the average user it is chaos. Most people do not have time to "surf the Web." They want information they feel they need, and they want it quickly and efficiently. They demand the kind of structure that makes that possible. In fact, the Internet would not have grown to the size it is now had it not been for the introduction of that kind of structure.

Media, groups, and government offer that structure. As they have in the past, people will turn to the familiar to make sense of the unfamiliar, in this case the Internet. Media organizations, particularly, are acutely aware of the service they can provide in organizing the news and information presentation to the new Internet user. As Robert Iger, ABC-TV president, stated "In a world in which there is massive choice, there's still going to be a need for someone to create order."[3]

The online access services (Compuserve, Prodigy, America Online) offered the very orderliness the early Internet lacked. They categorized the Internet for users. The programs they offered users were the subjects the users wanted, such as sports, stock reports, or entertainment. These organizational tools even dished up specific news categories. Yet, the future is with smaller, more local access providers who offer an entrance ramp to the Internet at much lower costs. However, these providers lack the order of the larger global companies. As a result, a vacuum is created that the megasites offered by news media organizations or groups can fill.

Yet, the structure these sites provide also carries its own biases. Such structure will serve as a new form of mediation, not merely in terms of the information the individual receives, but also as it concerns the nature of the feedback the individual gives to elites. As a result, the notion that the public will take control of agenda setting is absurd. The agenda-setting function will not suddenly devolve to the masses. Someone must organize the discussion and frame the alternatives. Then, and only then, can the public respond intelligently. The existence of a vacuum in agenda setting does not mean the public fills it. Rather, it means anarchy prevails, and, as a result, the public's role ultimately is reduced, not enhanced.

British commentator Ian McLean addresses the problem that arises if agenda setting is assumed to be held in abeyance:

> Today we will vote on how much to spend on the NHS (National Health Service), tomorrow on how to divide it up between hospitals, GPs (general practitioners), and anti-smoking propaganda, on Wednesday we will vote on animal experiments, and on Thursday we will vote on the Sunday trading laws.
>
> What can we do about the awkward character who says, "The issues are wrongly posed. I think it is worth spending a lot on hospitals only if the State permits medical experiments on animals to continue. So I cannot vote on Monday because I do not know the outcome of Wednesday's vote?"
>
> It is no use reversing the order, because then another awkward customer will say "I favour animal experiments if and only if NHS spending is high enough to allow the results to be used in a socialized health system."[4]

Setting the agenda and framing the options will remain in the hands of elites. Such framing will carry with it its own biases. For example, during the 1996 congressional debate over term limits, Senator John Ashcroft invited visitors to his site to register their opinions on the topic. The hot link for supporting term limits was much larger and more prominent than the one for opposition. Not surprisingly, 80 percent of votes registered were for term limits.[5]

Reliability

Only days after the tragic car accident that took the life of Princess Diana, a California-based Web site published a photograph purportedly of the car wreck with a bloodied Diana inside. The photograph was quickly branded a fraud. However, the incident again raised the issue of reliability of Web information.[6] The Internet will become a useful political tool for interested citizens only when its utility is proved to everyday users. The user does not want to continually question whether the information provided is actually reliable.

Established sources of information—media, groups, government—already offer these advantages. If interested citizens know those sources are also on the Internet, then the move to online information becomes more familiar for them and, hence, more attractive. Moreover, the presence of one source, such as the media or interest groups, has enhanced the others as these established sources transfer their symbiotic relationship with each other onto the Web. Offline, this relationship serves all parties. News stories quote official government sources or highly recognized groups. Groups refer to news media stories and editorials in their literature. Government institutions establish formal contacts with interest groups and offer extensive services to the press. This reliance upon each other meets the traditional media's definition of news—what official and quasi-official sources say and do—and it also enhances the reliability of news in the minds of the audience. The news audience comes to expect that news occurs from certain sources. New sources unknown to the public do not carry the same sort of legitimacy.

This also occurs on the Net. Not only are stories on the Net written similarly to those published offline, but the links embedded in the story or connected to it are going to be links to established organizations—government institutions or traditional groups. For example, a story about sexual harassment in the army will link to the army's official web site, where the user will hear the army's version of the story. Many groups include news stories or editorials about the group on their site. Many groups also link to each other, and many link to government agencies and Congress. In turn, government agencies link to sites of groups with similar issue interests. For example, the Department of Housing and Urban Development site links to sites such as the National Association of Realtors, the Mortgage Bankers Association, and the National Association of Home Builders. Even government reinforces the role of groups on the Net.

So why wouldn't users turn to new sites? New sites initially may seem attractive to users because they are novel, but the appeal can fade quickly as the users contemplate whether to trust the information they receive. As one journalist has commented: "OK, so a lot of Americans distrust the established news media? Are they likely to find that amateur Web sites maintained by people they don't know are more believable?"[7] Incidents such as the fake Diana photo remind Internet users of the dangers of relying on other types of sources. Traditional media will continue to be the most common news source on the Net and, in turn, they will continue to use as their sources the existing players generally viewed as reliable by the public.

Tool for Direct Democracy

Internet proponent Esther Dyson has predicted that the "Net will foster activity instead of passivity."[8] As demonstrated in chapter 1 the existence of communication technology does not transform people into political animals. Similarly, the Internet does not cause people to suddenly become politically active or even interested. Rather, American political behavior will remain essentially the same regardless of technological innovations designed to disseminate more political information.

This is especially true of the Internet. Despite the abundance of political information available on the Internet, it will not revolutionize public interest and knowledge. In fact, in some respects the Internet may well reduce the level of political knowledge held by Americans.

News Avoidance

Interest in politics reaches a peak (although not a very high one) during presidential election campaigns. For half of the eligible electorate who bother to vote in presidential elections, the campaign sparks interest in the electoral choices available. Otherwise, voters are not terribly interested in politics.

The Internet is not primarily a political tool. Most people who use the Internet do not do so for political purposes. Of those who go online, less than half do so for political news. This is among those who already belong to an upscale demographic and are more politically

interested than the general public. One evidence of this news avoidance, even on the Internet, is the fact that during the 1996 election
only 4 percent of the public consulted online sources for election
news.[9]

But, as Internet supporters reply, future elections will be different. As usage of the Internet increases, there will be more use for
political purposes. And younger people (those for whom the
Internet is more a part of the furniture than a sudden new appearance) will discover the Internet's political education role and use it
accordingly.

Admittedly, the future resides with an age group, people under
30, who, currently, are the most interested in utilizing the Internet.
However, people in this age group are no more interested in politics
than their elders, and, in fact, may actually be less so. A study released in early 1998 found that 76 percent of college students were
apathetic about politics.[10] A not surprising outcome is that young
people have been found to know far less than other age groups
about politics, particularly presidential candidates.[11] For example,
they visit political sites no more frequently than other age groups,
with the exception of those over 60. Among newspaper readers the
age group least likely to turn first to the news sections are readers
under 30.[12] Why would this nonpolitical group suddenly become
highly political, more so than older generations who have gradually
opted out of the political process?

Who Benefits?

If the Internet is not going to stimulate participation by the disinterested masses, will it have any benefit for anyone? The answer is yes.
The main beneficiaries will be those who are already politically interested. Even now, political Web sites are geared toward these people.
And those sites include special sections for even narrower audiences
such as the press, students of politics, and political insiders. As discussed earlier, the Internet has become a boon for specialists. This is
particularly true for the politically interested and active.

Particularized News

And what will happen to the average user? The existence of a
greater choice of information available on the Internet than on any

other existing mass medium quite possibly will lead citizens to become more narrowly informed than they were when there were fewer options available.

Up until the expansion of cable, the three major television networks united the country in a way that will never be repeated. For television viewers, early evening was dominated by news programs, with only one or two other viewing options. When the president spoke on television in a national address, or a presidential candidate debate occurred, the major networks preempted programming for this national event. The nation sat down together and watched common political information. At the height of network dominance, 76 percent of the television audience watched the 1976 debate.[13]

However, in 1996, only 66 percent of the audience watched the first presidential debate.[14] When given the choice, many television viewers chose to tune out a major political event in the heat of a presidential election campaign. This dip in public exposure has occurred despite the existence of more alternatives for acquiring political information (CNN, C-SPAN, prime-time network news programs), allowing the public more political data than ever before possible in the history of the nation.

The Internet is destined to have the same effect, but to an even greater degree. The body politic will be further fragmented. The practically infinite array of choices available on the Internet means that ignoring politics will become even easier. By using bookmarks or push services that grab preidentified subjects, people can avoid Internet political sites completely.

Offline, the audience can elicit political information without necessarily seeking it. Reading a newspaper or watching a television news broadcast may expose the less politically interested to stories they would not normally be drawn to but may glean useful information from. The front page is a measure of what the newspaper believes is important. Even readers who prefer sports or business news must get past the front page to do so. Something there may catch their eye and their interest.

However, that serendipity will be absent on the Web. People will more easily avoid information they do not want to encounter. For instance, increasingly, newspaper Web sites are making the front page only one in a menu of options. Push services may make them potentially obsolete for many people.

Through their usage of these selection tools, people will collect even more narrow strands of information, most of which will be nonpolitical. They will know even less about politics and policy than they would obtain from an evening news broadcast. As a consequence, rather than increasing the public's political knowledge, the Internet actually may contribute to information decline. The exception, as discussed above, would be the minority who are currently strongly politically interested.

The Participation Problem

But what about the claims the Internet will stimulate political participation? As the argument goes, this new tool will reinvigorate the public's interest in politics since people will see the potential for acquiring information and expressing opinions. John Seely Brown, chief scientist at Xerox, has described a newly enfranchised public: "Information technologies genuinely offer the chance to empower people . . . who for one reason or another have become either effectively disenfranchised or merely disenchanted."[15] Author Wayne Rash predicts that, through the Internet, "voters will have a voice that reaches directly to the highest levels of both parties and the government."[16]

And the Internet, it is claimed, could be used as a vehicle for voter participation. Technologically, the Internet offers the promise of an interactive communication tool facilitating public input and even direct democracy via formal electronic vote processes. Proponents point to the developments during the 1996 electoral campaign. A growing number of sites during the 1996 campaign highlighted voter registration materials. Voters were encouraged to register on an online form and then print the form to send in to local election boards. This could be only the beginning of a much more extensive usage.

Deliberation and the Net   Yet, the preponderance of evidence suggests the Internet will not only not motivate political activity on the part of the currently inactive, but it may contribute to further atomization of society. Concern over societal disconnectiveness, and the traditional media's role in that trend, has risen anew recently. Robert Putnam has charted the decline in communal activity in American life, both political and social, and concluded that "social capital"—the sense of connectiveness to each other—has diminished over the past two decades.[17] There is other evidence that people are associating less with each other and feeling less secure around others. One survey found that most people felt that you "can't be too careful" in dealing with other people while only one-third felt that "most people can be trusted."[18]

One explanation in this change of attitude may be behavioral— the way we spend our leisure time.[19] While two decades ago, people watched movies in theaters and chose from the programming of a handful of networks (ABC, CBS, NBC, and PBS), today they devote large blocks of leisure time to sitting in front of home entertainment centers including, in addition to the standard television receiver, videotape recorders, laser disc players, and home computers. Individual choice is a prominent component in mass entertainment. When a choice is available, increasingly the nod is toward individualized technological entertainment (videotapes, videodiscs, personal computers) rather than group entertainment, such as movie theaters, plays, bowling, and so on.

Where does the Internet fit into this trend? The Internet may be another step toward greater atomization. One hundred years ago, people received political information by attending rallies and standing in the public square to hear speeches by candidates or political activists. As mentioned previously, twenty years ago the nation jointly watched candidate debates.

But today the Internet has the potential of making those activities obsolete. The user can extract whatever political information he or she wants at any time of day without leaving the comfort of home or office. Candidates can even be questioned and opinions expressed without the citizen having to go to public meeting halls.

Yet, the vision (or nightmare) of a society of individuals who interact with each other only virtually is highly unlikely. Similar predictions were made about television replacing human interaction. Satellite and cable enhanced television's appeal and again made it the tool for society's atomization. But, despite Robert Putnam's fear that the United States is moving headlong toward social isolation, the felt need for human society (not computer-assisted society) is too strong.

However, television, particularly, has shaped both social and political behavior. While the pretelevision age of political campaigns centered on mass activity such as rallies, speeches, and street meetings, the television age has moved those activities into the living room, where one sits alone, or perhaps with a few family members, hearing speeches and watching political campaigns. Televised politics is strictly a spectator sport. While the public, communal activities in the pretelevision age featured citizens' interpersonal exchange of views, politics via television diminished that deliberative component.

Understandably, the Internet has been portrayed as the solution to this trend, a restoration of the deliberative component of political communication. David Thelen suggests citizens want ongoing communication with policy makers and with each other.[20] The Internet provides the mechanism for such deliberation. Ideally, citizens could use the Internet to debate the political issues of the day.

However, as this book has demonstrated, such a function is far more ideal than real. This broad vision of Internet civic participation is hampered by the absence of actual deliberation in Internet political discourse. The Internet is not the same as panels of citizens who meet and discuss until conclusions are reached and problems resolved.[21] Deliberative democracy, a concept fostered by James S. Fishkin in his "national caucus" during the 1996 presidential campaign, assumes voters engage in "thoughtful interaction," which is accomplished by providing voters with relevant materials.[22]

But the Internet does not accomplish that. In Usenet political discussions, people talk past one another, when they are not verbally attacking each other. The emphasis is not problem solving, but discussion dominance. Such behavior does not resemble deliberation and it does not encourage participation, particularly by the less politically interested.

Primary groups, such as families, neighborhoods, and community organizations are essential ingredients for Americans to move from faceless masses to participating individuals.[23] The Internet is supposed to duplicate that. Yet, there is concern that it actually displaces it. Robert Putnam admits his hunch that "meeting in an electronic forum is not the equivalent of meeting in a bowling alley."[24] Indeed, it is not. The Web is not a virtual community; it is a collection of isolated individuals.

Elite Response   Another missing element in the Internet participation scenario is the role of policy makers. Predictions of Internet-driven democracy assume not only that ordinary individuals are anxious to participate (a dubious claim), but also that policy makers want to listen. The evidence suggests otherwise. For example, government agencies are quick to allow users to send e-mail to the agency, but they don't encourage individuals to comment on specific pending agency decisions. Political party organizations rarely include bulletin boards on their Web sites.[25] Also, members of Congress actually place a lower priority on e-mail than on regular mail.

This policy maker response to e-mail actually was predicted more than a decade ago when political scientist Ithiel de Sola Pool, who described how though things change they also remain the same, wrote: Someone who "now laboriously writes a letter to his Congressman could on a computer network send an instantaneous personalized message to every member of Congress. It would, of course, not be listened to; it would perhaps have less effect than his present letter."[26]

Interactivity on the Internet is primarily an illusion. Interest groups, party organizations, and legislators seek to use the Web for information dissemination, but they are rarely interested in allowing their sites to become forums for the opinions of others. Ithiel de Sola Pool again correctly prophesied that interactivity would be mediated by these groups and individuals: "Somehow, by a combination of devices and customs, a protective shell will be created as fast as the flow of communication threatens to become overwhelming."[27]

Norman J. Vig concludes that communications technology has "enhanced some forms of political participation—notably by organized activist groups promoting particular interests or causes—while at the same time reducing the effectiveness of mass participation through traditional channels such as political parties."[28] The same can be said for the Internet alone. While the politically active are benefited, the politically inactive are left behind in the movement toward expression through this new technology.

The Ideal Citizen Moreover, the vision of the Internet as the forum of direct democracy assumes the existence of a certain ideal citizen. That ideal citizen seeks political information as well as a vehicle for expressing opinions on a wide range of issues. That citizen uses the Internet to keep abreast of news, search government documents, and express opinions through e-mail. And, eventually, that citizen uses the Internet to formally express opinions and actually influence policy.

But such an ideal citizen is more a rarity than commonplace. Most voters, much less most citizens, do not spend significant amounts of time collecting information about politics. In presidential elections, most voters only pay attention late in the campaign. For state and local elections, they may not attend to the campaign until the waning days. For most voters, information comes from snippets of newspaper stories or campaign brochures hung on the doorknob.

Formal Voting   The next step in the progression of the Internet-as-participation-mode argument is employment of the Internet as a mechanism for formal voting. That step would be a pivotal electoral system change, much like the introduction of the secret ballot was one hundred years ago. Given what has been presented here, it should be obvious that Internet voting would significantly benefit the politically interested and active. Electronic voting as a supplement to traditional voting would not disenfranchise others, but it would still disadvantage them vis-à-vis the more active. And *exclusive* Internet voting certainly shifts the bias toward the middle and upper classes, the already politically active.

Ironically, the politically interested are not in need of mobilization; it is the politically uninterested and inactive who need such mobilization. However, the Internet does not activate them. In fact, it may even have the effect of reducing public participation, particularly if the Internet becomes a formal process for public decision making.

Impediments to Participation

Rather than facilitating democratic participation, Internet democracy places impediments in the way of civic participation. Internet democracy requires voters to do more than they currently do in order to participate in the democratic process, a disturbing possibility in a society where voting has declined precipitously. The Internet forces voters to become technologically literate. It places the additional expectation of a commitment to political information gathering and involvement. Finally, it requires citizens to possess a high level of financial resources in order to participate.

Technological Literacy   One way the Internet may actually reduce public participation is through its requirement of technological competence in order to become involved in public opinion expression or even voting. The Internet, unlike any another prior medium for democratic participation, requires the public to possess a fairly sophisticated level of technological competence. In order to become informed and express opinions and even policy choices, voters must master a computer, as well as the Internet.

What does this mean for participation? For some citizens, such a technological requirement will be difficult to fulfill. Unlike the process of reading a ballot or pushing levers on a voting machine, this tool will screen out those who are unfamiliar with computer technology. Others, moreover, will view such a requirement as an unnecessary burden and refuse to participate.

No democratic society in modern history has ever placed such a high technological hurdle in the path of mass voting. In the United States, it is particularly ironic that in a time of increasing concern for facilitating public participation, we would create still more obstacles to participation. Such barriers do not deter the already politically active, but they do shrink the electorate even further by raising the bar of participation for those less interested or knowledgeable about politics.

Time Commitment   Another requirement the Internet imposes on public participation is the expectation of constant political involvement and awareness. The direct democracy vision of the Internet imposes a time requirement for participation beyond what most citizens are willing to devote. With Internet democracy, voters will be urged to do their civic duty and participate in the regular policy votes. Since these could occur monthly or even weekly, the voter will feel obliged to devote far more time to politics than he or she now does. Unlike radio, or television, or even cable, Internet democracy will require a high level of activity by the user. Choices must constantly be made, and the range of options is seemingly infinite.

That higher level of activity will not be a problem for the technologically literate or the politically active. But it can be a mind-boggling maze for many other users. Megasites with their one-stop approach will be tools for simplification. So will the creation of profiles for information retrieval, where people will have a preferred set of information automatically presented to them. These methods will reduce the number of choices and therefore help streamline the Internet information retrieval process for many people. However, the level of activity required to participate still will be quite high and perhaps overwhelming for many people.

Such participation cannot come without changes in many voters' approach to politics. Voting in elections (an activity shunned by most people anyway) will not be enough. Time now given to other activities of choice would have to be devoted to studying the issues. How many citizens will actually take that step?

The most politically interested and active will be those most prone to participate, while those who are willing to take the time every two or four years to acquire some information about candidates are likely to view this now requisite time commitment as too costly. Moreover, those who do not wish to take the time to participate now are not likely to do so when such participation comes at an even greater cost in terms of time and technological literacy.

The deterrence to participation caused by this new technoliterate component may be reduced over subsequent generations who are trained early in computer use. However, it is unrealistic to believe that Americans will undergo a dramatic attitude change leading to greater intensity of interest in things political. One example of the unlikelihood of people changing their behavior is the selection process for the Reform Party presidential candidate in 1996. In addition to other participation forums, Reform Party members could vote via e-mail in the party's presidential nomination processs. Some voters may have not participated because of the predictability of the outcome, that is, the almost certain nomination of Ross Perot. Nevertheless, only 5 percent of Reform Party members voted, despite the use of new technology such as e-mail.[29]

It could be argued that voters should be expected to devote this degree of effort to sustaining a representative democracy. It should be a requirement to be well informed and willing to sacrifice time and energy to participate. In fact, voters should welcome a direct democracy with the potential of bypassing, or at least more closely directing, representatives who without such constant guidance may not reflect public will.

Yet, the reality is people do not give that kind of attention and energy to politics. They do not spend time studying politics. Nor will they do so; nor should they be expected to do so. Raising expectations on voters lowers the numbers of those who actually participate, short of actual compulsion, while lowering expectations expands the number who will be drawn to participate.

Additional Financial Resources New communications technology historically has highlighted the income gap. Newspapers at first cost too much for the average person. In the 1700s and the early 1800s, the cost of a newspaper was $8 to 10 per year, far beyond the reach of the average person. Radio and television also initially shut out the poor.

Financing changes eventually lowered costs to include the previously excluded. The costs of owning a television set have fallen dramatically. Similarly, the costs of owning the hardware (computer, monitor, modem) essential for an Internet connection have already fallen and yet will.

Nevertheless, the Internet *does* now and continually *will* discriminate economically. Internet use requires Internet access, which costs money many people cannot pay. The integration of cable and the Internet may reduce the costs and increase the numbers of those who will purchase the services, but it will not eliminate the economic barrier.

Suggestions have been made to facilitate free access for the poor. However, such efforts have not been commercially profitable for either hardware makers or access services. Nor is it likely that legislation will be enacted to force such actions. Such enterprises would complain they are unfairly singled out.

People making over $75,000 annually are far more likely to own a computer, have access to the Internet, and use the Internet to visit political sites than those who make under $40,000.[30] In contrast, the average income nationally is approximately $32,000. Those numbers will change, but those at the lower end will lag behind, causing policy to be made by those at the upper end, as is currently true. As Langdon Winner has put it: "People equipped with personal computers, modems, cellular phones, and the like have begun to outshout those in our society for whom owning a telephone may conflict with paying the rent or the doctor."[31]

The Effects on Participation

Refuting the idea that new communications technology sweeps away mediating institutions, G. J. Mulgan argues that such technology "is not an end to mediation, but rather the emergence of more complex structures of mediation."[32] The same can be said for the Internet. However, the degree of complexity has reached new heights. The Internet is not like pushing a button or switching a dial. As a vehicle for political participation, it requires a level of technological literacy, interactivity, and financial resources unheard of in the history of democratic societies. Even as those requirements lessen somewhat with reduced costs for Internet-connected terminals or greater ease in reaching desired information, they will never go away completely.

Placing additional requirements on voters aids those who already participate in the process. Since the already active easily meet those requirements, they become the electorate, thus narrowing instead of expanding the numbers of those who participate in decisionmaking.

This phenomenon is nothing new. Today's politics are driven primarily, often exclusively, by a small percentage of politically interested activists. Even voting, which hovers around 50 percent of the eligible electorate (and far lower for nonpresidential elections), is dominated by the minority of the politically interested segment of the population. Internet voting will only maintain or perhaps increase slightly that dominance, not undermine it.

The point is that computer-assisted politics will not be radically different than today's politics. This notion stems from the incontrovertible fact that Americans will not be different people just because there are resources at their disposal to follow politics quite closely. Again, what differences exist will rest primarily with a small segment of citizens, those who are already politically interested. Those individuals will be able to participate with greater ease. They will be able, more readily, to express personal opinions; participate in group public opinion expression; and gain information about candidates, legislative action, executive decisions, current news, and even each other.

Hence, the Internet becomes a new, more efficient tool primarily for an elite of already politically interested activists.[33] The Internet's benefits for them have already been enumerated.[34] Obviously, these people do not need encouragement to participate, and they will find the process of articulating and mobilizing opinions even easier with the Internet.

But, the idea of the proverbial common citizen becoming active due to the Internet does not stand up under close scrutiny. Anecdotes used to demonstrate that common citizens are using the Internet to express themselves politically feature people who are already politically active or, unlike most people, possess uncommon resources for political activism.[35]

The gap between the politically active and the inactive will grow larger. The Internet will offer greater advantages to a political elite while simultaneously erecting another barrier to participation for those who are uninterested and uninvolved.

A Positive Role for the Internet

The conclusions of this book may be depressing to those who have hoped for the Internet to improve politics. The proposed revolution sounds appealing. The public would truly serve as the directors of public policy. Political participation would be reinvigorated. Elected representatives would be more accountable and less able to "get away" with bad, self-interested policy decisions.

Despite the fact that these things won't occur, the Internet does have the potential to be a positive force, although not necessarily a revolutionary one. It all depends on how the Internet is used. If the Internet serves primarily as an information source available at the times when voters want information, it might increase its utility to a large percentage of the public that is politically semiattentive. In 1996, a small percentage of voters actually used these sites to acquire candidate information. Of registered voters, 22 percent were online, and eight and a half million voters, or 9 percent of those who voted, said they relied on the Internet for election-related information during the campaign.[36] As mentioned earlier, political news sites were unprepared for the deluge of persons seeking to log on for election return information on election night in 1996. One exclaimed that "this is a defining moment for the Web as a part of public discourse."[37]

Interest in political sites dipped dramatically following the campaign. Not surprisingly, Webmasters of candidate sites found a dramatic decline in visitors to their sites. One popular site with political junkies, PoliticsNow, even shut down.

The numbers of Internet users extracting campaign-related information in all likelihood will increase in 1998 and, especially, in the presidential campaign of 2000. Yet, inevitably, interest will peak and then decline again. That surge and decline process is natural. When voters no longer need to make an immediate decision, they return to their regular (and likely far more interesting) activities.

Rather than suggest some flaw in the public or the system, this rhythm demonstrates that people are using the Internet rather than being used by it. They are seeking information when they need to make their judgments in a representative democracy. Then they go on with their lives, perhaps keeping one ear cocked occasionally for additional information. This cycle also suggests that individuals do not want such political information all the time, which would be essential for Internet democracy to work.

Moreover, in an age when voter turnout has declined steadily over the past four decades, the Internet should be able to play a positive role in facilitating voter turnout. With appropriate security checks against fraud, the Internet could be useful for facilitating the vote for those who are unable to go to a polling place on election day.

There is something wonderfully communal about walking to the local elementary school or other public building, or even someone's home, to stand in line with neighbors to cast a vote. Yet, with frequent business travel or immobility, not everyone can do so. Some states, pioneered by Oregon and Texas, have already moved toward the option of voting by mail. The Internet could be an option—allowing voting by those who wish to do so, but who are unable to go to the polls on a certain day. The frequent calls for weekend voting or establishing election day as a national holiday would become unnecessary.

The Internet will be a means to serve individuals' needs. Those who seek political information will find the Internet a fitting instrument. For those who wish to become politically involved, the Internet will be a valuable tool.

However, the Internet is not a panacea for our political system's flaws. Nor can it radically alter Americans' traditional disinterest in politics. As a tool for direct democracy, the Internet, like its predecessors, will fail in that expected role. In fact, the Internet is more likely to reduce participation and increase the political system's reliance on a small number of political activists than to actually represent public opinion. Though such reliance is not new, the danger comes from the illusion of broad public involvement. Such an illusion does not exist in a representative democracy since such extensive involvement is not expected.

Though this book will not be the last on the Web and politics, hopefully, it will be the last needed to place the Internet's political role in perspective. That is, the Internet, like its historical predecessors, is another new technology adapted to and dominated by traditional predominant forces in American politics in order to sustain existing power relationships, rather than a revolutionary force producing a long-sought-for unmediated direct democracy. That distinction is critical and, hopefully, seeing the Internet in this light will stimulate a future discussion of what the Internet is, rather than what it is not.

Rather than being new and different, the Internet is becoming quite familiar. One writer concluded that the new world of the Net is "all too much like the world we already live in."[38] That trend will merely accelerate in the years to come.

Methodology

Studying the Internet is not like reading a book or extracting data from a journal article. For one thing, replication is problematic. In fact, unless you download everything, even proving that you really saw what you claim to have seen on the Internet can be difficult. Content and even whole sites can come and go with great rapidity. Even citing information from the Internet is a new scholarly dilemma, that is, the dilemma of dealing with such a dynamic and transitory medium. Consequently, this research should be viewed as a first stab at systematic analysis of this new medium. Yet, despite the numerous difficulties a scholar faces in doing so, the Internet is a subject worth studying now and in the future. The main question for me and subsequent scholars will be how.

This study of the Internet was approached using three methods. One was *traditional content analysis.* Again, the problem with coding Internet sites is the difficulty in maintaining a dataset that does not change. I solved that problem by downloading most of my data, so at least it did not change. However, the data on the Internet does so and, quite naturally, did so in my case as well. So the reader must realize that the information I saw is not necessarily the same that he or she would see on those same sites currently, if the sites even exist.

Another method was *survey research.* Mail surveys of journalists, Webmasters of media organization sites, and Webmasters of interest group sites were conducted. These survey responses were invaluable in gauging current usage of the Internet as well as expectations of future use.

Still another method was *interviewing.* Interviewing was conducted primarily over the telephone or by e-mail. E-mail interviewing consists of sending a list of questions to the subject and then getting a response question by question. Occasionally, follow-up questions were asked. The Internet will affect the way interviewing is conducted, but that is another book.

The following explains the use of these methods in the organization of each chapter.

Chapter 2

A mail survey was sent to 200 journalists to determine individual reporters' usage of the Internet for newsgathering purposes. The intent was to create a sample of journalists who were more likely than not to have experience with the Web. Since such lists do not exist and a sample drawn from a list of journalists might well produce a small number of journalists who would be familiar with the Web, my effort was focused on journalists who were already on the Web. It was hoped that journalists whose stories are on the Web might be more familiar with the Web than others. Such journalists were identified through the newspapers whose Web pages are hot linked on the *American Journalism Review* Web site. For each state, we started at the first daily newspaper listed and then used every other newspaper in each state. Some newspapers selected had to be discarded because the web address was wrong, the site was under construction, or no stories were actually posted so, obviously, no bylines existed. Surveys were mailed during the month of July 1997 to the 200 journalists who were identified through this process. Fifty-four journalists (27 percent) responded. They represented a wide range of newspapers from large regional dailies to small local dailies.

A separate mail survey also was sent during the same time period to Webmasters of 200 media organizations. The Webmasters also were found through the *American Journalism Review* site, which includes a state-by-state listing of media organizations. The initial sample was stratified to include at least one media organization from each state, although the final sample obviously did not include such broad representation. Thirty-one Webmasters, representing radio and television stations and daily newspapers, responded to the survey.

Chapter 3

The most direct method of studying how groups are using the Internet is a systematic examination of their Internet products, that is, the groups' Web sites. A content analysis of 80 interest group sites was conducted. The sites were selected from a Yahoo! list of associations with Web sites. Preference was given to national associations. The list then included the following categories: Public Interest—41; Professional Associations—15; Trade Associations—12; Labor—10; Government Associations—2. Public interest groups may have been over-represented; however, they do represent a large and growing segment of organized groups.

The study was designed to be an in-depth analysis of sites, but not a particularly broad one. Therefore, there was no analysis of the groups in terms of categories as listed above. As a consequence, it is not possible in this study to differentiate in Internet usage between public interest groups, labor groups, trade associations, etc. That will have to be saved for some future study. Then addresses were found through Internet search engines. Sites difficult to access or not actually in existence were deleted to compile a workable group of sites. Sites were coded during May 1997.

The sites of the following groups were included in the sample of coded interest group Web sites as follows: National Abortion Rights Action League (NARAL), Planned Parenthood of America, Baptists for Life, Catholics United for Life, People for the American Way, Feminists for Life of America, National Right to Life, National Women's Coalition for Life, Pro Life Alliance of Gays & Lesbians, Stop FTR (Fetal Tissue Research), National Organization for Reform of Marijuana Laws, National Association of Social Workers, Environmental Defense Fund, National Parks & Conservation Association, Action on Smoking & Health, Amnesty International, Electronic Frontier Foundation, Fairness & Accuracy in Reporting, Feminist Majority Foundation, League of Conservation Voters, National Audubon Society, National Coalition for the Homeless, National Council of LaRaza, National Governor's Association, National PTA, National Rifle Association, Institute of Electrical and Electronics Engineers (IEEE), Network Professional Association, National Association for the Self-Employed, Home Office Association of America, American Institute of Architects, International Engineering Consortium (IEC), National Fire Prevention Association, American Chemical Society, American Geophysical Union, Amalgamated Transit Union, Computer Professionals for Social Responsibility, International Alliance of Theatrical Stage Employees, Moving Pictures Technicians, Artists and Allied Craft (IATSE), National Postal Mail Handlers Union, Office and Professional Employees International Union (OPEIU), Plumbers & Steamfitters Local 343, Stonecutters' Union of North America, Association of Veternarians for Animal Rights, World Wildlife Fund—U.S. Site, American Civil Liberties Union (ACLU), Justice on Campus, U.S. Chamber of Commerce, Voters Telecommunication Watch, Public Citizen, American Foundation for the Blind, National Urban League, Inc., National Congress for American Indians, AFL-CIO, American Conservative Union, American Heart Association, American Management Association, Children's Defense Fund, Council on State Governments, [Chicago] Council on Foreign Relations, Earth First, National Resources Defense Council, National Employment Lawyers Association (NELA), International Association of Bridge, Ornamental and Structural Ironworkers, Sheet Metal Workers International Association, Experimental Aircraft Association, Alliance for Public Technology, Institute of Management Consultants, Recreational Vehicle Industry Association (RIVA), [American] Physical Therapy Association, The American Leather Chemists Association, American Arbitration Association, National Association of Real Estate Publishers, International Wood Products Association, American Philological Association, Newspaper Association of America, American Geophysical Union (AGU), United Mineworkers of America (UMWA), American Postal Workers Union (APWU), Service Employees International Union (SEIU), Society of Stage Directors and Choreographers.

The *Associations Yellow Book* Spring 1997[1] was used to identify groups in various budget categories. The sample of groups in the three budget categories was selected by taking every fifteenth association with a budget of less than one million and every fifteenth association with a budget of more than one but less than five million. The procedure was altered slightly for those over five million, due to the possibility that an adequate sample of that group could not be obtained. Actually the opposite occurred. Only 4 groups with budgets under $1 million were included. We found 25 in the $1–5 million category and 25 in the over $5 million group. For that group every tenth association was used. Then an Internet search was conducted for the groups' Web sites.

Chapter 4

Three studies were conducted to collect data on Web sites of candidates. First, a search of three candidate Web site lists immediately following the November general election was conducted to determine how many major party candidates for Congress had Web pages. The Web site lists were Project Vote Smart 96 at *http://www.votesmart.org/campaign_96/cong_links.html*; GTE. Net at *http://www.gte.net/election96/*; and Campaign 96 Online at *http://96.com/cc.htm*. Duplicate listings across the three lists were deleted. One particular site, *http://96.com/cc./tm*, was used to examine incumbency and party affiliation.

Also, a content analysis of selected Web sites was conducted. One hundred candidate Web sites from the 1996 campaign were content analyzed. They were selected from the above megasites listing links to candidate Web sites and among sites that still existed and were completely workable when downloading occurred in January 1997. They were chosen to represent a range of offices, types of races, and party ID. Forty-six candidates identified themselves on their Web sites as Democrats, 34 as Republicans, 4 as Libertarians. Six other candidates represented themselves as from other minor parties. The rest of the candidates did not mention their party affiliation on their site either because they did not wish it known or they were independents. Sixty-nine of the candidates explained on their sites they were challengers, while 12 said they were incumbents. An additional 9 mentioned on the site that there was no incumbent in the race, 10 did not indicate that information on their site.

The oversampling of Democrats and challengers may be partly attributable at the federal level to Republican incumbents' reliance on government Web sites, which were not included in this study. No government sites were included because they were qualitatively different from campaign sites.

The candidates with the offices they ran for and their states are arranged below in alphabetical order: Michela Aliota, U.S. House (CA); Deborah Arnesen, U.S. House (NH); Peter Ashy, U.S. Senate (SC); Larrie Bailey, Governor (WV); Jim Baize, U.S. House (CA); Mary Lynn Bates, U.S. House (AL); Richard Borg, U.S. House (CA); Ben Brink, U.S. House (CA); Susan Brooks, U.S. House (CA); Ken Brown, U.S. House (GA); Tyrone Butler, U.S. House (NY); Tom

Campbell, U.S. House (CA); Walter Capps, U.S. House (CA); Jim Chapman, U.S. Senate (TX); Hank Chapot, U.S. House (CA); Beverly Clarke, U.S. House (TX); Bill Clarke, U.S. Senate (ME); John Cooksey, U.S. House (LA); Bud Cramer, U.S. House (AL); Richard Cunningham, Judge of Recorder's Court, Detroit (MI); Natalie Davis, U.S. Senate (AL); Dave Dawson, U.S. House (WY); Diana DeGette, U.S. House (CO); Joe Dehn, U.S. House (CA); John Divine, U.S. House (KS); Jill Docking, U.S. Senate (KA); Teresa Doggett, U.S. House (TX); Anna Eshoo, U.S. House (CA); Mike Fisher, State Attorney General (PA); Ernie Fletcher, U.S. House (KY); Errol Flynn, U.S. House (PA); Stephen Goldsmith, Governor (IN); Abe Gutmann, U.S. Senate (NM); Robin Hayes, Governor (NC); Kate Hirning, U.S. House (CA); Joe Hoeffel, U.S. House (PA); Tom Horton, U.S. House (VA); Gordon Houston, U.S. Senate (TN); Duane Hughes, U.S. House (CA); Jay Inslee, Governor (WA); Bill Jenkins, U.S. House (TN); Jay Johnson, U.S. House (WI); Tad Jude, U.S. House (MN); Jeffrey Kitchen, U.S. House (OH); Mina Baker Knoll, State Treasurer (PA); Russell Lacasse, U.S. House (ME); Nick Lampson, U.S. House (TX); George Landrith, U.S. House (VA); Dick Lane, U.S. House (CA); David Levering, U.S. House (CA); Georgianna Lincoln, U.S. House (AK); Gary Locke, Governor (WA); Carolyn Maloney, U.S. House (NY); Posten McCracken, U.S. House (GA); Dolly Madison McKenna, U.S. House (TX); Bonnie McKnight, U.S. House (MN); Kevin Meara, U.S. House (NJ); Jim Miller, U.S. Senate (VA); Walter Minnick, U.S. Senate (ID); Don Mooers, U.S. House (MD); Wayne Parker, U.S. House (AL); Bill Pascrell, U.S. House (NJ); Tom Peterson, U.S. House (TX); Mike Petyo, U.S. House (IN); John Place, U.S. House (CA); Norman Reece, U.S. House (CA); Jack Reed, U.S. Senate (RI); Bob Riley, U.S. House (AL); Mike Robinson, U.S. House (CO); Jay Rockefeller, U.S. Senate (WV); Jack Rodriguez, U.S. House (TX); Bob Ruch, U.S. House (IO); August St. John, Governor (VT); Todd Schmitz, State Legislature (WI); Pete Sessions, U.S. House (TX); Byron Sher, State Legislature (CA); Brad Sherman, U.S. House (CA); Bob Smith, U.S. Senate (NH); Matthew Sperling, U.S. House (NY); Pete Stark, U.S. House (CA); Sheila Stein, State Legislature (NY); Joe Susnhara, State Legislature (AZ); Jane Swift, U.S. House (MA); Rita Tamerius, U.S. House (CA); Ellen Tauscher, U.S. House (CA); Ed Teague, U.S. House (MA); Charlie Thompson, U.S. Senate (SC); John Thume, U.S. House (SD); Strom Thurmond, U.S. Senate (SC); Bob Torricelli, U.S. Senate (NJ); Jim Turner, U.S. House (TX); Richard Vinroot, Governor (NC); Dave

Walker, U.S. House (NC); Zack Wamp, U.S. House (TN); Paul Weissman, U.S. Senate (CO); Paul Wellstone, U.S. Senate (MN); Randy Whitman, U.S. House (OH); Joshua Williams, State Legislature (OK); Bill Witt, U.S. House (OR); and Deborah Wright, U.S. House (CA).

In addition, interviews were conducted with candidates or Webmasters from an additional 26 campaigns using the Internet for campaign communication. (One unintentional overlap was Beverly Clarke, Democratic congressional candidate from Texas.) These campaigns ranged from presidential to state legislative, with the greatest number including candidates for U.S. Congress. The candidates or Webmasters interviewed were identified from various political megasites containing campaign lists. Candidates were chosen to represent a cross section in terms of region, office sought, and political party.

Again, incumbency was not a variable because incumbents usually did not create campaign Web sites. Most used their government sites. Only 2 of the 24 campaigns were those run by incumbents (Peter Torkildson and Tom Campbell).

Telephone or e-mail interviews were conducted with either the candidate or the Webmaster or, in two cases, another aide responsible for the campaign site. Telephone interviews were conducted with 12 candidates and 10 Webmasters or other campaign aides responsible for the Internet. Candidates interviewed were, in alphabetical order, Brian Baird, Democratic congressional candidate from Washington; Representative Tom Campbell (R-California); Representative Chris Cannon (R-Utah); Beverly Clarke, Democratic congressional candidate from Texas; Jeff Gittelman, Independent candidate for New Mexico state legislature; Valli Sharpe Geisler, Reform Party congressional candidate from California; Representative Rick Hill, (R-Montana); Richard Osness, Libertarian candidate for State Senate in Minnesota; Ken Poston, Democratic congressional candidate from Georgia; Michael Robinson, Democratic congressional candidate from Colorado; Richard Swett, U.S. Senate Democratic candidate from New Hampshire; and Sue Wittig, Republican congressional candidate from New York. Webmasters or other aides responsible for the Internet included Michael Armini, Peter Torkildson for Congress (Massachusetts); Troy Bettinger, Joe Rogers for Congress (Colorado); Daniel Mai, Lamar Alexander for President; Gary Morello, Ed Munster for Congress (Connecticut);

Darek Newby, David Price for Congress (North Carolina); Ken Owen, Walter Capps for Congress (California); Joshua Ross, Campbell for Congress (California); Mark Sullivan, Tom Allen for Congress (Maine); Jim Thatcher, Cannon for Congress (Utah); and Eric Woolhiser, Susan Gallagher for U.S. Senate (Massachusetts).

Additionally, e-mail interviews were conducted with two other candidates and three other Webmasters. These candidates included Mark Jones, Libertarian U.S. Senate candidate from Delaware; and Thomas Lehman, Libertarian congressional candidate from Indiana. Webmasters or other aides included Wilson E. Allen, Julia Carson for Congress (Indiana); John Baker, Lamontagne for Governor (New Hampshire); and Mark Ellis, Susan Collins for U.S. Senate (Maine).

Chapter 5

The first method employed for this chapter was a survey of congressional offices regarding use of e-mail and the Internet. The survey, conducted during the summer of 1996, was sent to the offices of all members of Congress. Eighty-two responded—65 members of the House and 17 members of the Senate. This level of response represented 15 percent of the total members of Congress, but 19 percent of the members who maintained Web sites at that time.

The second method involved a content analysis of official congressional Web sites. Between mid-August and the end of December 1996, all existing Web sites for members of Congress were downloaded and coded. In total, 266 sites were coded, 100 for the Senate and 166 for the House. These sites were coded for presence of types of information, such as casework assistance, member legislative activity, issue emphasis, links to other sites, and so on.

Chapter 6

The sheer number of Usenet groups and the volume of message traffic over them is overwhelming. Therefore, I selected only three Usenet groups to serve as a case study. Selecting a small number of groups offers the opportunity to analyze the exchange of messages therein with greater depth.

However, such a small sample of groups raises another problem—generalization. It is hard to know whether the discussion of these groups is typical of political Usenet groups. That is a question that cannot be answered here. It will come as others conduct similar studies of other groups.

One attempt to address the generalization problem was the inclusion of representatives of differing types of groups, including the more mainstream as well as the radical fringe, the personality oriented as well as the ideological, the political left and the political right. The groups selected were *alt.politics.Clinton, alt.politics.usa. constitution,* and *alt.politics.radical-left.* The first group is a person-oriented group and was expected to attract more Usenet participants from the political center-left. The second was chosen to represent the political right and is a vaguely titled group. The third group was expected to attract people who are on the American radical left.

All posted messages during a one-week period (June 14 through June 20, 1997) were downloaded for each of these groups. The posted messages were identified and coded. This week's worth of message traffic for each group resulted in 743 messages coded for *alt.politics.Clinton;* 212 on *alt.politics.usa.constitution;* and 711 on *alt.politics.radical-left.* These were posted by 723 individuals—323 on the *alt.politics.Clinton;* 126 on *alt.politics.usa.constitution;* and 274 on *alt.politics.radical-left.*

Notes

Notes to Introduction

1. Jonathan Vankin and John Whalen, "How a Quack Becomes a Canard," *New York Times Magazine*, November 17, 1996, pp. 56–57. See also Matthew L. Wald, "Cyber-Mice That Roar, Implausibly," *New York Times*, November 10, 1996, p. 5.

2. I use the terms "Internet," "Net," "Web," and "World Wide Web" interchangeably, even though the Net purist would suggest a distinction. I realize that the Internet has been more than the World Wide Web. It also includes gopher, FTP, Usenet, BBBs, etc. But the Web has become, by far, the primary and most significant part of the Internet, thus making the terms virtually interchangeable. It is also used to apply to the services of the online access companies, such as Prodigy, CompuServe, America Online, etc., who both connect to the Internet and create their own virtual world smaller than, but quite similar to, the Internet.

3. John V. Pavlik, *New Media Technology: Cultural and Commercial Perspectives*, Boston: Allyn and Bacon, 1996, p. 139.

4. Kim Girard and Barb Cole-Gomolski, "Hold that thought, IS tells E-mailers," *Computerworld*, April 21, 1997, p. 1.

5. "Technology in the American Household," Times Mirror Center for the People & the Press report, May 1994, p. 4.

6. See American Internet User Survey, *http://etrg.findsvp.com/Internet/hightlights.html;* and O'Reilly Research, "Defining the Internet Opportunity," *http://www.ora.com/research/*

7. See CyberAtlas Market Size, at *http://www.cyberatlas.com/market.html*

8. Seventh WWW User Survey, Graphic, Visualization, & Usability Center, Georgia Tech University, June 1997; and "The Superhighway: 50 Million People on the Net . . . " *dot.COM*, April 1, 1997.

9. Ithiel de Sola Pool, *Technologies Without Boundaries*, edited by Eli M. Noam, Cambridge, Mass.: Harvard University Press, 1990, p. 7; John Doerr quoted in "Larry King on the Internet at the Robertson Stephens Technology Conference," *PR Newswire*, February 27, 1996.

10. Everett M. Rogers, *Communication Technology: The New Media in*

Society, New York: Free Press, 1986, pp. 27–32; and de Sola Pool, *Technologies Without Boundaries.*

11. Anthony Corrado and Charles M. Firestone, eds., *Elections in Cyberspace: Toward a New Era in American Politics,* Washington, D.C.: The Aspen Institute, 1996, p.16. For similar arguments, see Richard E. Sclove, *Democracy and Technology,* New York: Guilford Press, 1995.

12. Quoted in Lawrence Grossman, *The Electronic Republic,* New York: Penguin Books, 1995, p. 147.

13. Howard Fineman, "Who Needs Washington?" *Newsweek,* January 27, 1997, p. 50.

14. Rogers, *Communication Technology,* p. 183.

Notes to Chapter One

1. See, for example, Neil Randall, *The Soul of the Internet: Net Gods, Netizens and the Wiring of the World,* London; Boston: International Thomson Computer Press, 1997; Rick Smolan and Jennifer Erwitt, *24 Hours in Cyberspace: Painting on the Walls of the Digital Cave,* New York: Que Macmillan Publishing, 1996; Stephen Doheny-Farina, *The Wired Neighborhood,* New Haven: Yale University Press, 1996; Mark Derry, *Escape Velocity: Cyberculture at the End of the Century,* New York: Grove Press, 1996. Steve Talbott, *The Future Does Not Compute: Transcending the Machines in Our Midst,* Sebastopol, Calif. O'Reilly & Associates, 1995; and Howard Rheingold, *The Virtual Community: Homesteading on the Electronic Frontier,* Reading, Mass.: Addison-Wesley, 1993.

2. Don Tapscott, *The Digital Economy: Promise and Peril in the Age of Networked Intelligence,* New York: McGraw-Hill, 1996.

3. Eighth WWW User Survey, Graphic, Visualization, & Usability Center, Georgia Tech University, December 1997.

4. David S. Jackson, "AOL Buys Some Time," *Time,* February 10, 1997, p. 50; and Matthew McAllester, "New Scrutiny for Troubled AOL," *Newsday,* January 24, 1997, p. A6.

5. "One-in-Ten Voters Online for Campaign '96," Pew Research Center for the People & the Press, Technology '96— Summary, at *http://www.people-press.org/tech96sum.htm*

6. John V. Pavlik, *New Media Technology: Cultural and Commercial Perspectives,* Boston: Allyn and Bacon, 1996, pp. 55–56.

7. Sixth WWW User Survey, Graphic, Visualization, & Usability Center, Georgia Tech University, December 1996.

8. Pew Research Center Survey, January 23, 1998; and Harris Poll, February 18, 1998.

9. "Survey Profiles Voters' Use of Media," Media Studies Center, Freedom Forum News Advisory at *http://www.mediastudies.org/new.html*

10. U.S. Census Bureau, "Computer Use and Ownership," *http://www.census.gov/population/www/socdemo/computer.html*

11. "Technology in the American Household," Times Mirror Center for the People & the Press report, May 1994, p. 4.

12. "Going Mainstream: The Internet and the U.S. Mass Market," *Computer Industry Report,* January 15, 1998, p. 4."Dad-dy, Mom-my, Compu-ter," *PC Magazine,* June 10, 1997, p. 9.

13. Michael P. Niemara, "What's Hot, What's Not: A Look at Consumer Buying Patterns," *Chain Store Age,* April 1, 1998, p. 30.

14. Sixth WWW User Survey.

15. Francine Sommer quoted in Pavlik, *New Media Technology,* p. xii.

16. Everett M. Rogers, *Communication Technology: The New Media in Society,* New York: Free Press, 1986, p. 31.

17. See CyberAtlas data, at *http://www.cyberatlas.com/market.html*

18. See Network Wizards, at *http://www.nw.com/zone*

19. Pavlik, *New Media Technology,* pp. 51–2.

20. Search of Nexus "Major Newspapers" file for the period September 1–November 5, 1994 and September 1–November 5, 1996.

21. See, for example, "24 Hours in Cyberspace," *U.S. News & World Report,* October 21, 1996, p. 70.

22. Malcolm Fitch, "Cruise the Web to Land the Job of Your Dreams," *Money,* May 1997, p. 29.

23. CommerceNet/Nielsen Internet Demographics Survey, Spring '97 at *http://www.commerce.net/work/pilot/nielsen_96/*

24. "Surf's up for New-Wave Bankers." *The Economist,* October 7, 1995, pp. 77–8.

25. *The Electronic Marketplace 1997: Strategies for Connecting Buyers and Sellers,* Stamford, Conn.: Cowles/Simba Information, 1997; "Advertsing Revenues Keep Rising," *New Media Age,* April 9, 1998, p. 11.

26. Martha E. Mangelsdorf, "Low-Tech Winners in an On-line World," *Inc.,* June 1995, pp. 52–57; Ellen Stark, "How to Shop the Internet to Find the Highest Yields," *Money,* May 1997, p. 43; and Michael Krantz, "Amazonian Challenge: Can the Darling of Web Retailers Survive when the Big Boys Move In? *Time,* April 14, 1997, p. 71.

27. Ira Hellman, "Cut Your Costs by 85% Trading on the Internet," *Money,* August 1996, p. B7.

28. For a sample of such literature, see Alfred and Emily Glossbrenner, *Making Money on the Internet,* New York: McGraw-Hill, 1995; and David Cook, *Launching a Business on the Web,* Indianapolis, Ind.: Que, 1995.

29. "Business Spurs Online Commerce—Corporate Transactions to Total $2.2 Billion by 2000," *Traffic World,* February 10, 1997, p. 41.

30. CommerceNet/Nielsen Internet Demographics Survey, Spring '97 at *http://www.commerce.net/work/pilot/nielsen_96/*

31. Milton P. Huang and Norman E. Alessi, "The Internet and the Future of Psychiatry," *American Journal of Psychiatry,* July 1996, pp. 861–869.

32. Edward L. F. Gonzalez and Helen J. Seaton, "Internet Sources for Nursing and Allied Health," *Database,* June/July 1995, pp. 46–49.

33. Mark Ebell, "The Internet as a Resource for Family Physicians," *American Family Physician,* February 15, 1996, p. 850+.

34. "In His Own Words," *New York Times,* October 11, 1996, p. A26.

35. Diane Ravitch, "When School Comes to You," *The Economist,* September 11, 1993, p. 43.

36. For a discussion of online courses, see, for example, Yvette Cabrera, "On-Line Classes Answering Needs of Working Students," *Daily News* (Los Angeles), May 19, 1997, p. N3; and Robert Moskowitz, "Go To Virtual College, Get a Real Education," *Investor's Business Daily,* May 18, 1995, p. A1.

37. Stephen G. Jones, *Cybersociety: Computer-Mediated Communication and Community,* Thousand Oaks, CA: Sage, 1995, p. 11.

38. Malcolm R. Parks and Kory Floyd, "Making Friends in Cyberspace," *Journal of Communication,* Winter 1996, pp. 80–97; and Christine Ogan, "Listserver Communication during the Gulf War: What Kind of Medium is the Electronic Bulletin Board?" *Journal of Broadcasting and Electronic Media,* Winter 1993, pp. 177–196.

39. Pavlik, *New Media Technology,* pp. 310–311.

40. Sixth WWW User Survey.

41. For examples, see Clifford Stoll, *Silicon Snake Oil: Second Thoughts on the Information Superhighway,* New York: Doubleday, 1995; and Dinty W. Moore, *The Emperor's Virtual Clothes: The Naked Truth about Internet Culture,* Chapel Hill, NC: Algonquin Books, 1995.

42. Sherry Turkle, *Life on the Screen: Identity in the Age of the Internet,* New York: Simon and Schuster, 1995, p. 26.

43. Nina Bernstein, "Inmate Accused of Collecting Internet Child Pornography," *New York Times,* March 28, 1997, p. A16.

44. Princeton Survey Research Associates survey, February 16–17, 1995. "How concerned are you about . . . people being harassed by 'virtual stalking' through unwanted messages . . . very concerned, somewhat concerned, not too concerned, or not at all concerned?" Very—57%; Somewhat—23%; Not too—10%; Not at all—7%; Don't know—3%; also "How concerned are you about . . . people being harassed by real stalking from someone they first meet on the Internet . . . very concerned, somewhat concerned, not too concerned, or not at all concerned?" Very—52%; Somewhat—24%; Not too—11%; Not at all—9%; Don't know—4% "Cookie Trials on the Internet," *Consumers Research Magazine,* May 1987, p. 2.

45. John M. Broder, "Gore to Announce Electronic Bill of Rights Aimed at Privacy," *New York Times,* May 13, 1998, p. A16; "Forget 'Big Brother,'" *PR Newswire,* May 13, 1997.

46. Malcolm Fitch, "Here's How to Protect Your Wallet (And Your Privacy)," *Money,* April 1997, p. 32.

47. Lee Hawkins, Jr., "Security Firms See Opportunity in Crime," *Milwaukee Journal,* March 17, 1997, Monday Business, p. 7.

48. "The Superhighway: 50 Million People on the Net . . . " *dot.COM,* April 1, 1997.

49. "Children Online: Is Your Kid Caught Up in the Web?" *Consumer Reports,* May 1997, p. 27.

50. McAllester, "New Scrutiny for Troubled AOL," p. A6.

51. For a refutation of the argument of widespread, invasive pornography on the Net, see Daniel J. Barrett, *Bandits on the Information Superhighway,* Bonn: O'Reilly & Associates, 1995, pp. 144–153.

52. Randall E. Stross, "Sex Sells. But Internet Filtering Systems Are Thriving Too," *U.S. News & World Report,* March 17, 1997, p. 45.

53. Princeton Survey Research Associates survey, February 16–17, 1995. Two-thirds were "very concerned" about pornography being too available through the Internet. Another 18 percent were somewhat concerned.

54. Daphne Merkin, "A Fatal Step into Twilight," *U.S. News & World Report,* November 25, 1996, pp. 88–89.

55. Reno, Attorney General of the United States et al. v. American Civil Liberties Union et al., 117 S. ct. 2329 (1997).

56. Pam Belluck, "Stuck on the Web; Symptoms of Internet Addiction," *New York Times,* December 1, 1996, section 4, p. 5; and Nicole Bondi, "Warning: Internet Can be Habit-Forming," *Detroit News,* January 14, 1997, p. C6. For a contrary view asserting that Internet addiction does not exist, see Steven Levy, "Breathing is Also Addictive," *Newsweek,* December 30, 1996—January 6, 1997, p. 52.

57. Hubert H. Humphrey III, "Virtual Casinos, Real Stakes," *New York Times,* November 19, 1996, p. A13.

58. Richard Louv, "Downside of Teens On-Line is Isolation," *San Diego Union--Tribune,* October 7, 1995, p. E-1; and "Children Online," p. 27.

59. See, for example, Barrett, *Bandits on the Information Superhighway.*

60. Doheny-Farina, *The Wierd Neighborhood,* p. 37.

61. Moore, *The Emperor's Virtual Clothes,* p. 25.

62. Pavlik, *New Media Technology,* p. 335.

63. "One-in-Ten Voters Online for Campaign '96," Pew Research Center for the People & the Press, Technology '96— Summary, at *http://www.people-press.org/tech96sum.htm*

64. "Teenagers and Technology," p. 86.

65. Eighth WWW User Survey; and "The Superhighway: 50 Million People on the Net . . . " *dot.COM*, April 1, 1997.

66. "Survey Profiles Voters' Use of Media," Media Studies Center, Freedom Forum News Advisory at *http://www.mediastudies.org/new.html*

67. Fred Colman, "A Great Lost Cause: France vs. The Internet," *U.S. News & World Report*, April 21, 1997, p. 57.

68. Lawrence Grossman, *The Electronic Republic*, New York: Penguin Books, 1995, p. 149.

69. See Anthony Corrado and Charles M. Firestone, eds, *Elections in Cyberspace: Toward a New Era in American Politics*, Washington, D.C.: The Aspen Institute, 1996; and Pavlik, *New Media Technology*, p. 313.

70. Hans K. Klein, " Grassroots Democracy and the Internet: The Telecommunications Policy Roundtable—Northeast (TPR-NE), paper presented at the Internet Society 1995 International Networking Conference, Honolulu, Hawaii, 28–30 June 1995. For a copy of the paper, see *http://ralph.gmu.edu/~pbaker/klein.txt*

71. Edward Schwartz, *Netactivism: How Citizens Use the Internet*, Sebastopol, Calif.: Songline Studios, 1996, p. 5.

72. Corrado and Firestone, eds., *Elections in Cyberspace*, pp. 6–7.

73. See, for example, Bruce Maxwell, *How to Access the Federal Government on the Internet 1997*, Washington, D.C.: CQ Press, 1996; Carol Briggs-Erickson and Toni Murphy, *Environmental Guide to the Internet*, 2nd ed., Rockville, MD: Government Institutes, 1996. Bill Mann, *Politics on the Net*, Indianapolis, IN: Que, 1995; The Federal Internet source, Washington, D.C.: National Journal, Inc.: NetWeek, 1995; Randy Reddick, *The Online Journalist: Using the Internet and Other Electronic Resources*, Fort Worth, TX: Harcourt Brace College, 1995; Josh Blackman, *How to Use the Internet for Legal Research*, New York: Find/SVP, 1996. However, these how-to books date quickly due to the rapid change seemingly endemic in the Internet.

74. Speech to the International Telecommunications Union, March 21, 1994. Reprinted in Deborah G. Johnson and Helen Nissenbuam, eds., *Computers, Ethics & Social Values*, Englewood Cliffs, NJ: Prentice Hall, 1995, p. 621.

75. "Speech to the International Telecommunications Union," p. 625.

76. "Who Speaks for Cyberspace?" *The Economist*, January 14, 1995, p. 69.

77. Allison Mitchell,"They See the Future and It Works for Them," *New York Times*, October 11, 1996, p. A26.

78. Quoted in Benjamin Sheffner, "Term Limits Lobbying, on the Net With Just Two Weeks to Go Before Senate Vote, Advocates Shun Big-Money Media Effort in Favor of Ashcroft's Low-Key Push on the World Wide Web," *Roll Call*, April 11, 1996.

79. Corrado and Firestone, eds., *Elections in Cyberspace*, p. 29.

80. Howard Fineman, *"Who Needs Washington?" Newsweek*, January 27, 1997, p. 50.

81. Rogers, *Communication Technology, p. 237.*

82. *Pavlik, New Media Technology*, pp. 168–169. Gore has gravitated toward such new media firsts. He was the first member of the House of Representatives to give a speech on C-SPAN in 1979, as well as the first member of the Senate to do so when C-SPAN was introduced there in 1986. Stephen Frantzich and John Sullivan, *The C-SPAN Revolution*, Norman: University of Oklahoma Press, 1996, p. 60.

83. See, for example, "Voters Can Take Chat with Candidates via Cyberspace," *Miami Herald*, October 22, 1995; and "Schools, Libraries Access the Internet, *Hartford Courant*, October 3, 1996.

84. Grossman, *The Electronic Republic*, p. 146. Though most Internet users do not employ this new technology for political communication, a minority do. One survey in late 1996 found that 17 percent of Internet users had sent e-mail to groups, organizations, or public officials. See "One-in-Ten Voters Online for Campaign '96," Pew Research Center for the People & the Press, Technology '96—Summary, at *http://www.people-press.org/tech96sum.htm*

85. Grossman, *The Electronic Republic*, p. 149.

86. Grossman, *The Electronic Republic*, pp. 237–254.

87. Corrado and Firestone, eds., *Elections in Cyberspace*, p. 29.

88. W. Russell Neuman, *The Future of the Mass Audience*, Cambridge, Eng.: Cambridge University Press, 1991, p. 109.

89. Lightner was a founder of MADD (Mothers Against Drunk Driving) after her own child was killed by a drunk driver, while Walsh, whose son was kidnapped and later killed in a highly public incident, lobbied agressively for a federal database on missing children and later hosted a program on crime.

90. Princeton Survey Research Associates survey, February 20–23, 1997. (Question: "I'd like to know how often you watch certain TV programs or read certain publications. For each item that I read, tell me if you watch or read it regularly, sometimes, hardly ever, or never. How often do you . . . watch the national nightly network news on CBS, ABC, or NBC . . . regularly, sometimes, hardly ever, or never? This is different from local news shows about the area where you live." Regularly—41%, Sometimes—31%, Hardly Ever—14%, Never—14%.

91. John Consoli, "Good News, Bad News," *Editor & Publisher,* May 3, 1997, p. 18.

92. "Survey Profiles Voters' Use of Media," Media Studies Center, Freedom Forum News Advisory, at *http://www.mediastudies.org/new.html*

93. NBC News, *Wall Street Journal* survey, September 12–15, 1996. The

question is: "(For each of the following descriptions I read, please tell me if this applies to you personally.) Regularly use the Internet or other on-line computer services, either at home or at work . . . does that apply to you or doesn't it?" 18–29: applies—38%; does not apply—60%, not sure—2%; and Voter News Service Exit Survey, November 5, 1996. The question is: "Do you regularly use the Internet?" 18–29: Yes—38%; No—62%.

94. See the U.S. Census Bureau, *Current Population Reports*, Series P20-495, "Household and Family Characteristics," March 1996; and S.M.A.R.T. (Systems for Measuring and Reporting Television), "T.V. Ownership Survey," Statistical Research, Inc., June 16, 1997.

95. "Survey Profiles Voters' Use of Media."

96. Eighth WWW User Survey.

97. "One-in-Ten Voters Online for Campaign '96," Pew Research Center for the People & the Press, Technology '96— Summary, at *http://www.people-press.org/tech96sum.htm*

98. "One-in-Ten Voters Online for Campaign '96."

99. "One-in-Ten Voters Online for Campaign '96."

100. Wirthlin Worldwide and WSI, "Internet Market Share Size and Demographics," September 1996.

101. See All Things Political at *http://www.federal.com/Political.html*; and "Survey Profiles Voters' Use of Media."

102. In fairness, some research has reached contrary conclusions. One study found users hold party preferences and vote much like non-users. See Douglas Muzzio and David Birdsell, "The 1996 'Net Voter," *The Public Perspective*, December/January 1997, pp. 42–43.

103. Sixth WWW User Survey.

104. "One-in-Ten Voters Online for Campaign '96."

105. For a discussion of the political activity of the Internet users, as compared with the general public and users of other new media, see Richard Davis and Diana Owen, *New Media and American Politics*, New York: Oxford University Press, 1998, pp.164–185.

106. See Davis and Owen, *New Media and American Politics.*

107. Pavlik, *New Media Technology*, pp. 310–311. For a comparison of online users with the total population, see also "One-in-Ten Voters Online for Campaign '96."

108. Pavlik, *New Media Technology*, pp. 337–340.

109. Erik Barnouw, *A Tower in Babel: A History of Broadcasting in the United States*, Volume 1. New York: Oxford University Press, 1966, p. 3.

110. Rogers, *Communication Technology*, p. 187.

111. For examples of this argument, see Kenneth C. Laudon,

Communications Technology and Democratic Participation, New York: Praeger, 1977.

112. For an example of the former, see Jacques Ellul, *The Technological Society*, New York: Vintage, 1967. Ellul does not limit his argument to mass communications technology. For examples of the latter point, see Neil Postman, *Amusing Ourselves to Death: Public Discourse in the Age of Show Business*, New York; Penguin, 1985; Postman, *Technopoly*, New York: Alfred A. Knopf, 1992; and Nathan Rotenstreich, "Technology and Politics," in Carl Mitcham and Robert Mackey, eds., *Philosophy and Technology: Readings in the Philosophical Problems of Technology*, New York: Free Press, 1972.

113. Robert W. Desmond, *The Information Process: World News Reporting to the Twentieth Century*, Iowa City: University of Iowa Press, 1978, pp. 57, 432–433.

114. Charles F. Briggs and Augustus Maverick, *The Story of the Telegraph and the History of the Great Atlantic Cable*, New York: Rudd and Carleton, 1858, p. 26.

115. Quoted in Irwin Lebow, *Information Highways and Byways: From the Telegraph to the 21st Century*, New York: IEEE Press, 1995, p. 1.

116. This has even prompted several book titles: Sarah Goddard Power, *The Communications Revolution*, Washington, D.C.: U.S. Dept. of State, Bureau of Public Affairs, Office of Public Communication, Editorial Division, 1981; Frederick Williams, *The Communications Revolution*, Beverly Hills: Sage Publications, 1982; and George N. Gordon, *The Communications Revolution: A History of Mass Media in the United States*, New York: Hastings House, 1977.

117. Desmond, *The Information Process*, p. 370.

118. Quoted in Jeff Kisseloff, *The Box: An Oral History of Television, 1920–1961*, New York: Penguin, 1995, pp. 51, 171.

119. Ralph Lee Smith, *The Wired Nation*, New York: Harper & Row, 1972, p. 2.

120. Regis McKenna, "Stalking the Information Society," *Upside*, January 1995, p. 36.

121. Christopher H. Sterling and John M. Kittross, *Stay Tuned: A Concise History of American Broadcasting*, Belmont, CA: Wadsworth, 1978, pp. 92, 182.

122. Barnouw, *A Tower in Babel*, p. 207; and George E. Lott, Jr. "The Press-Radio War of the 1930s," *Journal of Broadcasting*, Summer 1970, p. 279.

123. Robert W. McChesney, "Conflict, Not Consensus: The Debate over Broadcast Communication Policy" in William S. Solomon and Robert W. McChesney, eds., *Ruthless Criticism: New Perspectives in U.S. Communication History*, Minneapolis: University of Minnesota Press, 1993, p. 233.

124. For a discussion of this, see McChesney, "Conflict, Not Consensus," in Solomon and McChesney, eds., *Ruthless Criticism*.

125. Sterling and Kittross, *Stay Tuned*, pp. 62–66.

126. Barnouw, *A Tower in Babel*, p. 209.

127. Robert W. McChesney, "The Battle for the U.S. Airwaves, 1928–1935," *Journal of Communication*, Autumn 1990, pp. 36–42.

128. For a discussion of the battle by one group, labor, to establish a national radio network, see Robert. W. McChesney, "Labor and the Marketplace of Ideas," *Journalism Monographs* 134 (August 1992).

129. Sterling and Kittross, *Stay Tuned*, p. 292.

130. Herbert H. Howard, *Multiple Ownership in Television Broadcasting*, New York: Arno Press, 1979, pp. 131–200.

131. Howard, *Multiple Ownership in Television Broadcasting*, pp. 181–185.

132. For histories of cable in the United States, see Timothy Hollins, *Beyond Broadcasting: Into the Cable Age*, London: BFI Publishing, 1984, pp. 113–124; and Smith, *The Wired Nation*.

133. "Bandwidth Evolution," *Digital Kids Report*, October 1, 1996.

134. Erik Barnouw, *The Image Empire: A History of Broadcasting in the United States*, Volume 3—from 1953, New York: Oxford University Press, 1966, p. 248.

135. Smith, *The Wired Nation*, p. 55.

136. Hollins, *Beyond Broadcasting*, p. 128.

137. Quoted in Howard, *Multiple Ownership in Television Broadcasting*, p. 219.

138. Richard Davis, *The Press and American Politics: The New Mediator*, Upper Saddle River, NJ: Prentice-Hall, 1996, pp. 9–11.

139. For a brief discussion of the history of the Internet, see Robert E. Kahn, "The Role of the Government in the Evolution of the Internet," in National Academy of Engineering, *Revolution in the U.S. Information Structure*, Washington: National Academy Press, 1995, pp. 13–24; and *Realizing the Information Future: The Internet and Beyond*, Washington: National Academy Press, 1994, pp. 20–30.

140. Pavlik, *New Media Technology*, p. 151.

141. "Where You Can Connect," *Time*, February 10, 1997.

142. For evidence of the trend, see "One-in-Ten Voters Online for Campaign '96."

143. Merrill Morris and Christine Ogan, "The Internet as Mass Medium," *Journal of Communication*, Winter 1996, p. 42.

144. Ian McLean, *Democracy and New Technology*, Cambridge, U.K.: Polity Press, 1989, p. 94.

145. Corrado and Firestone, *Elections in Cyberspace*, p. 22.

146. Doheny-Farina, *The Wired Neighborhood*, p. 77.

147. Kenneth C. Laudon, *Communications Technology and Democratic Participation*, New York: Praeger, 1977, p. 19.

148. John Newhagen and Sheizaf Rafaeli, "Why Communication Researchers Should Study the Internet," *Journal of Communication*, Winter 1996, p. 5.

149. Charles McGrath, "The Internet's Arrested Development," *New York Times Magazine*, December 8, 1996, p. 82.

150. "Solid Clinton Lead, Small Gain for Congressional Democrats," Pew Research Center for the People & the Press, News Release, September 13, 1996.

151. McGrath, "The Internet's Arrested Development," pp. 80–85.

Notes to Chapter Two

1. John V. Pavlik, *New Media Technology: Cultural and Commercial Perspectives*, Boston: Allyn and Bacon, 1996, p. 5.

2. For a discussion of this tendency to adapt, see Pavlik, *New Media Technology*, ch. 3.

3. Anthony Corrado and Charles M. Firestone, eds., *Elections in Cyberspace: Toward a New Era in American Politics*, Washington, D.C.: The Aspen Institute, 1996, p. 26.

4. Margie Wylie, "Electronic Newspaper Is an Oxymoron," *ASAP*, May 10, 1995, p. 14.

5. Helen Kennedy, "Oh, What a Wicked Web: Internuts Wired into Weird World," (New York) *Daily News*, April 13, 1997, p. 21.

6. "Newspapers Wrestle With the Online Bear, part 3," *Seybold Report on Publishing Systems*, April 22, 1996.

7. See *www.rotten.com* for a discussion of the incident on the site that originally displayed the photograph.

8. Dennis Wagner, "Conspiracy Buffs Love Case of Missing Plane," *Arizona Republic*, April 10, 1997, p. A1.

9. See, for example, James Brooke, "Military Pilot Went Down with Plane, Air Force Says," *New York Times*, April 26, 1997, p. 8; Patrick J. Lyons, "Taking in the Sites; UFO Believers and Debunkers Thrive on the Web," *New York Times*, June 30, 1997, p. D8; George Johnson, "Death in a Cult: The Signal; Comets Breed Fear, Fascination, and Web Sites," *New York Times*, March 28, 1997, p. A18; and Tim Weiner, "One Source, Many Ideas in Foster Case," *New York Times*, August 13, 1995, p. 19.

10. Rita Ciolli, "For Media, Scoops Turn to Oops," *Newsday*, February 2, 1998, p. A4.

11. Phil Noble, "Net the Vote," *Campaigns and Elections*, July 1996, at *http://www.caelect.com/july96/net.the.vote.html*

12. "The Feats of 1995 That Have Changed Our Lives," *U.S. News &*

World Report, December 25, 1995/January 1, 1996, p. 101; and Debra A. Velsmid, "Newspapers Online," *ASAP*, July 1996, p. 8.

13. See Newspaper Association of America, at *http://www.naa.org/ info/facts/09.html*; and John Consoli, "Good News, Bad News," *Editor &Publisher*, May 3, 1997, p. 18.

14. Pavlik, *New Media Technology*, pp. 151–152.

15. Bruce Garrison, "Online Newsgathering Trends in 1994–96," paper presented at the spring conference of the Communication Technology and Policy Division, Association for Education in Journalism and Mass Communication, St. Petersburg, Florida, February 8, 1997, at *http://www. miami.edu/com/car/stpete.htm*; and Paul Eisenberg, "Most Journalists Wired; Rely More on Net for Sourcing, Financial News," at *http://www. freedomforum.org/technology/1998/2/12netjour.asp*

16. Joe Abernathy, "Casting the Internet; A New Tool for Electronic News Gathering," *Columbia Journalism Review* (January/February 1993), p. 56.

17. Guy Berger, "The Internet: A Goldmine for Editors and Journalists," Presentation to the World Editors Forum, May 1996 at *http://www.ru.ar. za/departments/journ/gold.html internet*

18. Berger, "The Internet: A Goldmine for Editors and Journalists."

19. See, for example, A Reporter's Internet Survival Guide, *at http:// www.qns.net/~casey/* and *St. Louis Journalism Review*, at *http://www. ccrc.wustl.edu/spj/resources.html*

20. The American Reporter, at *http://www.newslink.org/*

21. Reporter's Internet Guide, at *http://www.crl.com:80/~jshenry/ rig.html*

22. Berger, "The Internet: A Goldmine for Editors and Journalists."

23. Anthony Corrado and Charles M. Firestone, *Elections in Cyberspace*, p. 25.

24. For a survey of managing editors asking this question, see NAA Presstime, April 1997, *at ttp://www.naa.org/presstime/9704/p497surv. html*

25. Laurence Zuckerman, "Don't Stop the Presses: Newspapers Balk at Scooping Themselves," *New York Times*, January 6, 1997, at *http://www.nytimes.com/library/cyber/week/010697/newspapers.html*

26. Pavlik, *New Media Technology*, p. 152.

27. See Newspaper Association of America, at *http://www.naa.org/ info/facts/09.html*

28. Zuckerman, "Don't Stop the Presses: Newspapers Balk at Scooping Themselves."

29. Pavlik, *New Media Technology* , p. 142.

30. "One-in-Ten Voters Online for Campaign '96," Pew Research

Center for the People & the Press, Technology '96—Summary, at *http://www.people-press.org/tech96sum.htm*

31. "One-in-Ten Voters Online for Campaign '96."
32. "One-in-Ten Voters Online for Campaign '96."
33. "One-in-Ten Voters Online for Campaign '96."
34. "One-in-Ten Voters Online for Campaign '96."
35. "One-in-Ten Voters Online for Campaign '96."
36. "Technology in the American Household," Times-Mirror Center for the People & the Press report, May 1994, p. 38
37. "One-in-Ten Voters Online for Campaign '96."

Notes to Chapter Three

1. Anthony Corrado and Charles M. Firestone, eds., *Elections in Cyberspace: Toward a New Era in American Politics,* Washington, D.C.: The Aspen Institute, 1996, p. 12.
2. Craig Karmin, "'Third Wave' Lobbyists Battle On-Line Over Smut Ban Proposal," *The Hill,* December 20, 1995, p. 7.
3. E. E. Schattschneider, *Party Government,* New York: Country Life Press, 1942, p. 202.
4. Corrado and Firestone, eds., *Elections in Cyberspace.* p. 10.
5. Jeffrey M. Berry, *Lobbying for the People: The Political Behavior of Public Interest Groups,* Princeton, N.J.: Princeton University Press, 1977, p. 235.
6. For a sample of this literature, see Kay Lehman Schlozman and John T. Tierney, *Organized Interests and American Democracy,* New York: Harper & Row, 1986; Graham K. Wilson, *Interest Groups in the United States,* Oxford,: Clarendon Press, 1981; Jeffrey M. Berry, *The Interest Group Society,* Boston: Little, Brown, 1984; and Berry, *Lobbying for the People.*
7. David B. Truman, *The Governmental Process,* New York: Knopf, 1958, p. 213.
8. See Jack L. Walker, Jr., *Mobilizing Interest Groups in America: Patrons, Professions, and Social Movements,* Ann Arbor: The University of Michigan Press, 1991, p. 192.
9. Schlozman and Tierney, *Organized Interests,* p. 170.
10. Walker, *Mobilizing Interest Groups in America,* p. 12.
11. For a discussion of the latter, see Schlozman and Tierney, *Organized Interests,* pp. 170–199; and Berry, *Lobbying for the People,* pp. 243–250.
12. Charlotte Ryan, *Prime Time Activism: Media Strategies for Grassroots Organizing,* Boston: South End Press, 1991, p. 4.
13. Schlozman and Tierney, *Organized Interests,* p. 185.
14. Ibid., pp. 191–193.
15. Kevin W. Hula, "Linking the Network: Interest Group Electronic

Coalitions in the Policy Process," paper presented at the annual meeting of the Southern Political Science Association, November 1–4, 1995, Tampa, Florida, p. 15.

16. Hula, "Linking the Network," p. 15.

17. Schlozman and Tierney, *Organized Interests*, p. 185.

18. Eileen Simpson, "Lobbyists Are Tapping into the Internet to Sway Votes of Members of Congress," *Rocky Mountain News*, January 5, 1997, p. 5A.

19. Simpson, "Lobbyists Are Tapping into the Internet."

20. Obviously, this information could well have multiple uses—reassuring the members that the group is active, educating others about the group's role, and offering participation-designated information to activist members or others. Given the fact that most people who read this material are not activists, the first and second purposes are probably the more common.

21. Berry, *The Interest Group Society*, p. 143.

22. Schlozman and Tierney, *Organized Interests*, pp. 193–194.

23. Alice A. Love, "The Age of CyberLobbying: 'Electronic Advocacy' Field About to Launch Hill Lobbying Revolution," *Roll Call*, March 13, 1995.

24. Thomas Goetz, "Lobby Links: Mr. Web Site Goes to Washington," *The Village Voice*, June 10, 1997, p. 31.

25. Craig Karmin, "'Third Wave' Lobbyists Battle On-Line Over Smut Ban Proposal," *The Hill*, December 20, 1995, p. 7.

26. Telephone interview with Representative Tom Campbell (R-California), December 19, 1996.

27. Richard Davis, Diana Owen, and Vincent James Strickler, "Congress and the Internet," paper presented at the annual meeting of the International Communication Association, Montreal, Quebec, May 22–26, 1997.

28. See E. E. Schattschneider, *The Semi-Sovereign People: A Realist's View of Democracy in America*, New York: Holt, Rinehart and Winston, 1960, p. 35.

29. The National Rifle Association has been declining in membership in recent years due to controversy over the group's more hardline political approach. See Dana Milbank, "NRA Must Decide Whether to Refocus its Aim as its Membership Shrinks to Smaller Caliber," *Wall Street Journal*, April 13, 1996, p. A14; and Katherine Q. Seelye, "Gun Lobby in Bitter Power Struggle," *New York Times*, January 30, 1997, p. 6.

30. Hula, "Linking the Network."

31. Allan J. Cigler and Burdett A. Loomis, *Interest Group Politics*, 3rd ed., Washington: CQ Press, 1991, p. 396.

Notes to Chapter Four

1. See the July 1996 issue in particular.

2. Edmund L. Andrews, "The '96 Race on the Internet: Surfer Beware," *New York Times*, October 23, 1995, p. A1.

3. Douglas Muzzio and David Birdsell, "The 1996 'Net Voter," *The Public Perspective*, December/January 1997, pp. 42–43.

4. "One-in-Ten Voters Online for Campaign '96," Pew Research Center for the People & the Press, Technology '96—Summary at *http://www.people-press.org/tech96sum.htm*

5. "One-in-Ten Voters Online for Campaign '96."

6. Douglas and Birdsell, "The 1996 'Net Voter."

7. For this argument, see Anthony Corrado and Charles M. Firestone, eds., *Elections in Cyberspace: Toward a New Era in American Politics*, Washington, D.C.: The Aspen Institute, 1996, pp. 10–12.

8. Corrado and Firestone, *Elections in Cyberspace*, p. 12.

9. Telephone interview with Beverly Clarke, Democratic congressional candidate from Texas, November 20, 1996.

10. Telephone interview with Ken Poston, Democratic congressional candidate from Georgia, March 3, 1997.

11. Telephone interview with Richard Osness, Minnesota State Senate candidate, November 22, 1996.

12. Telephone interview with Eric Woolhiser, Webmaster for Susan Gallagher for U.S. Senate Campaign in Massachusetts, November 14, 1996.

13. This is one reason the number of "hits" is an innaccurate measure of user interest because avid candidate or party supporters frequently visiting the site for campaign updates or just reinforcement effectively boosted the numbers.

14. Judith S. Trent and Robert V. Friedenberg, *Political Campaign Communication*, 2nd ed., New York: Praeger, 1991, p. 13; and Edie N. Goldenberg and Michael W. Traugott, *Campaigning for Congress*, Washington, D.C.: CQ Press, 1984, p. 112.

15. For a matrix of communication techniques, see Goldenberg and Traugott, *Campaigning for Congress*, pp. 113–114.

16. Find/SVP at *http://wtrg.finsvp.com/index.html;* and "Internet Market Share Size and Demographics," A Survey by Wirthlin Worldwide and WSI, September 1996; and "One-in-Ten Voters Online for Campaign '96."

17. For example, see the site for Conservative Internet Cybertext at *http://walden.mo.net/~ths/cic.htm*

18. E-mail correspondence with Wilson E. Allen, Webmaster for the Julia Carson for Congress Committee, November 14, 1996.

19. Telephone interview with Michael Armini, Press Secretary to former Representative Peter Torkildsen (R-Massachusetts), November 20, 1996.

20. Chris Gray, "1996 Races Running Online; Candidates Log onto Internet," *Times-Picayune*, July 28, 1996, p. A1.

21. E-mail correspondence with Wilson E. Allen, Webmaster for the Julia Carson for Congress Committee, November 14, 1996.

22. Telephone interview with Valli Sharpe-Geisler, Reform congressional candidate from California, November 20, 1996.

23. Telephone interview with Troy Bettinger, Webmaster for the Joe Rogers for Congress Campaign, November 11, 1996.

24. E-mail correspondence with Wilson E. Allen, Webmaster for the Julia Carson for Congress Committee, November 14, 1996.

25. Thomas Holbrook suggests this is one of four reasons campaigns matter in his *Do Campaigns Matter?* Thousand Oaks, CA: Sage, 1996.

26. For a discussion of the importance of name recognition and familiarity, particularly for challengers, see, for example, Gary C. Jacobson, *The Politics of Congressional Elections*, 3rd ed., New York: Harper Collins, 1992; and Barbara Hinckley, *Congressional Elections*, Washington: CQ Press, 1981.

27. E-mail correspondence with Wilson E. Allen, Webmaster for the Julia Carson for Congress Committee, November 14, 1996.

28. Telephone interview with Eric Woolhiser, Webmaster for Susan Gallagher for U.S. Senate Campaign in Massachusetts, November 14, 1996.

29. Telephone interview with Representative-elect Chris Cannon of Utah, December 20, 1996.

30. Telephone interview with Eric Woolhiser, Webmaster for Susan Gallagher for U.S. Senate Campaign in Massachusetts, November 14, 1996.

31. Telephone interview with Joshua Ross, Webmaster for Tom Campbell for Congress Campaign, November 20, 1996.

32. Telephone interview with Representative-elect Chris Cannon (R-Utah), December 20, 1996.

33. For a discussion of the distinctions between these types of messages, see Barbara G. Salmore and Stephen A. Salmore, *Candidates, Parties, and Campaigns*, 2nd ed., Washington, D.C.: CQ Press, 1989, pp. 145–149.

34. Telephone interview with Michael Armini, Press Secretary to former Representative Peter Torkildsen (R-Massachusetts), November 20, 1996.

35. Telephone interview with Troy Bettinger, Webmaster for the Joe Rogers for Congress Campaign, November 11, 1996.

36. Telephone interview with Troy Bettinger.

37. Telephone interview with Michael Robinson, Republican congressional candidate from Colorado, November 20, 1996.

38. Paul S. Herrnson, *Congressional Elections: Campaigning at Home and in Washington, D.C.*, Washington: CQ Press, 1995, pp. 161–164.

39. Telephone interview with Representative Tom Campbell (R-California), December 19, 1996.

40. Curtis J. Sitomer, "Jesse Unruh, A Devotee of Politics and Power," *Christian Science Monitor*, August 13, 1987, p. 17.

41. Rajiv Chandrasekaran, "Politics Finding a Home on the Net," *Washington Post*, November 22, 1996, p. A4.

42. Telephone interview with Troy Bettinger, Webmaster for the Joe Rogers for Congress Campaign, November 11, 1996.

43. Telephone interview with Michael Robinson, Republican congressional candidate from Colorado, November 20, 1996.

44. Telephone interview with Gary Torello, president of QGM and Webmaster for the campaign site of Ed Munster who ran in the 2nd Congressional District in Connecticut, November 20, 1996.

45. Telephone interview with Gary Torello.

46. See "Election Crush Creates Internet Logjam," CNN Interactive, at *http://cnn.com/TECH9611/06/Internet.crush.ap/index.html*

47. "One-in-Ten Voters Online for Campaign '96."

48. E-mail correspondence with John Baker, Webmaster of the Lamontagne for Governor Campaign, December 21, 1996.

49. E-mail correspondence with Wilson E. Allen, Webmaster for the Julia Carson for Congress Committee, November 14, 1996.

50. Telephone interview with Eric Woolhiser, Webmaster for Susan Gallagher for U.S. Senate Campaign in Massachusetts, November 14, 1996.

51. Muzzio and Birdsell, "The 1996 'Net Voter."

52. John Doerr quoted in "Larry King on the Internet at the Robertson Stephens Technology Conference," *PR Newswire*, February 27, 1996.

53. Telephone interview with Representative-elect Chris Cannon (R-Utah), December 20, 1996.

54. "Parties on the Net; Will the New Media be a Bust or a Boon for Politics?" *Time*, November 11, 1996.

Notes to Chapter Five

1. Lawrence Grossman, *The Electronic Republic*, New York: Penguin Books, 1995, p. 159.

2. *Congressional Record*, January 4, 1995, vol. 141, no. 1, p. 1400.

3. Mark Lewyn and John Carey, "Will America Log on to Internewt?" *Business Week*, December 5, 1994, p. 38.

4. See *http://hillsource.house.gov* for House Republican Conference site.

5. E-mail response from Rob Patton, Systems Administrator for Senator Barbara Boxer (D-California), June 15, 1995.

6. Quoted in Graeme Browning, "Return to Sender," *National Journal,* April 1, 1995, p. 794.

7. Browning, "Return to Sender," p. 797.

8. Charles McGrath, "The Internet's Arrested Development," *New York Times Magazine,* December 8, 1996, p. 85.

9. Interview with Representative Tom Campbell (R-California), December 19, 1996.

10. See Richard Fenno's classic *Homestyle: Members in Their Districts,* New York: Little Brown, 1978; and also Glenn R. Parker, *Homeward Bound: Explaining Changes in Congressional Behavior,* Pittsburgh: University of Pittsburgh Press, 1986.

11. David Mayhew, *Congress: The Electoral Connection,* New Haven: Yale University Press, 1974.

12. Diana Evans Yiannakis, "House Members' Communication Styles: Newsletters and Press Releases, *Journal of Politics,* August–November 1982, pp. 1049–1071.

13. Alice A. Love, "Five Steps to a Higher-Tech House: Gingrich's Technology Revolution Includes Internet for All," *Roll Call,* January 23, 1995.

14. Gary Chapman, "Sending a Message to the White House," *Technology Review,* July 1993, p. 16.

15. Chapman, "Sending a Message to the White House," p. 17.

16. E-mail message from Stephen K. Horn, Director, Presidential E-Mail, White House Office of Correspondence, August 14, 1997.

17. Lorien Golaski, "Taking the Cyber Plunge: White House Sets Good Example," *Business Marketing,* April 1995, p. T-2.

18. Telephone interview with Charles D. Benjamin, Associate Director, White House Information Systems and Technology Division, August 18, 1996.

19. Edwin Diamond and Robert A. Silverman, *White House to Your House: Media and Politics in Virtual America,* Cambridge, MA: MIT Press, 1997, p. 150.

20. "Radio Address of the President and the Vice President to the Nation," White House Office of the Press Secretary, April 19, 1997, at *http://www.whitehouse.gov*

21. Diamond and Silverman, *White House to Your House,* p. 148.

22. See Stephen Doheny-Farina, *The Wired Neighborhood,* New Haven: Yale University Press, 1996.

23. Bruce Maxwell, *How to Access the Federal Government on the Internet 1997,* Washington, D.C.: CQ Press, 1996, p. 4.

Notes to Chapter Six

1. "White House Firm on Medical Records," UPI Wire Story, September 12, 1996.

2. U.S. Congress, House, *A bill to prevent and punish acts of terrorism, and for other purposes,* Public L. 104-132, 104th Cong., 2nd sess., April 24, 1996.

3. For a brief early history of Usenet, see Michael Hauben and Ronda Hauben, *Netizens: On the History and Impact of Usenet and the Internet,* Los Alamitos, Calif.: IEEE Computer Society Press, 1997, pp. 39–46.

4. Brendan P. Kehoe, "Zen and the Art of the Internet: A Beginner's Guide to the Internet, 1st ed., January 1992, at *http://sundance.cso. uiuc.edu/Publications/Other/Zen/zen-1.0__toc.html*

5. Mark Harrison, *The Usenet Handbook: A User's Guide to Netnews,* Sebastopol, CA: O'Reilly & Associates, 1995, pp. 9–10.

6. Hauben and Hauben, *Netizens: On the History and Impact of Usenet and the Internet.*

7. Margaret L. McLaughlin et al., "Standards of Conduct on Usenet," in *Stephen G. Jones, en., Cybersociety: Computer-Mediated Communication and Community,* Thousand Oaks, CA: Sage, 1995, p. 102.

8. Anthony Corrado and Charles M. Firestone, eds., *Elections in Cyberspace: Toward a New Era in American Politics,* Washington, D.C.: The Aspen Institute, 1996, p.17.

9. Hauben and Hauben, *Netizens,* p. 243.

10. Hauben and Hauben, *Netizens,* p. 243.

11. Hauben and Hauben, *Netizens,* pp. 243–244.

12. Charles McGrath, "The Internet's Arrested Development," *New York Times Magazine,* December 8, 1996, p. 84.

13. Stephen Doheny-Farina, *The Wired Neighborhood,* New Haven: Yale University Press, 1996, p. 55.

14. McGrath, "The Internet's Arrested Development," p. 84.

15. "The Superhighway: 50 Million People on the Net . . . " *dot.COM,* April 1, 1997.

16. "Survey Profiles Voters' Use of Media," Media Studies Center, Freedom Forum News Advisory, at *http://www.mediastudies.org/new.html*

17. McLaughlin et al., "Standards of Conduct on Usenet," pp. 90–111.

18. Langdon Winner, "Privileged Communications," *Technology Review,* May/June 1995, p. 70.

19. Dinty W. Moore, *The Emperor's Virtual Clothes: The Naked Truth about Internet Culture,* Chapel Hill, N.C.: Algonquin Books, 1995, p. 19.

20. Moore, *The Emperor's Virtual Clothes,* p. 24.

21. Hauben and Hauben, *Netizens,* p. 3.

22. Harrison, *The Usenet Handbook,* p. 198.

23. John V. Pavlik, *New Media Technology: Cultural and Commercial Perspectives,* Boston: Allyn and Bacon, 1996, p. 103.

Notes to Chapter Seven

1. John V. Pavlik, *New Media Technology: Cultural and Commercial Perspectives,* Boston: Allyn and Bacon, 1996, p. 140.

2. Peter McGrath, "The Web: Infotopia or Marketplace?" *Newsweek,* January 27, 1997, p. 82.

3. Quoted in Pavlik, *New Media Technology,* p. 56.

4. Iain McLean, *Democracy and New Technology,* Cambridge, U.K.: Polity Press, 1989, p. 113.

5. Paul Starobin, "On the Square," *National Journal,* May 25, 1996, pp. 1145–1149.

6. Amy Harmon, "Diana Photo Restarts Debate Over Lack of Restrictions on Internet Postings," *New York Times,* September 22, 1997, p. C9.

7. Starobin, "On the Square," pp. 1148–1149.

8. Esther Dyson, *Release 2.0: A Design for Living in the Digital Age,* New York: Broadway, 1997, p. 36.

9. Pew Research Center for the People & the Press, "News Attracts Most Internet Users," Washington, D.C.: Pew Research Center, December 16, 1996. The study was a reinterview telephone survey of 1,003 adults who were identified in previous surveys as online users. The questionnaire was administered between October 21 and October 31, 1996.

10. "Freshman Apathy Continues, U.S. College Survey Shows," *Minneapolis Starr Tribune,* January 12, 1998, p. A7.

11. Andrew Kohut, "The Age of Indifference: A Study of Young Americans and How They View the News," Times Mirror Center for the People & the Press, June 28, 1990, p. 23.

12. Public Opinion Online, February 7, 1996. Yankelovich Clancy Shulman survey, July 8–9, 1992.

13. *Time,* Yankelovich, Skelly and White poll, Sept. 29, 1976.

14. CBS News/New York Times survey, Oct. 15, 1996.

15. Quoted in Lawrence Grossman, *The Electronic Republic,* New York: Penguin, 1995, p. 147.

16. Wayne Rash, *Politics on the Nets,* New York: W.H. Freeman, 1997, p. 181.

17. Robert Putnam, "Bowling Alone: America's Declining Social Capital," *Journal of Democracy,* January 1995, pp. 65–78.

18. "Trust in Government Survey," January 1996, Princeton Survey Research Associates survey conducted for the Kaiser Foundation, Harvard University, and the *Washington Post,* November 28–December 4, 1995.

19. Putnam, "Bowling Alone."

20. David Thelen, *Becoming Citizens in the Age of Television*, Chicago: University of Chicago Press, 1996.

21. Thelen, *Becoming Citizens in the Age of Television*, pp. 206–207.

22. See James S. Fishkin, *Democracy and Deliberation: New Directions for Democratic Reform*, New Haven: Yale University Press, 1991, pp. 1–13.

23. Thelen, *Becoming Citizens in the Age of Television*, pp. 177–192.

24. Putnam, "Bowling Alone," p. 76.

25. Scott Parker, "Mastering the Tool of Political Web Sites: Rating the State Republican Party Web Sites," unpublished manuscript.

26. Ithiel de Sola Pool, *Technologies Without Boundaries*, edited by Eli M. Noam, Cambridge, Mass.: Harvard University Press, 1990, p. 261.

27. de Sola Pool, *Technologies Without Boundaries*.

28. Michael E. Kraft and Norman J. Vig, eds., *Technology and Politics*, Durham: Duke University Press, 1988, p. 25.

29. For discussions of the Reform Party's nomination process, see Sam Fulwood III, "Perot Wins Reform Party Nomination; Politics: Dallas Billionaire Easily Outpolls Ex-Colo. Gov. Lamm to Gain Second Run at White House. Weeklong Balloting Process Confused Many, Created Wait Until Accountants Verify the Results," *Los Angeles Times*, Aug. 18, 1996, p. 1; James Toedtman, "Longshots Convention/Perot, Lamm Lament Deficit, Attack Democrats, GOP, "*Newsday*, Aug. 12, 1996, p. A04; and Vincent J. Schodolski, "Lamm Accuses Perot of Divisive Power Play; Reform Party Convention May be Explosive," *Chicago Tribune*, Aug. 11, 1996. p. 11C.

30. "Survey Profiles Voters' Use of Media," Media Studies Center, Freedom Forum News Advisory, at *http://www.mediastudies.org/new.html*

31. Langdon Winner, "Privileged Communications," *Technology Review*, May/June 1995, p. 70.

32. G. J. Mulgan, *Communication and Control: Networks and the New Economies of Communication*, Cambridge, Eng.: Polity Press, 1991, p. 7.

33. See also Kenneth Laudon, *Communications Technology and Democratic Participation*, New York: Praeger, 1977, pp. 110–111.

34. See, for example, Edward Schwartz, *Netactivism: How Citizens Use the Internet*, Sebastopol, Calif.: Songline Studios, 1996.

35. See, for example, Starobin, "On the Square."

36. David Winston, "Voter Decision Making and the Internet," presentation at the Politics Online Conference, November 21, 1996, Washington, D.C. See *http://www.flyingkite.com/main/*

37. See "Election Crush Creates Internet Logjam," CNN Interactive, at *http://cnn.com/TECH9611/06/Internet.crush.ap/index.html*

38. Charles McGrath, "The Internet's Arrested Development," *New York Times Magazine*, December 8, 1996, p. 80.

Note to Methodology

1. *Associations Yellow Book,* New York: Leadership Directories Inc., 1997.

Index

RVARD UNIVERSITY